PhysioEx™ 8.0
for A&P
Laboratory Simulations in Physiology

Peter Zao
North Idaho College

Timothy Stabler
Indiana University Northwest

Lori Smith
American River College

Greta Peterson
Middlesex Community College

Marcia C. Gibson
University of Wisconsin—Madison
(Histology Review Supplement)

Nina Zanetti
Siena College

Andrew Lokuta
University of Wisconsin—Madison

PEARSON

Benjamin
Cummings

San Francisco Boston New York
Cape Town Hong Kong London Madrid Mexico City
Montreal Munich Paris Singapore Sidney Tokyo Toronto

Editor-in-Chief: Serina Beauparlant
Project Editor: Sabrina Larson
Media Editor: Erik Fortier
Managing Editor: Wendy Earl
Editorial Assistant: Nicole Graziano
Production Supervisor: Leslie Austin
Media Developers: Cadre Design
Marketing Manager: Gordon Lee
Cover Design: Riezebos Holzbaur Design Group
Senior Manufacturing Buyer: Stacey Weinberger

Benjamin Cummings gratefully acknowledges Carolina Biological Supply for the use of numerous histology images found on the PhysioEx™ CD-ROM.

The Authors and Publisher believe that the lab experiments described in this publication, when conducted in conformity with the safety precautions described herein and according to the school's laboratory safety procedures, are reasonably safe for the student to whom this manual is directed. Nonetheless, many of the described experiments are accompanied by some degree of risk, including human error, the failure or misuses of laboratory or electrical equipment, mismeasurement, chemical spills, and exposure to sharp objects, heat, bodily fluids, blood, or other biologies. The Authors and Publishers disclaim any liability arising from such risks in connection with any of the exeriments contained in the manual. If students have any questions or problems with materials, procedures, or instructions on any experiment, they should always ask the instructor for help before proceeding.

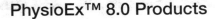

PhysioEx™ 8.0 Products

For the Anatomy & Physiology Course

PhysioEx 8.0 for A&P: Laboratory Simulations in Physiology
order ISBN 0-321-54856-6

Instructor Guide for PhysioEx 8.0 for A&P
order ISBN 0-321-54898-1

For the Human Physiology Course

PhysioEx 8.0 for Human Physiology: Laboratory Simulations in Physiology
order ISBN 0-321-54857-4

Instructor Guide for PhysioEx 8.0 for Human Physiology
order ISBN 0-321-54899-X

To locate the Benjamin Cummings sales representative nearest you, visit http://www.aw.com/replocator

ISBN 0-321-54856-6 (package with CD)
ISBN 978-0-321-54756-6 (package with CD)

ISBN 0-321-54893-0 (book only)
ISBN 978-0-321-54893-1 (book only)

4 5 6 7 8 9 10—MAL—12 11 10 09
www.aw-bc.com

Contents

Preface

PhysioEx™ version 8.0 consists of 11 exercises containing 79 physiology lab activities that may be used to supplement or replace wet labs. This easy-to-use software allows you to repeat labs as often as you like, perform experiments without harming live animals, and conduct experiments that may be difficult to perform in a wet lab environment due to time, cost, or safety concerns. You also have the flexibility to change the parameters of an experiment and observe how outcomes are affected. In addition, PhysioEx includes an extensive histology tutorial that allows you to study histology images at various magnifications. This manual will walk you through each lab step-by-step. You will also find Review Sheets following each exercise to test your understanding of the key concepts in each lab.

New to Version 8.0

Note to instructors: If you have used previous versions of PhysioEx, here is a summary of what you will find new to version 8.0:

• New data in Activities 1–4, Hormones and Metabolism, to demonstrate a more dramatic difference in metabolic rate.

• An examination of how estrogen and calcitonin affect bone density in Activity 5, Hormone Replacement Therapy.

• A glucose tolerance test in Activity 7, Insulin and Diabetes, Part II, to strengthen the correlation between types of diabetes and diagnosis.

• A new activity, Measuring Cortisol and Adrenocorticotropic Hormone (Activity 8), that explores the relationship between the levels of these two hormones and a variety of endocrine disorders.

PhysioEx 8.0 also includes revisions to the Blood Typing, BMR Measurement, Cardiovascular Physiology, and Cell Transport videos. All seven videos are available on the CD-ROM.

Topics in This Edition

Exercise 1 Cell Transport Mechanisms and Permeability. Explores how substances cross the cell's membrane. Simple and facilitated diffusion, osmosis, filtration, and active transport are covered.

Exercise 2 Skeletal Muscle Physiology. Provides insights into the complex physiology of skeletal muscle. Electrical stimulation, isometric contractions, and isotonic contractions are investigated.

Exercise 3 Neurophysiology of Nerve Impulses. Investigates stimuli that elicit action potentials, stimuli that inhibit action potentials, and factors affecting nerve conduction velocity.

Exercise 4 Endocrine System Physiology. Investigates the relationship between hormones and metabolism; the effect of estrogen replacement therapy; the diagnosis of diabetes; and the relationship between the levels of cortisol and adrenocorticotropic hormone and a variety of endocrine disorders.

Exercise 5 Cardiovascular Dynamics. Topics of inquiry include vessel resistance and pump (heart) mechanics.

Exercise 6 Frog Cardiovascular Physiology. Variables influencing heart activity are examined. Topics include setting up and recording baseline heart activity, the refractory period for cardiac muscle, and an investigation of physical and chemical factors that affect enzyme activity.

Exercise 7 Respiratory System Mechanics. Investigates physical and chemical aspects of pulmonary function. Students collect data simulating normal lung volumes. Includes a new activity on comparative spirometry. Other activities examine factors such as airway resistance and the effect of surfactant on lung function.

Exercise 8 Chemical and Physical Processes of Digestion. Turns the student's computer into a virtual chemistry lab where enzymes, reagents, and incubation conditions can be manipulated (in compressed time) to examine factors that affect enzyme activity.

Exercise 9 Renal System Physiology. Simulates the function of a single nephron. Topics include factors influencing glomerular filtration, the effect of hormones on urine function, and glucose transport maximum.

Exercise 10 Acid/Base Balance. Topics include respiratory and metabolic acidosis/alkalosis, as well as renal and respiratory compensation.

Exercise 11 Blood Analysis. Covers hematocrit determination, erythrocyte sedimentation rate determination, hemoglobin determination, blood typing, and total cholesterol determination.

Histology Atlas and Review Supplement. Includes over 200 histology images viewable at various magnifications, with accompanying descriptions and labels.

Getting Started

To use PhysioEx, your computer should meet the following minimum requirements (regardless of whether you are using the CD or accessing PhysioEx via the Web):

Windows:

• OS: Windows® XP, Vista™

• Resolution: 1024 × 768

• Latest version of Adobe® Flash® Player

• Latest version of Adobe Reader®

- Browsers: Internet Explorer 6.0 (XP only); Internet Explorer 7.0; FireFox 2.0

- Internet Connection: 56K modem minimum for website

- Printer

Macintosh:

- OS: 10.3.x, 10.4.x

- Resolution: 1024 × 768

- Latest version of Adobe Flash Player

- Latest version of Adobe Reader

- Browsers: Safari 1.3 (10.3.x only); Safari 2.0 (10.4.x only); FireFox 2.0

- Internet Connection: 56K modem minimum for website

- Printer

Instructions for Getting Started—Mac Users (CD version)

1. Put the PhysioEx CD in the CD-ROM drive. Double-click the PhysioEx CD icon on your desktop, and then double-click the **StartHere.html** file.

2. Although you do not need a live Internet connection to run PhysioEx, you do need to have a browser (such as Firefox or Safari) installed on your computer.

3. Click **License Agreement** to read the License Agreement, then close the License Agreement window.

4. In the PhysioEx window, click **Enter.**

Instructions for Getting Started—IBM/PC Users (CD version)

1. Put the PhysioEx CD in the CD-ROM drive. The program should launch automatically. If autorun is disabled on your machine, double click the My Computer icon on your Windows desktop, double-click the PhysioEx CD icon, and then double-click the **StartHere.html** file.

2. Although you do not need a live Internet connection to run PhysioEx, you do need to have a browser (such as Firefox or Internet Explorer) installed on your computer.

3. Click **License Agreement** to read the License Agreement.

4. In the PhysioEx window, click **Enter.**

5. From the Main Menu, click on the lab you wish to enter.

Instructions for Getting Started—Web Users

Follow the instructions for accessing www.physioex.com that appear at the very front of your lab manual.

Technical Support

If you need technical support, please contact the Benjamin Cummings Product Support Center at http://247.aw.com.

Cell Transport Mechanisms and Permeability

The molecular composition of the plasma membrane allows it to be selective about what passes through it. It allows nutrients to enter the cell but keeps out undesirable substances. By the same token, valuable cell proteins and other substances are kept within the cell, and excreta, or wastes, pass to the exterior. This property is known as **differential,** or **selective, permeability.** Transport through the plasma membrane occurs in two basic ways. In **active processes,** the cell provides energy (ATP) to power the transport. In the other, **passive processes,** the transport process is driven by concentration or pressure differences between the interior and exterior of the cell.

Passive Processes

The two key passive processes of membrane transport are diffusion and filtration. Diffusion is an important transport process for every cell in the body. By contrast, filtration usually occurs only across capillary walls. Each of these will be considered in turn.

Diffusion

Recall that all molecules possess *kinetic energy* and are in constant motion. As molecules move about randomly at high speeds, they collide and ricochet off one another, changing direction with each collision. For a given temperature, all matter has about the same average kinetic energy. Because kinetic energy is directly related to both mass and velocity (KE $= \frac{1}{2} mv^2$), smaller molecules tend to move faster.

When a **concentration gradient** (difference in concentration) exists, the net effect of this random molecular movement is that the molecules eventually become evenly distributed throughout the environment—in other words, the process called diffusion occurs. Hence, **diffusion** is the movement of molecules from a region of their higher concentration to a region of their lower concentration. Diffusion's driving force is the kinetic energy of the molecules themselves.

The diffusion of particles into and out of cells is modified by the plasma membrane, which constitutes a physical barrier. In general, molecules diffuse passively through the plasma membrane if they are small enough to pass through its pores (and are aided by an electrical and/or concentration gradient), or if they can dissolve in the lipid portion of the membrane as in the case of CO_2 and O_2.

The diffusion of solute particles dissolved in water through a differentially permeable membrane is called **simple diffusion.** The diffusion of water through a differentially permeable membrane is called **osmosis.** Both simple diffusion and osmosis involve movement of a substance from an area of its higher concentration to one of its lower concentration, that is, down its concentration gradient.

Solute Transport Through Nonliving Membranes

This computerized simulation provides information on the passage of water and solutes through semipermeable membranes, which may be applied to the study of transport mechanisms in living membrane-bounded cells.

ACTIVITY 1

Simulating Dialysis (Simple Diffusion)

Choose **Exercise 5B: Cell Transport Mechanisms and Permeability** from the drop-down menu and click **GO.** Watch the **Cell Transport** video to see an actual dialysis experiment performed. Then click **Simple Diffusion.** The opening screen will appear in a few seconds (Figure 1.1). The primary features on the screen when the program starts are a pair of glass beakers perched atop a solutions dispenser, a dialysis membranes cabinet at the right side of the screen, and a data collection unit at the bottom of the display.

The beakers are joined by a membrane holder, which can be equipped with any of the dialysis membranes from the cabinet. Each membrane is represented by a thin colored line suspended in a gray supporting frame. The solute concentration of dispensed solutions is displayed at the side of each beaker. As you work through the experiments, keep in mind that membranes are three-dimensional; thus what appears as a slender line is actually the edge of a membrane sheet.

The solutions you can dispense are listed beneath each beaker. You can choose more than one solution, and the amount to be dispensed is controlled by clicking (+) to increase concentration or (−) to decrease concentration. The chosen solutions are then delivered to their beaker by clicking the **Dispense** button on the same side. Clicking the **Start** button opens the membrane holder and begins the experiment. The **Start** button will become a **Pause** button after it is clicked once. To clean the beakers and prepare them for the next run, click **Flush.** Clicking **Pause** and then **Flush** during a run stops the experiment and prepares the beakers for another run. You can adjust the timer for any interval between 5 and 300 minutes; the elapsed time is shown in the small window to the right of the timer.

To move dialysis membranes from the cabinet to the membrane holder, click and hold the mouse on the selected membrane, drag it into position between the beakers, and then release the mouse button to drop it into place. Each membrane possesses a different molecular weight cutoff (MWCO), indicated by the number below it. You can think of

MWCO in terms of pore size; the larger the MWCO number, the larger the pores in the membrane.

The **Run Number** window in the data collection unit at the bottom of the screen displays each experimental trial (run). When you click the **Record Data** button, your data is recorded in the computer's memory and is displayed in the data grid at the bottom of the screen. Data displayed in the data grid include the solute (Solute) and membrane (MWCO) used in a run, the starting concentrations in the left and right beakers (Start Conc. L. and Start Conc. R.), and the average diffusion rate (Avg. Diff. Rate). If you are not satisfied with a run, you can click **Delete Run.** *Note:* Remember that sodium chloride (NaCl) does not move as a molecule. It dissociates to Na^+ and Cl^- ions in water.

1. Click and hold the mouse on the 20 MWCO membrane, and drag it to the membrane holder between the beakers. Release the mouse button to lock the membrane into place.

2. Now increase the NaCl concentration to be dispensed by clicking the (+) button under the left beaker until the display window reads 9.00 m*M*. Click **Dispense** to fill the left beaker with 9.00 m*M* NaCl solution.

3. Click the **Deionized Water** button under the right beaker and then click **Dispense** to fill the right beaker with deionized water.

4. Adjust the timer to 60 minutes (compressed time), then click the **Start** button. When Start is clicked, the barrier between the beakers descends, allowing the solutions in each beaker to have access to the dialysis membrane separating them. Recall that the Start button becomes a Pause button that allows you to momentarily halt the progress of the experiment so you can see instantaneous diffusion or transport rates.

5. Watch the concentration windows at the side of each beaker for any activity. A level above zero in NaCl concentration in the right beaker indicates that Na^+ and Cl^- ions are diffusing from the left into the right beaker through the semipermeable dialysis membrane. Record your results in Chart 1. Record (—) for no diffusion. If diffusion occurred, record

CHART 1	Dialysis Results (average diffusion rate in m*M*/min)		
	Membrane (MWCO)		
Solute	20	50	100	200
NaCl				
Urea				
Albumin				
Glucose				

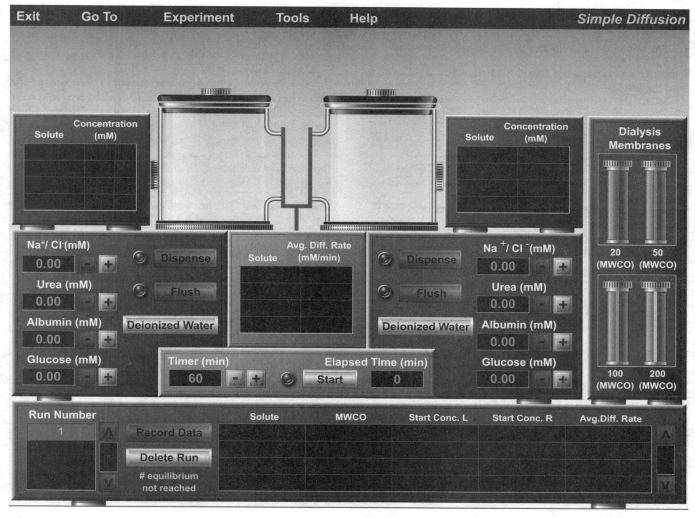

(a)

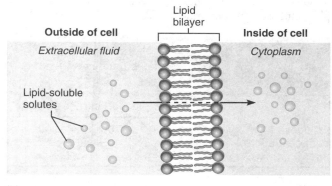

(b)

FIGURE 1.1 Simple diffusion. (a) Opening screen of the Simple Diffusion experiment. (b) Simple diffusion through the phospholipid bilayer.

the average diffusion rate in Chart 1. Click the **Record Data** button to keep your data in the computer's memory.

6. Click the 20 MWCO membrane (in the membrane holder) again to automatically return it to the membranes cabinet and then click **Flush** beneath each beaker to prepare for the next run.

7. Drag the next membrane (50 MWCO) to the holder and repeat steps 2 through 6. Continue the runs until you have tested all four membranes. (Remember: Click **Flush** beneath each beaker between runs.)

8. Now repeat the same experiment three times for urea, albumin, and glucose, respectively. In step 2 you will be dis-

pensing first urea, then albumin, and finally glucose, instead of NaCl.

9. Click **Tools** → **Print Data** to print your data.

Which solute(s) were able to diffuse into the right beaker from the left?

_____

Which solute(s) did not diffuse?

_____

If the solution in the left beaker contained both urea and albumin, which membrane(s) could you choose to selectively remove the urea from the solution in the left beaker? How would you carry out this experiment?

_____

_____

_____

Assume that the solution in the left beaker contained NaCl in addition to the urea and albumin. How could you set up an experiment so that you removed the urea, but left the NaCl concentration unchanged? *Hint:* Assume that you also have control of the contents in the right beaker.

_____

_____

_____ ▬

Facilitated Diffusion

Some molecules are lipid insoluble or too large to pass through plasma membrane pores; instead, they pass through the membrane by a passive transport process called **facilitated diffusion.** In this form of transport, solutes combine with carrier protein molecules in the membrane and are then transported *along* or *down* their concentration gradient. Because facilitated diffusion relies on carrier proteins, solute transport varies with the number of available membrane transport proteins.

ACTIVITY 2

Simulating Facilitated Diffusion

Click the **Experiment** menu and then choose **Facilitated Diffusion.** The opening screen will appear in a few seconds

(Figure 1.2). The basic screen layout is similar to that of the previous experiment with only a few modifications to the equipment. You will notice that only NaCl and glucose solutes are available in this experiment, and you will see a Membrane Builder on the right side of the screen.

The (+) and (−) buttons underneath each beaker adjust solute concentration in the solutions to be delivered into each beaker. Similarly, the buttons in the Membrane Builder allow you to control the number of carrier proteins implanted in the membrane when you click the **Build Membrane** button.

In this experiment, you will investigate how glucose transport is affected by the number of available carrier molecules.

1. The Glucose Carriers window in the Membrane Builder should read 500. If not, adjust to 500 by using the (+) or (−) button.

2. Now click **Build Membrane** to insert 500 glucose carrier proteins into the membrane. You should see the membrane appear as a slender line encased in a support structure within the Membrane Builder. Remember that we are looking at the edge of a three-dimensional membrane.

3. Click on the membrane and hold the mouse button down as you drag the membrane to the membrane holder between the beakers. Release the mouse to lock the membrane into place.

4. Adjust the glucose concentration to be delivered to the left beaker to 2.00 m*M* by clicking the (+) button next to the Glucose window until it reads 2.00.

5. To fill the left beaker with the glucose solution, click the **Dispense** button just below the left beaker.

6. Click the **Deionized Water** button below the right beaker, and then click the **Dispense** button. The right beaker will fill with deionized water.

7. Set the timer to 60 minutes, and click **Start.** Watch the concentration windows next to the beakers. When the 60 minutes have elapsed, click the **Record Data** button to display glucose transport rate information in the grid at the

CHART 2	Facilitated Diffusion Results (glucose transport rate, m*M*/min)		
	No. of glucose carrier proteins		
Glucose concentration (m*M*)	500	700	900
2.00			
8.00			

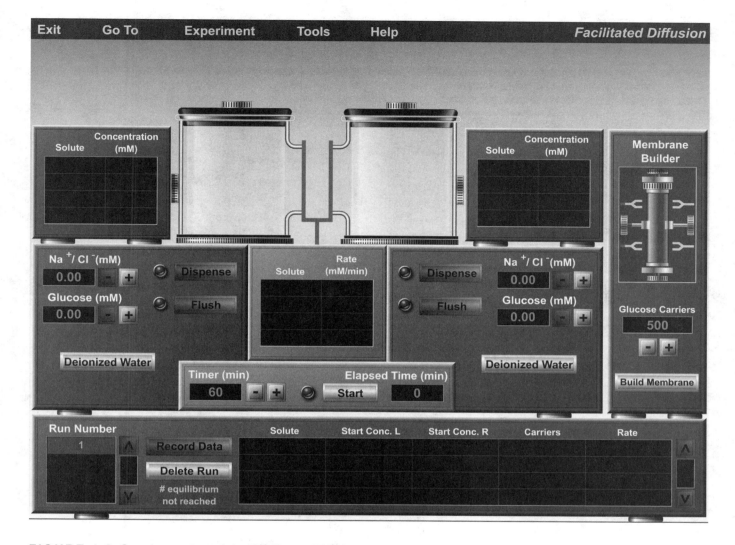

FIGURE 1.2 Opening screen of the Facilitated Diffusion experiment.

lower edge of the screen. Record the glucose transport rate in Chart 2.

8.   Click the **Flush** button beneath each beaker to remove any residual solution.

9.   Click the membrane's holder to return it to the Membrane Builder. Increase the glucose carriers, and repeat steps 2 through 8 using membranes with 700 and then 900 glucose carrier proteins. Record the glucose transport rate in Chart 2 each time.

10. Repeat steps 1 through 9 at 8.00 m*M* glucose concentration. Record your results in Chart 2.

11. Click **Tools → Print Data** to print your data.

What happened to the rate of facilitated diffusion as the number of protein carriers increased? Explain your answer.

_____

_____

_____

What do you think would happen to the transport rate if you put the same concentration of glucose into both beakers instead of deionized water in the right beaker?

_____

_____

Should NaCl have an effect on glucose diffusion? Explain your answer. Use the simulation to see if it does.

_____

_____

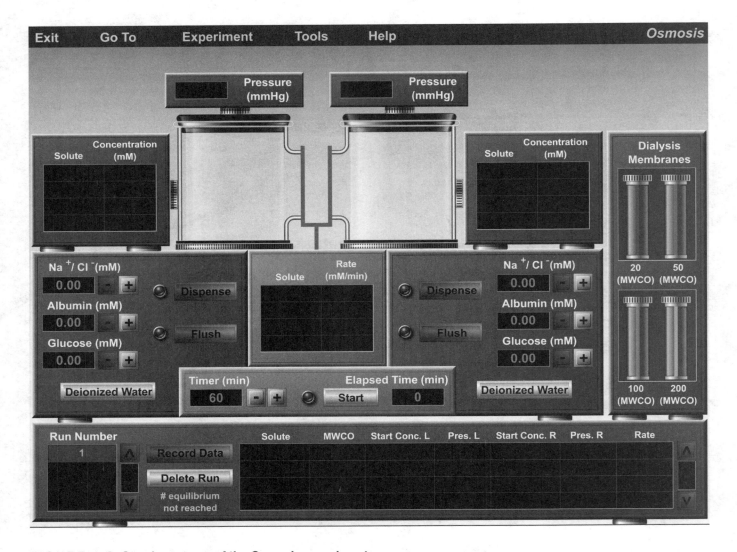

FIGURE 1.3 Opening screen of the Osmosis experiment.

Osmosis

A special form of diffusion, the diffusion of water through a semipermeable membrane, is called **osmosis.** Because water can pass through the pores of most membranes, it can move from one side of a membrane to another relatively unimpeded. Osmosis occurs whenever there is a difference in water concentration on the two sides of a membrane.

If we place distilled water on both sides of a membrane, *net* movement of water will not occur; however, water molecules would still move between the two sides of the membrane. In such a situation, we would say that there is no *net* osmosis. The concentration of water in a solution depends on the number of solutes present. Therefore, increasing the solute concentration coincides with a decrease in water concentration. Because water moves down its concentration gradient, it will always move toward the solution with the highest concentration of solutes. Similarly, solutes also move down their concentration gradient. If we position a *fully* permeable membrane (permeable to solutes and water) between two solutions of differing concentrations, then all substances—solutes and water—will diffuse freely, and an equilibrium will be reached

between the two sides of the membrane. However, if we use a semipermeable membrane that is impermeable to the solutes, then we have established a condition where water will move but solutes will not. Consequently, water will move toward the more concentrated solution, resulting in a volume increase. By applying this concept to a closed system where volumes cannot change, we can predict that the pressure in the more concentrated solution would rise.

ACTIVITY 3

Simulating Osmotic Pressure

Click the **Experiment** menu, and then select **Osmosis.** The opening screen will appear in a few seconds (Figure 1.3). The most notable difference in this experiment screen concerns meters atop the beakers that measure pressure changes in the beaker they serve. As before, (+) and (−) buttons control solute concentrations in the dispensed solutions.

1. Drag the 20 MWCO membrane to the holder between the two beakers.

2. Adjust the NaCl concentration to 8.00 m*M* in the left beaker, and then click the **Dispense** button.

3. Click **Deionized Water** under the right beaker, and then click **Dispense.**

4. Set the timer to 60 minutes, and then click **Start** to run the experiment. Pay attention to the pressure displays. At the end of the run, click the **Record Data** button to retain your data in the computer's memory, and also record the osmotic pressure in Chart 3.

5. Click the membrane to return it to the membrane cabinet.

6. Repeat steps 1 through 5 with the 50, 100, and 200 MWCO membranes.

Do you see any evidence of pressure changes in either beaker, using any of the four membranes? If so, which membrane(s)?

_____

_____

Does NaCl appear in the right beaker? If so, which membrane(s) allowed it to pass?

_____

_____

7. Now perform the same experiment for albumin and glucose by repeating steps 1 through 6 for each solute. For albumin, dispense 9.00 m*M* albumin in step 2 (instead of NaCl). For glucose, dispense 10.00 m*M* glucose in step 2 (instead of NaCl).

8. Click **Tools → Print Data** to print your data.

Answer the following questions using the results you recorded in Chart 3. Use the simulation if you need help formulating a response.

CHART 3	Osmosis Results (pressure in mm Hg)			
	Membrane (MWCO)			
Solute	20	50	100	200
Na$^+$Cl$^-$				
Albumin				
Glucose				

Explain the relationship between solute concentration and osmotic pressure.

_____

_____

Will osmotic pressure be generated if solutes are able to diffuse? Explain your answer.

_____

_____

Because the albumin molecule is much too large to pass through a 100 MWCO membrane, you should have noticed the development of osmotic pressure in the left beaker in the albumin run using the 100 MWCO membrane. What do you think would happen to the osmotic pressure if you replaced the deionized water in the right beaker with 9.00 m*M* albumin in that run? (Both beakers would contain 9.00 m*M* albumin.)

_____

_____

What would happen if you doubled the albumin concentration in the left beaker using any membrane?

_____

_____

In the albumin run using the 200 MWCO membrane, what would happen to the osmotic pressure if you put 10 m*M* glucose in the right beaker instead of deionized water? Explain your answer.

_____

_____

_____

_____

What if you used the 100 MWCO membrane in the albumin/glucose run described in the previous question?

_____

_____

Simulating Filtration

Filtration is the process by which water and solutes pass through a membrane (such as a dialysis membrane) from an area of higher hydrostatic (fluid) pressure into an area of lower hydrostatic pressure. Like diffusion, it is a passive process. For example, fluids and solutes filter out of the capillaries in the kidneys into the kidney tubules because blood pressure in the capillaries is greater than the fluid pressure in the tubules. Filtration is not a selective process. The amount

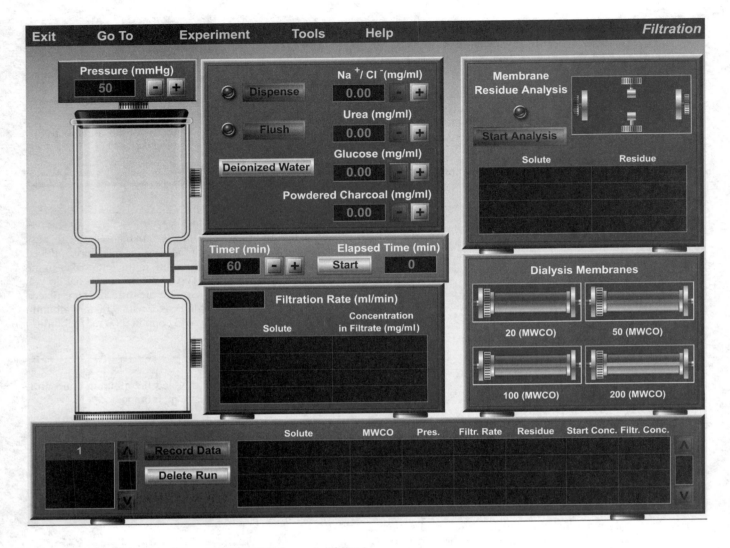

FIGURE 1.4 Opening screen of the Filtration experiment.

of filtrate—fluids and solutes—formed depends almost entirely on the pressure gradient (the difference in pressure on the two sides of the membrane) and on the size of the membrane pores.

Click the **Experiment** menu, and then choose **Filtration.** The opening screen will appear in a few seconds (Figure 1.4). The basic screen elements resemble the other simulations but in a different arrangement. The top beaker can be pressurized to force fluid through the filtration membrane into the bottom beaker. Any of the filtration membranes can be positioned in the holder between the beakers by drag-and-drop as in the previous experiments. The solutions you can dispense are listed to the right of the top beaker and are adjusted by clicking the (+) and (−) buttons. The selected solutions are then delivered to the top beaker by clicking **Dispense.** The top beaker is cleaned and prepared for the next run by clicking **Flush.** You can adjust the timer for any interval between 5 and 300; the elapsed time is shown in the window to the right of the timer. When you click the **Record Data** button, your data is recorded in the computer's memory and is displayed in the data grid at the bottom of the screen.

Solute concentrations in the filtrate are automatically monitored by the *Filtration Rate Analysis unit* to the right of the bottom beaker. After a run you can detect the presence of any solute remaining on a membrane by using the *Membrane Residue Analysis* unit located above the membranes cabinet.

1. Click and hold the mouse on the 20 MWCO membrane, and drag it to the holder below the top beaker. Release the mouse button to lock the membrane into place.

2. Now adjust the NaCl, urea, glucose, and powdered charcoal windows to 5.00 mg/ml each, and then click **Dispense.**

3. If necessary, adjust the pressure unit atop the beaker until its window reads 50 mm Hg.

4. Set the timer to 60 minutes, and then click **Start.** When the Start button is clicked, the membrane holder below the top beaker retracts, and the solution will flow through the membrane into the beaker below.

5. Watch the Filtration Rate box for any activity. A rise in detected solute concentration indicates that the solute parti-

CHART 4	Filtration Results			
		Membrane (MWCO)		
Solute		20	50	100	200
	Filtration rate (ml/min)				
NaCl	In filtrate (mg/ml)				
	Membrane residue (+/−)				
Urea	In filtrate (mg/ml)				
	Membrane residue (+/−)				
Glucose	In filtrate (mg/ml)				
	Membrane residue (+/−)				
Powdered charcoal	In filtrate (mg/ml)				
	Membrane residue (+/−)				

cles are moving through the filtration membrane. At the end of the run, record the filtration *rate* and the amount of each solute present in the *filtrate* (mg/ml) in Chart 4.

6. Now drag the 20 MWCO membrane to the holder in the Membrane Residue Analysis unit. Click **Start Analysis** to begin analysis (and cleaning) of the membrane. Record your results for solute *residue* presence on the membrane (+ for present, − for not present) in Chart 4, and click the **Record Data** button to keep your data in the computer's memory.

7. Click the 20 MWCO membrane again to automatically return it to the membranes cabinet, and then click **Flush** to prepare for the next run.

8. Repeat steps 1 through 7 three times using 50, 100, and 200 MWCO membranes, respectively.

9. Click **Tools → Print Data** to print your data.

How did the membrane's MWCO affect the filtration rate?

_____

_____

Which solute did not appear in the filtrate using any of the membranes?

_____

_____

What would happen if you increased the driving pressure? Use the simulation to arrive at an answer.

_____

_____

Explain how you can increase the filtration rate through living membranes.

_____

_____

By examining the filtration results, we can predict that the molecular weight of glucose must be

greater than _____ but less than _____. ▪

Active Transport

Whenever a cell expends cellular energy (ATP) to move substances across its membrane, the process is referred to as an *active transport process*. Substances moved across cell membranes by active means are generally unable to pass by diffusion. There are several possible reasons why substances may not be able to pass through a membrane by diffusion: they may be too large to pass through the membrane channels, they may not be lipid soluble, or they may have to move against rather than with a concentration gradient.

In one type of active transport, substances move across the membrane by combining with a protein carrier molecule; the process resembles an enzyme-substrate interaction. ATP provides the driving force, and in many cases the substances move against concentration or electrochemical gradients or both. Some of the substances that are moved into the cells by such carriers, commonly called **solute pumps,** are amino acids and some sugars. Both solutes are lipid insoluble and too large to pass through the membrane channels but are necessary for cell life. On the other hand, sodium ions (Na^+) are ejected from the cells by active transport. There is more Na^+ outside the cell than inside, so the Na^+ tends to remain in the cell unless actively transported out. In the body, the most common type of solute pump is the coupled Na^+-K^+ (sodium-potassium) pump that moves Na^+ and K^+ in opposite directions across cellular membranes. Three Na^+ are ejected for every two K^+ entering the cell.

Engulfment processes such as pinocytosis and phagocytosis also require ATP. In **pinocytosis,** the cell membrane sinks beneath the material to form a small vesicle, which then pinches off into the cell interior. Pinocytosis is most common for taking in liquids containing protein or fat.

In **phagocytosis** (cell eating), parts of the plasma membrane and cytoplasm expand and flow around a relatively large or solid material such as bacteria or cell debris and engulf it, forming a membranous sac called a *phagosome.* The phagosome is then fused with a *lysosome* and its contents are digested. In the human body, phagocytic cells are mainly found among the white blood cells and macrophages that act as scavengers and help protect the body from disease-causing microorganisms and cancer cells.

You will examine various factors influencing the function of solute pumps in the following experiment.

ACTIVITY 5

Simulating Active Transport

Click the **Experiment** menu and then choose **Active Transport.** The opening screen will appear in a few seconds (Figure 1.5). This experiment screen resembles the osmosis experiment screen except that an ATP dispenser is substituted for the pressure meters atop the beakers. The (+) and (−) buttons control NaCl, KCl, and glucose concentrations in the dispensed solutions. You will use the Membrane Builder to build membranes containing glucose (facilitated diffusion) carrier proteins and active transport Na^+-K^+ (sodium-potassium) pumps.

In this experiment, we will assume that the left beaker represents the cell's interior and the right beaker represents the extracellular space. The Membrane Builder will insert the Na^+-K^+ (sodium-potassium) pumps into the membrane so Na^+ will be pumped toward the right (out of the cell) while K^+ is simultaneously moved to the left (into the cell).

1. In the Membrane Builder, adjust the number of glucose carriers and the number of sodium-potassium pumps to 500.

2. Click **Build Membrane,** and then drag the membrane to its position in the membrane holder between the beakers.

3. Adjust the NaCl concentration to be delivered to the left beaker to 9.00 m*M*, then click the **Dispense** button.

4. Adjust the KCl concentration to be delivered to the right beaker to 6.00 m*M*, then click **Dispense.**

5. Adjust the ATP dispenser to 1.00 m*M*, then click **Dispense ATP.** This action delivers the chosen ATP concentration to both sides of the membrane.

6. Adjust the timer to 60 min, and then click **Start.** Click **Record Data** after each run.

7. Click **Tools → Print Data** to print your data.

Watch the solute concentration windows at the side of each beaker for any changes in Na^+ and K^+ concentrations. The Na^+ transport rate stops before transport has completed. Why do you think that this happens?

_____

What would happen if you did not dispense any ATP?

_____

8. Click either **Flush** button to clean both beakers. Repeat steps 3 through 6, adjusting the ATP concentration to 3.00 m*M* in step 5. Click **Record Data** after each run.

Has the amount of Na^+ transported changed?

_____

What would happen if you decreased the number of sodium-potassium pumps?

_____

Explain how you could show that this phenomenon is not just simple diffusion. (Hint: Adjust the Na^+ concentration in the right beaker.)

_____

_____

9. Click either **Flush** button to clean both beakers. Now repeat steps 1 through 6, dispensing 9.00 m*M* NaCl into the left beaker and 10.00 m*M* NaCl into the right beaker (instead of 6.00 m*M* KCl). Is Na^+ transport affected by this change? Explain your answer.

_____

_____

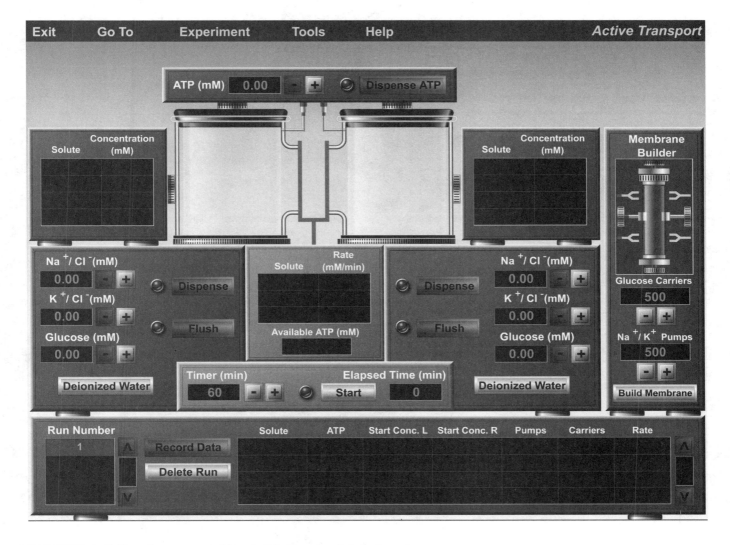

FIGURE 1.5 Opening screen of the Active Transport experiment.

What would happen to the rate of ion transport if we increased the number of sodium-potassium pump proteins?

_____

_____

Would Na$^+$ and K$^+$ transport change if we added glucose solution?

_____

_____

10. Click **Tools → Print Data** to print your recorded data.

Try adjusting various membrane and solute conditions and attempt to predict the outcome of experimental trials. For example, you could dispense 10 mM glucose into the right beaker instead of deionized water. ▬

NAME _____

LAB TIME/DATE _____

Cell Transport Mechanisms and Permeability

Simple Diffusion

1. The following refer to Activity 1: Simulating Dialysis (Simple Diffusion).

Which solute(s) were able to pass through the 20 MWCO membrane?

_____

According to your results, which solute had the highest molecular weight? _____

Which solute displayed the highest rate of diffusion through the 200 MWCO membrane? _____

Using the data from Chart 1, explain the relationship between the rate of diffusion and the size of the solute.

_____

Facilitated Diffusion

2. The following refer to Activity 2: Simulating Facilitated Diffusion.

Did any of the substances travel against their concentration gradient? Explain why or why not.

_____

_____

Using your results from Chart 2, what was the fastest rate of facilitated diffusion recorded? _____. Describe

the conditions that were used to achieve this rate. _____

_____

Name two ways to increase the rate of glucose transport. _____

_____

Did NaCl affect glucose transport? _____

Did NaCl require a transport protein for diffusion? Why or why not? _____

_____

Osmotic Pressure

3. The following refer to Activity 3: Simulating Osmotic Pressure.

For NaCl, which MWCO membrane(s) provided for the net movement of water without movement of NaCl?

_____

Explain how you determined this. (*Hint*: Correlate your results to the data in Chart 3.) _____

_____

For glucose, which MWCO membrane(s) provided for the net movement of glucose without net movement of water?

_____

Explain how you determined this. _____

_____

Is osmotic pressure generated if solutes diffuse freely? _____

Explain how the solute concentration affects osmotic pressure. _____

_____

Filtration

4. The following refer to Activity 4: Simulating Filtration.

Using your results in Chart 4, which MWCO membrane had the greatest filtration rate? _____

Explain the relationship between pore size and filtration rate. _____

_____

Which solute did not appear in the filtrate using any of the membranes? _____

What is your prediction of the molecular weight of glucose compared to the other solutes in the solution? _____

What happened when you increased the driving pressure? _____

_____

Explain why fluid flows from the capillaries of the kidneys into the kidney tubules.

_____

_____

How do you think a decrease in blood pressure would affect filtration in the kidneys? _____

_____

5. The following refer to Activity 5: Simulating Active Transport.

With 1 mM ATP added to the cell interior (left beaker) and the extracellular space (right beaker), was all of the Na$^+$ moved

into the extracellular space? Why or why not? _____

_____

Describe the effect of decreasing the number of sodium-potassium pumps. _____

Describe how you were able to show that the movement of sodium was due to active transport. _____

_____

Skeletal Muscle Physiology

O B J E C T I V E S

1. To define these terms used in describing muscle physiology: *multiple motor unit summation, maximal stimulus, treppe, wave summation,* and *tetanus.*
2. To identify two ways that the mode of stimulation can affect muscle force production.
3. To plot a graph relating stimulus strength and twitch force to illustrate graded muscle response.
4. To explain how slow, smooth, sustained contraction is possible in a skeletal muscle.
5. To graphically understand the relationships between passive, active, and total forces.
6. To identify the conditions under which muscle contraction is isometric or isotonic.
7. To describe in terms of length and force the transitions between isometric and isotonic conditions during a single muscle twitch.
8. To describe the effects of resistance and starting length on the initial velocity of shortening.
9. To explain why muscle force remains constant during isotonic shortening.
10. To explain experimental results in terms of muscle structure.

Skeletal muscles are composed of hundreds to thousands of individual cells, each doing their share of work in the production of force. As their name suggests, skeletal muscles move the skeleton. Skeletal muscles are remarkable machines; while allowing us the manual dexterity to create magnificent works of art, they are also capable of generating the brute force needed to lift a 100-lb. sack of concrete. When a skeletal muscle from an experimental animal is electrically stimulated, it behaves in the same way as a stimulated muscle in the intact body, that is, in vivo. Hence, such an experiment gives us valuable insight into muscle behavior.

This set of computer simulations demonstrates many important physiological concepts of skeletal muscle contraction. The program graphically provides all the equipment and materials necessary for you, the investigator, to set up experimental conditions and observe the results. In student-conducted laboratory investigations, there are many ways to approach a problem, and the same is true of these simulations. The instructions will guide you in your investigation, but you should also try out alternate approaches to gain insight into the logical methods used in scientific experimentation.

Try this approach: As you work through the simulations for the first time, follow the instructions closely and answer the questions posed as you go. Then try asking "What if . . . ?" questions to test the validity of your hypotheses. The major advantages of these computer simulations are that the muscle cannot be accidentally damaged, lab equipment will not break down at the worst possible time, and you will have ample time to think critically about the processes being investigated.

Because you will be working with a simulated muscle and an oscilloscope display, you need to watch both carefully during the experiments. Think about what is happening in each situation. You need to understand how you are experimentally manipulating the muscle in order to understand your results.

Electrical Stimulation

A contracting skeletal muscle will produce force and/or short-ening when nervous or electrical stimulation is applied. The force generated by a whole muscle reflects the number of mo-tor units firing at a given time. Strong muscle contraction im-plies that many motor units are activated and each unit has maximally contracted. Weak contraction means that few motor units are active; however, the activated units are maximally contracted. By increasing the number of motor units firing, we can produce a steady increase in muscle force, a process called **recruitment** or **multiple motor unit summation.**

Regardless of the number of motor units activated, a sin-gle contraction of skeletal muscle is called a muscle twitch (Figure 2.1b). A tracing of a muscle twitch is divided into three phases: latent, contraction, and relaxation. The **latent period** is a short period between the time of stimulation and the beginning of contraction. Although no force is generated during this interval, chemical changes occur intracellularly in preparation for contraction, such as the release of calcium from the sarcoplasmic reticulum. During contraction, the myofilaments are sliding past each other, and the muscle shortens. Relaxation takes place when contraction has ended and the muscle returns to its normal resting state and length.

The first activity you will conduct simulates an **isometric,** or **fixed length, contraction** of an isolated skeletal muscle. This activity allows you to investigate how the strength and fre-quency of an electrical stimulus affect whole muscle function. Note that these simulations involve indirect stimulation by an electrode placed on the surface of the muscle. This differs from the situation in vivo where each fiber in the muscle receives di-rect stimulation via a nerve ending. In other words, increasing the intensity of the electrical stimulation mimics how the ner-vous system increases the number of motor units activated.

Single Stimulus

Choose **Exercise 2**: **Skeletal Muscle Physiology** from the drop-down menu and click **GO.** Before you perform the ac-tivities, watch the **Skeletal Muscle** video to gain an appreci-ation for the preparation required for these experiments. Then click **Single Stimulus.** The opening screen will appear in a few seconds (Figure 2.1a). The oscilloscope display, the grid at the top of the screen, is the most important part of the screen because it graphically displays the contraction data for analysis. Time is displayed on the horizontal axis. A full sweep is initially set at 200 msec. However, you can adjust the sweep time from 200 msec to 1000 msec by clicking and dragging the **200** msec button at the lower right corner of the oscilloscope display to the left to a new position on the time axis. The force (in grams) produced by muscle contraction is displayed on the vertical axis. Clicking the **Clear Tracings** button at the bottom right of the oscilloscope erases all mus-cle twitch tracings from the oscilloscope display.

The *electrical stimulator* is the equipment seen just be-neath the oscilloscope display. Clicking **Stimulate** delivers the electrical shock to the muscle through the electrodes lying on the surface of the muscle. Stimulus voltage is set by clicking the (+) or (−) buttons next to the voltage window. Three small windows to the right of the Stimulate button dis-play the force measurements. *Active force* is produced during muscle contraction, while *passive force* results from the mus-cle being stretched (much like a rubber band). The *total force* is the sum of active and passive forces. The red arrow at the

left of the oscilloscope display is an indicator of passive force. After the muscle is stimulated, the **Measure** button at the right edge of the electrical stimulator becomes active. When the Measure button is clicked, a vertical orange line will be displayed at the left edge of the oscilloscope display. Clicking the arrow buttons below the Measure button moves the orange line horizontally across the screen. The Time win-dow displays the difference in time between the zero point on the X-axis and the intersection between the orange measure line and the muscle twitch tracing.

The muscle is suspended in the support stand to the left of the oscilloscope display. The hook through the upper ten-don of the muscle is part of the force transducer, which mea-sures the force produced by the muscle. The hook through the lower tendon secures the muscle in place. The weight cabinet just below the muscle support stand is not active in this ex-periment; it contains weights you will use in the isotonic con-traction part of the simulation. You can adjust the starting length of the muscle by clicking the (+) or (−) buttons lo-cated next to the Muscle Length display window.

When you click the **Record Data** button in the data col-lection unit below the electrical stimulator, your data is recorded in the computer's memory and is displayed in the data grid at the bottom of the screen. Data displayed in the data grid include the voltage, muscle length, and active, passive, and total force measurements. If you are not satisfied with a single run, you can click **Delete Line** to erase a single line of data. Clicking the **Clear Table** button will remove all accumu-lated data in the experiment and allow you to start over.

ACTIVITY 1

Practicing Generating a Tracing

1. Click the **Stimulate** button once. Because the beginning voltage is set to zero, no muscle activity should result. You will see a blue line moving across the bottom of the oscillo-scope display. This blue line will indicate muscle force in the experiments. If the tracings move too slowly across the screen, click and hold the **200** button at the lower right corner of the oscilloscope and drag it to the left to the 40 msec mark and release it. This action resets the total sweep time to 1000 msec to speed up the display time.

2. Click and hold the (+) button beneath the Stimulate but-ton until the voltage window reads 3.0 volts. Click **Stimulate** once. You will see the muscle react, and a contraction tracing will appear on the screen. Notice that the muscle tracing color alternates between blue and yellow each time the Stimulate button is clicked to enhance the visual difference between twitch tracings. You can click the **Clear Tracings** button as needed to clean up the oscilloscope display. To retain your data, click the **Record Data** button at the end of each stimulus.

3. Change the voltage to 5.0 volts, and click **Stimulate** again. Notice how the force of contraction also changes. Identify the latent, contraction, and relaxation phases in the tracings.

4. You may print your data by clicking **Tools → Print Data.** You may also print out hard copies of the graphs you generate by clicking on **Tools → Print Graph.**

Feel free to experiment with anything that comes to mind to get a sense of how whole muscle responds to an electrical stimulus. ▪

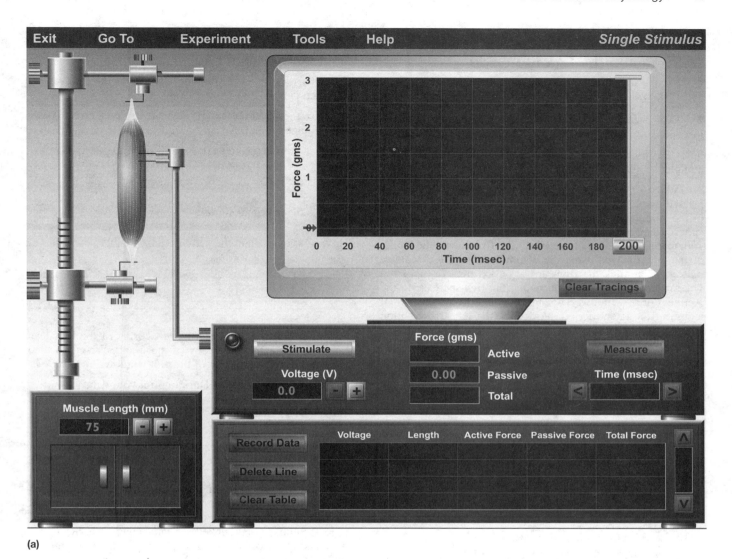

(a)

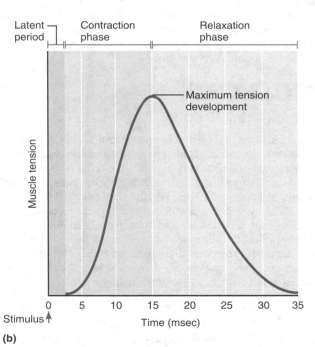

(b)

FIGURE 2.1 Single stimulus and muscle twitch.
(**a**) Opening screen of the Single Stimulus experiment. (**b**) The muscle twitch: myogram of an isometric twitch contraction.

Determining the Latent Period

1. Click **Clear Tracings** to erase the oscilloscope display. The voltage should be set to 5.0 volts.

2. Drag the **200** msec button to the right edge of the oscilloscope.

3. Click the **Stimulate** button once, and allow the tracing to complete.

4. When you measure the length of the latent period from a printed graph, you measure the time between the application of the stimulus and the beginning of the first observable response (increase in force). The computer can't "look ahead," anticipating the change in active force. To measure the length of the latent period using the computer, click the **Measure** button. Then click the right arrow button next to the **Time** window repeatedly until you notice the first increase in the Active Force window. This takes you beyond the actual length of the latent period. Now click the left arrow button next to the **Time** window until the Active Force window again reads zero. At this point the computer is measuring the time between the application of the stimulus and the last point where the active force is zero (just prior to contraction).

How long is the latent period? _____ msec

What occurs in the muscle during this apparent lack of activity?

_____

_____   ▪▪

The Graded Muscle Response to Increased Stimulus Intensity

As the stimulus to a muscle is increased, the amount of force produced by the muscle also increases. As more voltage is delivered to the whole muscle, more muscle fibers are activated and the total force produced by the muscle is increased. Maximal contraction occurs when all the muscle cells have been activated. Any stimulation beyond this voltage will not increase the force of contraction. This experiment mimics muscle activity in vivo where the recruitment of additional motor units increases the total force produced. This phenomenon is called *multiple motor unit summation* or *recruitment*.

Investigating Graded Muscle Response to Increased Stimulus Intensity

1. Click **Clear Tracings** if there are tracings on your screen.

2. Set the voltage to 0.0, and click **Stimulate.**

3. Click **Record Data.** If you decide to redo a single stimulus, choose the data line in the grid and click **Delete Line** to erase that single line of data. If you want to repeat the entire experiment, click the **Clear Table** button to erase all data recorded to that point.

4. Repeat steps 2 and 3, increasing the voltage by 0.5 each time until you reach the maximum voltage of 10.0. Be sure to select **Record Data** each time.

5. Observe the twitch tracings. Click on the **Tools** menu and then choose **Plot Data.**

6. Use the slider bars to display Active Force on the Y-axis and Voltage on the X-axis.

7. Use your graph to answer the following questions:

What is the minimal, or threshold, stimulus? _____ V

What is the maximal stimulus? _____ V

How can you explain the increase in force that you observe?

_____

_____

8. Click **Print Plot** at the top left corner of the Plot Data window to print a hard copy of the graph. When finished, click the X at the top right of the plot window.

9. Click **Tools → Print Data** to print your data. ▪▪

Multiple Stimulus

Choose **Multiple Stimulus** from the **Experiment** menu. The opening screen will appear in a few seconds (Figure 2.2).

The only significant change to the on-screen equipment is found in the electrical stimulator. The measuring equipment has been removed and other controls have been added: The **Multiple Stimulus** button is a toggle that allows you to alternately start and stop the electrical stimulator. When Multiple Stimulus is first clicked, its name changes to Stop Stimulus, and electrical stimuli are delivered to the muscle at the rate specified in the Stimuli/sec window until the muscle completely fatigues or the stimulator is turned off. The stimulator is turned off by clicking the **Stop Stimulus** button. The stimulus rate is adjusted by clicking the (+) or (−) buttons next to the Stimuli/sec window.

Investigating Treppe

When a muscle first contracts, the force it is able to produce is less than the force it is able to produce in subsequent contractions within a relatively narrow time span. A myogram, a recording of a muscle twitch, reveals this phenomenon as the **treppe,** or staircase, effect. For the first few twitches, each successive stimulation produces slightly more force than the previous contraction as long as the muscle is allowed to fully relax between stimuli, and the stimuli are delivered relatively close together. Treppe is thought to be caused by increased efficiency of the enzyme systems within the cell and increased availability of intracellular calcium.

1. The voltage should be set to 8.2 volts, and the muscle length should be 75 mm.

2. Drag the **200** msec button to the center of the X-axis time range.

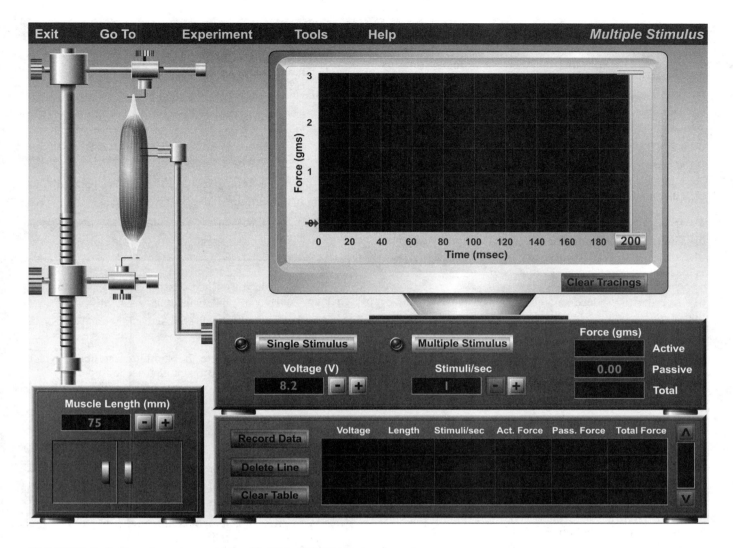

FIGURE 2.2 Opening screen of the Multiple Stimulus experiment.

3. Be sure that you fully understand the following three steps before you proceed.

- Click **Single Stimulus.** Watch the twitch tracing carefully.

- After the tracing shows that the muscle has completely relaxed, immediately click **Single Stimulus** again.

- When the second twitch completes, click **Single Stimulus** once more and allow the tracing to complete.

4. Click **Tools → Print Graph.**

What happens to force production with each subsequent stimulus?

_____

_____ ▬

A C T I V I T Y   5

Investigating Wave Summation

As demonstrated in Activity 3 with single stimuli, multiple motor unit summation is one way to increase the amount of force produced by muscle. Multiple motor unit summation relied on increased stimulus *intensity* in that simulation. Another way to increase force is by wave, or temporal, summation. **Wave summation** is achieved by increasing the stimulus *frequency,* or rate of stimulus delivery to the muscle. Wave summation occurs because the muscle is already in a partially contracted state when subsequent stimuli are delivered.

Tetanus can be considered an extreme form of wave summation that results in a steady, sustained contraction. In effect, the muscle does not have any chance to relax because it is being stimulated at such a high frequency. This fuses the force peaks so that we observe a smooth tracing.

1. Click **Clear Tracings** to erase the oscilloscope display.

2. Set and keep the voltage at the maximal stimulus (8.2 volts) and the muscle length at 75 mm.

3. Drag the **200** msec button to the right edge of the oscilloscope display unless you are using a slow computer.

4. Click **Single Stimulus,** and then click **Single Stimulus** again when the muscle has relaxed about halfway. Unlike the previous experiment, we will not allow the muscle to completely relax.

You may click **Tools → Print Graph** any time you want to print graphs generated during this activity.

Is the peak force produced in the second contraction greater

than that produced by the first stimulus? _____

5. Try stimulating again at greater frequencies by clicking the **Single Stimulus** button several times in rapid succession.

Is the total force production even greater? _____

6. In order to produce smooth, sustained muscle contraction at Active Force = 2 gms, do you think you will need to increase or decrease the voltage?

_____

_____

Change the voltage to test your hypothesis and try rapidly clicking **Single Stimulus** several times.

At what voltage were you able to achieve Active Force = 2 gms?

_____

_____

7. How does the frequency of stimulation affect the amount of force generated by the muscle? *Hint:* Compare the force generated from a single click and from rapidly clicking **Single Stimulus** several times.

_____

_____

_____

ACTIVITY 6

Investigating Fusion Frequency/Tetanus

1. Click **Clear Tracings** to erase the oscilloscope display.

2. The voltage should be set to 8.2 volts, and the muscle length should be 75 mm.

3. Adjust the stimulus rate to 30 stimuli/sec.

4. The following steps constitute a single "run." Become familiar with the procedure for completing a run before continuing.

- Click **Multiple Stimulus.**
- When the tracing is close to the right side of the screen, click **Stop Stimulus** to turn off the stimulator.
- Click **Record Data** to retain your data in the grid at the bottom of the screen and in the computer's memory. Click **Tools → Print Graph** to print a hard copy of your graph at any point during this activity.

If you decide to redo a single run, choose the data line in the grid and click **Delete Line** to erase that single line of data. If you want to repeat the entire experiment, click the **Clear Table** button to erase all data recorded thus far.

Describe the appearance of the tracing.

_____

_____

5. Repeat steps 3 and 4, increasing the stimulation rate by 10 stimuli/sec each time up to 150 stimuli/sec.

How do the tracings change as the stimulus rate is increased?

_____

6. When you have finished observing the twitch tracings, click the **Tools** menu, and then choose **Plot Data.**

7. Set the Y-axis slider to display Active Force and the X-axis slider to display Stimuli/sec.

From your graph, estimate the stimulus rate above which there appears to be no significant increase in force.

_____ stimuli/sec

This rate is the *fusion frequency,* also called tetanus.

8. Click **Print Plot** at the top left of the Plot Data window. When finished, click the X at the top right of the plot window.

9. Reset the stimulus rate to the fusion frequency identified in step 7.

10. Try to produce a smooth contraction at Force = 2 gms and Force = 3 gms by adjusting only the stimulus intensity, or voltage, using the following procedure.

- Decrease the voltage to a starting point of 1.0 volt, and click **Multiple Stimulus.**
- Click **Stop Stimulus** to turn off the stimulator when the tracing is near the right side of the oscilloscope display.
- If the force produced is not smooth and continuous at the desired level of force, increase the voltage in 0.1-volt increments and stimulate as above until you achieve a smooth force at 2 gms and again at 3 gms.

What stimulus intensity produced smooth force at Force = 2 gms?

_____ V

Which intensity produced smooth contraction at Force = 3 gms?

_____ V

Explain what must happen to the intensity and frequency of the stimulus to achieve smooth contraction at different force levels.

_____

_____

_____

_____

_____ ▬

Investigating Muscle Fatigue

A prolonged period of sustained contraction will result in **muscle fatigue,** a condition in which the tissue has lost its ability to contract. Fatigue results when a muscle cell's ATP consumption is faster than its production. Consequently, increasingly fewer ATP molecules are available for the contractile parts within the muscle cell.

1. Click **Clear Tracings** to erase the oscilloscope display.

2. The voltage should be set to 8.2 volts, and the muscle length should be 75 mm.

3. Adjust the stimulus rate to 120 stimuli/sec.

4. Click **Multiple Stimulus,** allow the tracing to sweep through three screens, and then click **Stop Stimulus** to stop the stimulator.

Click **Tools → Print Graph** at any time to print graphs during this activity. Click **Tools → Print Data** to print your data.

Why does the force begin to decrease with time? Note that a decrease in force indicates muscle fatigue.

_____

_____

5. Click **Clear Tracings** to erase the oscilloscope display. Keep the same settings as before.

6. You will be clicking **Multiple Stimulus** on and off three times to demonstrate fatigue with recovery. Read the steps below before proceeding.

- Click **Multiple Stimulus.**

- When the tracing reaches the middle of the screen, briefly turn off the stimulator by clicking **Stop Stimulus,** then immediately click **Multiple Stimulus** again.

- You will see a dip in the force tracing where you turned the stimulator off and then on again. The force tracing will continue to drop as the muscle fatigues.

- Before the muscle fatigues completely, repeat the on/off cycle twice more without clearing the screen.

   Turning the stimulator off allows a small measure of recovery. The muscle will produce force for a longer period if the stimulator is briefly turned off than if the stimulations were allowed to continue without interruption. Explain why.

_____

7. To see the difference between continuous multiple stimulation and multiple stimulation with recovery, click **Multiple Stimulus** and let the tracing fall without interruption to zero force. This tracing will follow the original myogram exactly until the first "dip" is encountered, after which you will notice a difference in the amount of force produced between the two runs.

Describe the difference between the current tracing and the myogram generated in step 6.

_____

_____

_____

_____

_____

_____

_____ ▬

Isometric Contraction

Isometric contraction is the condition in which muscle length does not change regardless of the amount of force generated by the muscle (_iso_ = same, _metric_ = length). This is accomplished experimentally by keeping both ends of the muscle in a fixed position while stimulating it electrically. Resting length (length of the muscle before contraction) is an important factor in determining the amount of force that a muscle can develop. **Passive force** is generated by stretching the muscle and is due to the elastic properties of the tissue itself. This passive force is largely due to the protein titin, which acts as a molecular bungee cord. **Active force** is generated by the physiological contraction of the muscle. Think of the muscle as having two force properties: it exerts passive force when it is stretched (like a rubber band exerts passive force) and active force when it contracts. Total force is the sum of passive and active forces, and it is what we experimentally measure.

   This simulation allows you to set the resting length of the experimental muscle and stimulate it with individual maximal stimulus shocks. A graph relating the forces generated to the length of the muscle will be automatically plotted as you stimulate the muscle. The results of this simulation can then be applied to human muscles in order to understand how optimum resting length will result in maximum force production. In order to understand why muscle tissue behaves as it does, it is necessary to comprehend contraction at the cellular level. _Hint:_ If you have difficulty understanding the results of this exercise, review the sliding filament model of muscle contraction. Then think in terms of sarcomeres that are too short, those that are too long, and those that have the ideal length-tension relationship.

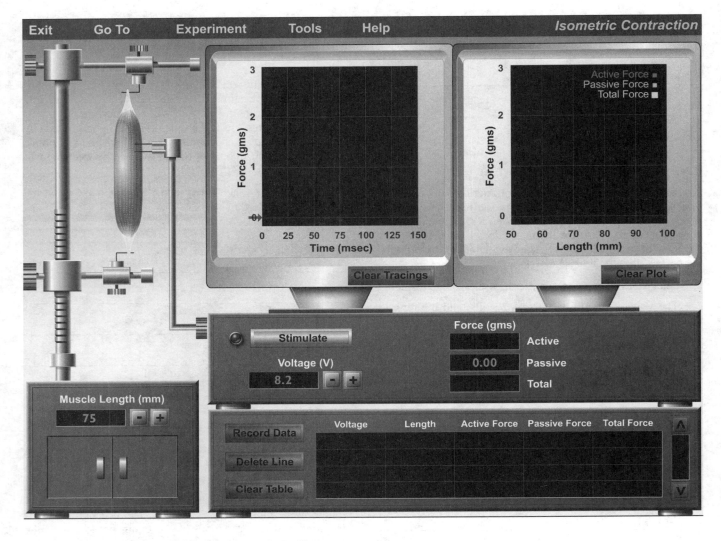

FIGURE 2.3 Opening screen of the Isometric Contraction experiment.

Choose **Isometric Contraction** from the **Experiment** menu. The opening screen will appear in a few seconds (Figure 2.3). Notice that the oscilloscope is now divided into two parts. The left side of the scope displays the muscle twitch tracing. The active, passive, and total force data points are plotted on the right side of the screen.

A C T I V I T Y   8

Investigating Isometric Contraction

1. The voltage should be set to the maximal stimulus (8.2 volts), and the muscle length should be 75 mm.

2. To see how the equipment works, stimulate once by clicking **Stimulate.** You should see a single muscle twitch tracing on the left oscilloscope display and three data points representing active, passive, and total force on the right display. The yellow box represents the total force and the red dot it contains symbolizes the superimposed active force. The green square represents the passive force data point.

3. Try adjusting the muscle length by clicking the (+) or (−) buttons located next to the Muscle Length window, and watch the effect on the muscle.

4. When you feel comfortable with the equipment, click **Clear Tracings** and **Clear Plot.**

5. Now stimulate at different muscle lengths using the following procedure.

-   Shorten the muscle to a length of 50 mm by clicking the (−) button next to the Muscle Length window.

-   Click **Stimulate** and, when the tracing is complete, click **Record Data.**

-   Repeat the **Stimulate** and **Record Data** sequence, increasing the muscle length by 2 mm each time until you reach the maximum muscle length of 100 mm.

6. Carefully examine the active, passive, and total force plots in the right oscilloscope display.

7. Click **Tools → Print Data** to print your data.

What happens to the passive and active forces as the muscle length is increased from 50 mm to 100 mm?

Passive force:

_____

_____

_____

Active force:

_____

_____

_____

Total force:

_____

_____

Explain the dip in the total force curve. (*Hint:* Keep in mind you are measuring the sum of active and passive forces.)

_____

_____

_____

_____

_____

Isotonic Contraction

During **isotonic contraction,** muscle length changes, but the force produced stays the same (*iso* = same, *tonic* = force). Unlike the isometric exercise in which both ends of the muscle are held in a fixed position, one end of the muscle remains free in the isotonic contraction exercise. Different weights can then be attached to the free end while the other end is fixed in position on the force transducer. If the weight is not too great, the muscle will be able to lift it with a certain velocity. You can think of lifting an object from the floor as an example: if the object is light it can be lifted quickly (high velocity), whereas a heavier weight will be lifted with a slower velocity. Try to transfer the idea of what is happening in the simulation to the muscles of your arm when you lift a weight. The two important variables in this exercise are starting length of the muscle and resistance (weight) applied. You have already examined the effect of starting length on muscle force production in the previous exercise. Now you will change both muscle length and resistance to investigate how such changes affect the speed of skeletal muscle shortening. Both variables can be independently altered, and the results are graphically presented on the screen.

Choose **Isotonic Contraction** from the **Experiment** menu. The opening screen will appear in a few seconds (Figure 2.4). The general operation of the equipment is the same as in the previous experiments. In this simulation, the weight cabinet doors are open. You will attach weights to the lower tendon of the muscle by clicking and holding the mouse on any weight in the cabinet and then dragging-and-dropping the

weight's hook onto the lower tendon. The Muscle Length window displays the length achieved when the muscle is stretched by hanging a weight from its lower tendon. You can click the (+) and (−) buttons next to the Platform Height window to change the position of the platform on which the weight rests. Click on the weight again to automatically return it to the weight cabinet. The electrical stimulator displays the initial velocity of muscle shortening in the Velocity window to the right of the Voltage control.

A C T I V I T Y   9

Investigating the Effect of Load on Skeletal Muscle

1. Set the voltage to the maximal stimulus (8.2 volts).

2. Drag-and-drop the 0.5-g weight onto the muscle's lower tendon.

3. Platform height should be 75 mm.

4. Click **Stimulate** and simultaneously watch the muscle action and the oscilloscope tracing.

5. Click the **Record Data** button to retain and display the data in the grid.

What do you see happening to the muscle during the flat part of the tracing? Click **Stimulate** to repeat if you wish to see the muscle action again.

_____

_____

Does the force the muscle produces change during the flat part of the tracing (increase, decrease, or stay the same)?

_____

6. Return the 0.5-g weight to the cabinet. Drag the 1.5-g weight to the muscle. Click **Stimulate,** and then click **Record Data.**

Which of the two weights used so far results in the highest initial velocity of shortening?

Weight _____ g

Velocity _____ mm/sec

7. Repeat step 6 for the remaining two weights.

Weight _____ g

Velocity _____ mm/sec

Weight _____ g

Velocity _____ mm/sec

8. Choose **Plot Data** from the **Tools** menu.

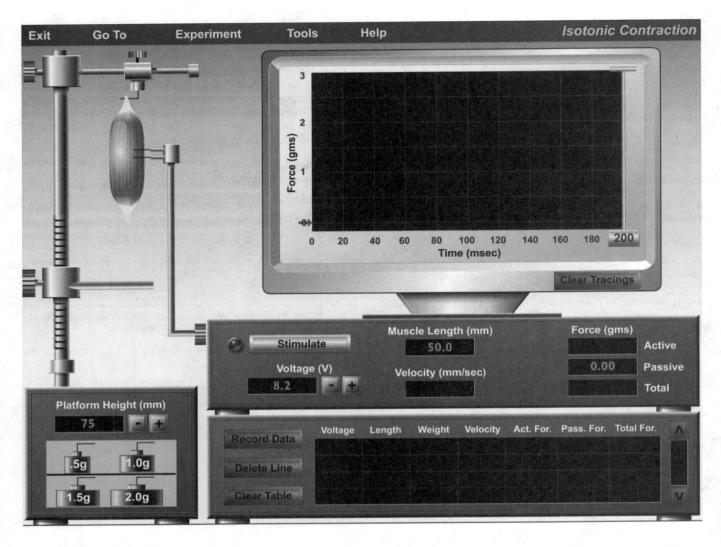

FIGURE 2.4 Opening screen of the Isotonic Contraction experiment.

9. Set Weight as the X-axis and Total Force as the Y-axis by dragging the slider bars. Click **Print Plot** if you wish to print the graph.

What does the plot reveal about the relationship between resistance and the initial velocity of shortening?

_____

_____

_____

10. Close the plot window. If you wish, click **Tools → Print Data** to print your data.

11. Click **Clear Table** in the data control unit at the bottom of the screen. Click **Yes** when you are asked if you want to erase all data in the table.

12. Return the current weight to the weight cabinet.

13. Attach the 1.5-g weight to the muscle and run through the range of starting lengths from 60–90 mm in 5-mm increments. Be sure to click **Record Data** after each stimulus.

14. After all runs have been completed, choose **Plot Data** from the **Tools** menu.

15. Set Length as the X-axis and Velocity as the Y-axis by dragging the slider bars. Click **Print Plot** if you wish to print the graph.

Describe the relationship between starting length and initial velocity of shortening.

_____

_____

_____

_____

Histology Review Supplement

For a review of skeletal muscle tissue, go to **Exercise H: Histology Atlas and Review** on the **PhysioEx website** to print out the **Skeletal Muscle Tissue Review** worksheet.

NAME _____

LAB TIME/DATE _____

Skeletal Muscle Physiology

Electrical Stimulation

1. Name each phase of a typical muscle twitch, and, on the following line, describe what is happening in each phase.

   a. _____

   _____

   b. _____

   _____

   c. _____

   _____

2. In Activity 2, how long was the latent period? _____ msec

   Describe the chemical changes that are occurring during this period. _____

   _____

   _____

The Graded Muscle Response to Increased Stimulus Intensity

3. From Activity 3, describe the effect of increasing the voltage. What happened to the force generated and why did this change

   occur? _____

   _____

   _____

4. How does this change occur in vivo? _____

   _____

   _____

5. In Activity 4, you looked at the effect of stimulating the muscle multiple times in a short period with complete relaxation between the stimuli.

Describe the force of contraction with each subsequent stimulus. _____

_____

_____

6. Describe the chemical changes that are thought to correlate to this change in vivo.

_____

_____

7. In Activity 5, what was the effect of increasing the frequency of stimulation?

_____

_____

8. Compare and contrast wave summation with recruitment (multiple motor unit summation). How are they similar? How was each achieved in the simulation?

_____

_____

_____

9. Explain how wave summation and recruitment are achieved in vivo.

_____

_____

10. For Activity 6, explain how you were able to achieve smooth contraction at a given force level. _____

_____

11. In Activity 7, explain why the force of the muscle decreased over time during uninterrupted stimulation. Describe the

multiple causes of this phenomenon, which occurs in vivo with prolonged use of a muscle. _____

_____

_____

Isometric Contraction

12. In Activity 8, at what length of the muscle does the passive force start to increase?

_____

13. Explain what happens to the active force with an increase in the muscle length.

_____

14. Explain what happens to the active force with a decrease in the muscle length.

_____

15. Explain what is happening in the sarcomere that results in the changes in total force when the muscle length changes. _____

_____

Isotonic Contraction

16. In Activity 9, which weight resulted in the highest initial velocity of shortening? _____

17. Explain the relationship between the amount of resistance and the initial velocity of shortening.

_____

18. Explain why it will take you longer to perform 10 repetitions lifting a 20-pound weight than it would to perform the same

number of repetitions with a 5-pound weight. _____

_____

Neurophysiology of Nerve Impulses

OBJECTIVES

1. To define the following terms: *irritability, conductivity, resting membrane potential, polarized, sodium-potassium pump, threshold stimulus, depolarization, action potential, repolarization, hyperpolarization, absolute refractory period, relative refractory period, nerve impulse, compound nerve action potential,* and *conduction velocity.*
2. To list at least four different stimuli capable of generating an action potential.
3. To list at least two agents capable of inhibiting an action potential.
4. To describe the relationship between nerve size and conduction velocity.
5. To describe the relationship between nerve myelination and conduction velocity.

Neurons have two major physiological properties: **excitability,** or the ability to respond to stimuli and convert them into nerve impulses, and **conductivity,** the ability to transmit an impulse (in this case, to take the neural impulse and pass it along the cell membrane). In the resting neuron (that is, a neuron that does not have any neural impulses), the exterior of the cell membrane is positively charged and the interior is negatively charged relative to the outside. This difference in electrical charge across the plasma membrane is referred to as the **resting membrane potential,** and the membrane is said to be **polarized.** The **sodium-potassium pump** in the membrane maintains the difference in electrical charge established by diffusion of ions. This active transport mechanism moves 3 sodium ions (Na^+) out of the cell while moving in 2 potassium ions (K^+). Therefore, the major cation (positively charged ion) outside the cell in the extracellular fluid is Na^+, and the major cation inside the cell is K^+. The inner surface of the cell membrane is more negative than the outer surface, mainly due to intracellular proteins, which, at body pH, tend to be negatively charged.

The resting membrane potential can be measured with a voltmeter by putting a recording electrode just inside the cell membrane with a reference, or ground,

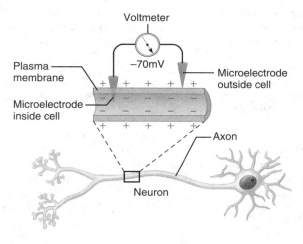

FIGURE 3.1 Resting membrane potential is measured with a voltmeter.

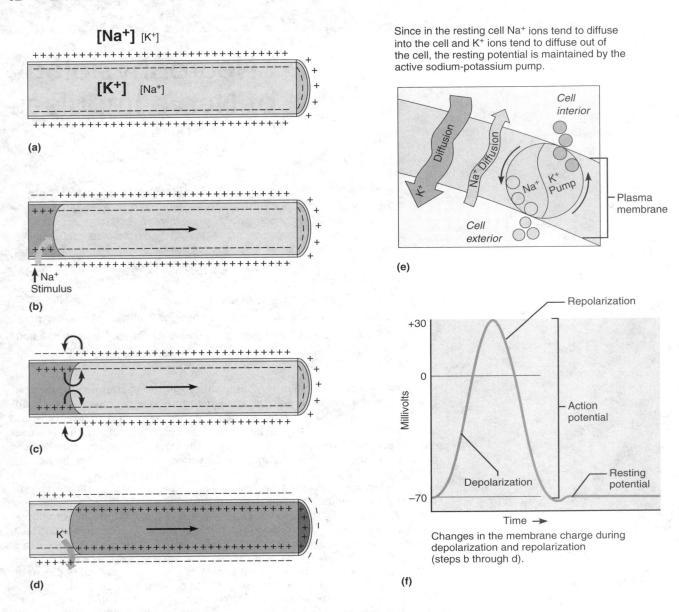

FIGURE 3.2 The nerve impulse. (a) Resting membrane potential (-70 mV). There is an excess of positive ions outside the cell, with Na$^+$ the predominant ion in extracellular fluid and K$^+$ the predominant intracellular ion. The plasma membrane has a low permeability to Na$^+$. **(b)** Depolarization—reversal of the resting potential. Application of a stimulus changes the membrane permeability, and Na$^+$ ions are allowed to diffuse rapidly into the cell. **(c)** Generation of the action potential or nerve impulse. If the stimulus is of adequate intensity, the depolarization wave spreads rapidly along the entire length of the membrane. **(d)** Repolarization—reestablishment of the resting potential. The negative charge on the internal plasma membrane surface and the positive charge on its external surface are reestablished by diffusion of K$^+$ out of the cell, proceeding in the same direction as in depolarization. **(e)** The original ionic concentrations of the resting state are restored by the sodium-potassium pump. **(f)** A tracing of an action potential.

electrode outside the membrane (see Figure 3.1). In the giant squid axon (on which most early neural research was conducted), or in the frog axon that will be used in this exercise, the resting membrane potential is measured at -70 millivolts (mV). (In humans, the resting membrane potential typically measures between -40 mV and -90mV.)

The Nerve Impulse

When a neuron is activated by a stimulus of adequate intensity, known as a **threshold stimulus,** the membrane at its *trigger zone,* typically the axon hillock, briefly becomes more permeable to Na$^+$ ions (sodium ion channels in the cell membrane open). Na$^+$ rushes into the cell, increasing the number of positive ions inside the cell and changing the membrane polarity. The interior surface of the membrane becomes less negative and the exterior surface becomes less positive, a phenomenon called **depolarization** (see Figure 3.2b). When depolarization reaches a certain point called **threshold,** an **action potential** is initiated (see Figure 3.2c) and the polarity of the membrane reverses.

When the membrane depolarizes, the resting membrane potential of -70 mV becomes less negative. When the membrane potential reaches 0 mV, indicating there is no charge difference across the membrane, the sodium ion channels start to close and potassium ion channels open. By the time the sodium ion channels finally close, the membrane potential has reached $+35$ mV. The opening of the potassium ion channels allows K^+ to flow out of the cell down its electrochemical gradient—remember, ions of like charge are repelled from each other. The flow of K^+ out of the cell causes the membrane potential to move in a negative direction. This is referred to as **repolarization** (see Figure 3.2d). This repolarization occurs within a millisecond of the initial sodium influx and reestablishes the resting membrane potential. Actually, by the time the potassium ion channels close, the cell membrane has undergone a **hyperpolarization,** slipping to perhaps -75 mV. With the channels closed, the membrane potential is quickly returned to the normal resting membrane potential.

When the sodium ion channels are open, the membrane is totally insensitive to additional stimuli, regardless of the force of stimulus. The cell is in what is called the **absolute refractory period.** During repolarization, the membrane may be stimulated if a very strong stimulus is used. This period is called the **relative refractory period.**

The action potential, once started, is self-propagating, spreading rapidly along the neuron membrane. The action potential is a *phenomenon, all-or-none,* in which the neuron membrane either depolarizes to threshold and the action potential is generated, or it does not. In neurons, the action potential is also called a **nerve impulse.** When it reaches the axon terminal, it triggers the release of neurotransmitters into the synaptic cleft. Depending on the situation, the neurotransmitter will either excite or inhibit the postsynaptic neuron.

In order to study nerve physiology, we will use a frog nerve and several electronic instruments. The first instrument is the *electronic stimulator*. Nerves can be stimulated by chemicals, touch, or electric shock. The electronic stimulator administers an electric shock that is pure direct current (DC), and allows duration, frequency, and voltage of the shock to be precisely controlled. The stimulator has two output terminals; the positive terminal is red and the negative terminal is black. Voltage leaves the stimulator via the red terminal, passes through the item to be stimulated (in this case, the nerve), and returns to the stimulator at the black terminal to complete the circuit.

The second instrument is the **oscilloscope,** an instrument that measures voltage changes over a period of time. The face of the oscilloscope is similar to a black-and-white television screen. The screen of the oscilloscope is the front of a tube with a filament at the other end. The filament is heated and gives off a beam of electrons that passes to the front of the tube. Electronic circuitry allows the electron beam to be brought across the screen in preset time intervals. When the electrons hit the phosphorescent material on the inside of the screen, a spot on the screen will glow. When we apply a stimulus to a nerve, the oscilloscope screen will display one of the following three results: no response, a flat line, or a graph with a peak. A graph with a peak indicates that an action potential has been generated.

While performing the following experiments, keep in mind that you are working with a nerve, which consists of many neurons—you are not working with just a single neuron. The action potential you will see on the oscilloscope screen reflects the cumulative action potentials of all the neurons in the nerve, called a **compound nerve action potential.** Although an action potential follows the all-or-none law within a single neuron, it does not necessarily follow this law within an entire nerve. When you electrically stimulate a nerve at a given voltage, the stimulus may result in the depolarization of most of the neurons but not necessarily all of them. To achieve depolarization of *all* of the neurons, a higher stimulus voltage may be needed.

Eliciting (Generating) a Nerve Impulse

In the following experiments, you will investigate what kinds of stimuli trigger an action potential. To begin, select **Exercise 3: Neurophysiology of Nerve Impulses** from the drop-down menu and click **GO.** Before you perform the activities, watch the **Nerve Impulses** video to see how ambient activitiy is measured. Then click **Eliciting a Nerve Impulse.** The opening screen will appear in a few seconds (see Figure 3.3). Note that a sciatic nerve from a frog has been placed into the nerve chamber. Leads go from the stimulator output to the nerve chamber, the vertical box on the left side. Leads also go from the nerve chamber to the oscilloscope. Notice that these leads are red and black. The current travels along the red lead to the nerve. When the nerve depolarizes, it will generate an electrical current that will travel along the red wire to the oscilloscope and back to the nerve along the black wire.

ACTIVITY 1

Electrical Stimulation

1. Set the voltage at 1.0 V by clicking the $(+)$ button next to the **Voltage** display.

2. Click **Single Stimulus.**

Do you see any kind of response on the oscilloscope screen? _____

If you saw no response, or a flat line indicating no action potential, click the **Clear** button on the oscilloscope, increase the voltage, and click **Single Stimulus** again until you see a trace (deflection of the line) that indicates an action potential.

What was the *threshold voltage,* that is, the voltage at which you first saw an action potential? _____ V

Click **Record Data** on the data collection box to record your results.

3. If you wish to print your graph, click **Tools** and then **Print Graph.** You may do this each time you generate a graph on the oscilloscope screen.

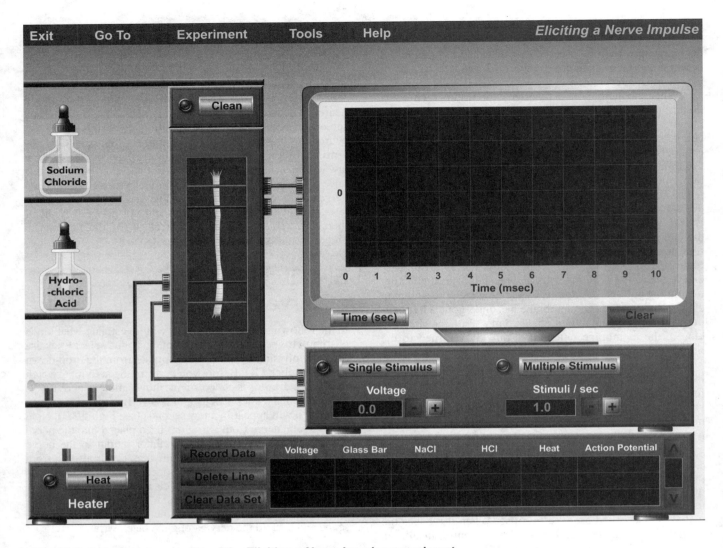

FIGURE 3.3 Opening screen of the Eliciting a Nerve Impulse experiment.

4. Increase the voltage by 0.5 V, and click **Single Stimulus.**

How does this tracing compare to the one trace that was generated at the threshold voltage? (Hint: Look very carefully at the tracings.)

_____

_____

What reason can you give for the change?

_____

_____

_____

Click **Record Data** on the data collection box to record your results.

5. Continue to increase the voltage by 0.5 V and to click **Single Stimulus** until you find the point beyond which no further increase occurs in the peak of the action potential trace.

Record this maximal voltage here: _____ V

Click **Record Data** to record your results. ▬▬▬

Now that we have seen that an electrical impulse can cause an action potential, let's try some other methods of stimulating a nerve.

Mechanical Stimulation

1. Click the **Clear** button on the oscilloscope.

2. Using the mouse, click the glass rod located on the bottom shelf on the left side of the screen, and drag it over to the nerve. When the glass rod is over the nerve, release the

mouse button to indicate that the rod is now touching the nerve. What do you see on the oscilloscope screen?

_____

How does this tracing compare with the other tracings that you have generated?

_____

_____

Click **Record Data** to record your results. Leave the graph on the screen so that you can compare it to the graph you will generate in the next activity. ▰

ACTIVITY 3

Thermal Stimulation

Click on the glass rod and drag it to the heater, releasing the mouse button. Click on the **Heat** button. When the rod turns red, indicating that it has been heated, click and drag the rod over the nerve and release the mouse button. What happens?

_____

_____

How does this trace compare to the trace that was generated with the unheated glass rod?

_____

_____

What explanation can you provide for this?

_____

_____

Click **Record Data** to record your results. Then click **Clear** to clear the oscilloscope screen for the next activity. ▰

ACTIVITY 4

Chemical Stimulation

1. Click and drag the dropper from the bottle of sodium chloride (salt solution) over to the nerve in the chamber and then release the mouse button to dispense drops.

Does this generate an action potential? _____

2. Look back at Activity 1 for the voltage you determined. Set the voltage at that level, and click **Single Stimulus** to stimulate the nerve.

Does this tracing differ from the original threshold stimulus

tracing?_____

Click **Record Data** to record your results.

3. Click the **Clean** button on top of the nerve chamber. This will return the nerve to its original (nonsalted) state. Click **Clear** to clear the oscilloscope screen.

4. Click and drag the dropper from the bottle of hydrochloric acid over to the nerve, and release the mouse button to dispense drops.

Does this generate an action potential?_____

Does this tracing differ from the one generated by the original

threshold stimulus? _____

Click **Record Data** to record your results.

5. Click on the **Clean** button on the nerve chamber to clean the chamber and return the nerve to its untouched state.

6. Click **Tools** → **Print Data** to print the data you have recorded for this experiment.

To summarize your experimental results, what kinds of stimuli can elicit an action potential?

_____

_____

_____ ▰

Inhibiting a Nerve Impulse

Numerous physical factors and chemical agents can impair the ability of nerve fibers to function. For example, deep pressure and cold temperature both block nerve impulse transmission by preventing local blood supply from reaching the nerve fibers. Local anesthetics, alcohol, and numerous other chemicals are also effective in blocking nerve transmission. In this experiment, we will study the effects of various agents on nerve transmission.

To begin, click the **Experiment** menu and select **Inhibiting a Nerve Impulse.** The display screen for this activity (Figure 3.4) is similar to the screen in the first activity. To the left are bottles of several agents that we will test on the nerve. Keep the tracings you printed out from the first activity close at hand for comparison.

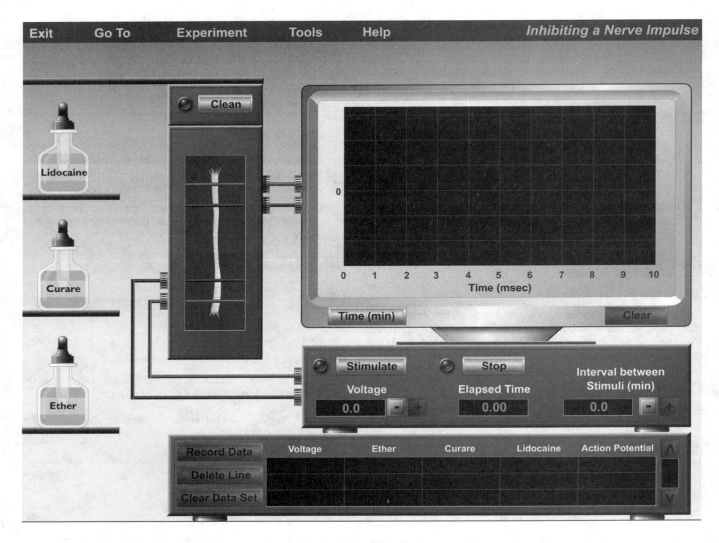

FIGURE 3.4 Opening screen of the Inhibiting a Nerve Impulse experiment.

ACTIVITY 5

Testing the Effects of Ether

1.   Using the mouse, click and drag the dropper from the bottle of ether over to the nerve in between the stimulating electrodes and recording electrodes. Release the mouse button to dispense drops.

2.   Look back at Activity 1 for the voltage you determined. Set the voltage at that level, and click **Single Stimulus** to stimulate the nerve. What sort of trace do you see?

_____

_____

What has happened to the nerve? _____

_____

Click **Record Data** to record your results.

3.   Click on the **Time (min)** button on the oscilloscope. This button toggles the time scale between minutes and milliseconds. The screen will now display activity over the course of 10 minutes (the space between each vertical line representing 1 minute). Because of the change in time scale, an action potential will look like a sharp vertical spike on the screen.

4.   Click the (+) button under **Interval between Stimuli** on the stimulator until the timer is set for 2.0 minutes. This will set the stimulus to stimulate the nerve every two minutes. Click on **Stimulate** to start the stimulations. Watch the **Elapsed Time** display. With the change in time scale, the action potential will look like a straight vertical line.

How long does it take for the nerve to return to normal?

_____

5.   Click on the **Stop** button to stop this action and to return the Elapsed Time to 0.0.

6. Click the **Time (msec)** button on the oscilloscope to return it to its normal millisecond display.

7. Click **Clear** to clear the oscilloscope for the next activity.

8. Click the (−) button under **Interval between Stimuli** until it is reset to 0.00. ▆▆

Testing the Effects of Curare

Curare is a well-known plant extract that South American Indians used to paralyze their prey. It is an alpha-toxin that binds to acetylcholine binding sites on the postsynaptic cell membrane, which will prevent the acetylcholine from acting. Curare blocks synaptic transmission by preventing the flow of neural impulses from neuron to neuron.

1. Click and drag the dropper from the bottle of curare and position the dropper on the nerve in between the stimulating and recording electrodes. Release the mouse button to dispense drops.

2. Look back at Activity 1 for the voltage you determined. Set the voltage at that level, and click Single Stimulus to stimulate the nerve. Does this generate an action potential?

_____

What explains this effect?_____

What do you think would be the overall effect of curare on the organism?

_____

_____

Click **Record Data** to record your results.

3. Click on the **Clean** button on the nerve chamber to remove the curare and return the nerve to its original untouched state.

4. Click **Clear** to clear the oscilloscope screen for the next activity. ▆▆

Testing the Effects of Lidocaine

Note: Lidocaine is a sodium-channel antagonist that prevents sodium channels from opening.

1. Click and drag the dropper from the bottle of lidocaine and position it over the nerve between the stimulating and recording electrodes. Release the mouse button to dispense drops. Does this generate a trace?

_____

2. Look back at Activity 1 for the voltage you determined. Set the voltage at that level, and click **Single Stimulus** to stimulate the nerve. What sort of tracing is seen?

_____

Why does lidocaine have this effect on nerve fiber transmission?

_____

_____

Click **Record Data** to record your results. Click **Tools →
Print Data** if you wish to print your data.

3. Click on the **Clean** button on the nerve chamber to remove the lidocaine and return the nerve to its original untouched state. ▆▆

Nerve Conduction Velocity

As has been pointed out, one of the major physiological properties of neurons is conductivity: the ability to transmit the nerve impulse to other neurons, muscles, or glands. The nerve impulse, or propagated action potential, occurs when Na^+ floods into the neuron, causing the membrane to depolarize. Although this event is spoken of in electrical terms, and is measured using instruments that measure electrical events, the **conduction velocity,** that is, the velocity of the action potential along a neural membrane, does not occur at the speed of light. Rather, this event is much slower. In certain nerves in the human, the velocity of an action potential may be as fast as 120 meters per second. In other nerves, conduction speed is much slower, occurring at a speed of less than 3 meters per second.

To see the setup for this experiment, click the **Experiment** menu and select **Nerve Conduction Velocity** (Figure 3.5). In this exercise, the oscilloscope and stimulator will be used along with a third instrument, the bio-amplifier. The **bio-amplifier** is used to amplify any membrane depolarization so that the oscilloscope can easily record the event. Normally, when a membrane depolarization sufficient to initiate an action potential is looked at, the interior of the cell membrane goes from −70 mV to about +40 mV. This is easily registered and viewable on an oscilloscope without the aid of an amplifier. However, in this experiment, it is the change in the membrane potential on the *outside* of the nerve that is being observed. The change that occurs here during depolarization will be so minuscule that it must be amplified in order to be visible on the oscilloscope.

A nerve chamber (similar to the one used in the previous two experiments) will be used. The design is basically a plastic box with platinum electrodes running across it. The nerve will be laid on these electrodes. Two electrodes will be used to bring the impulse from the stimulator to the nerve and three will be used for recording the membrane depolarization.

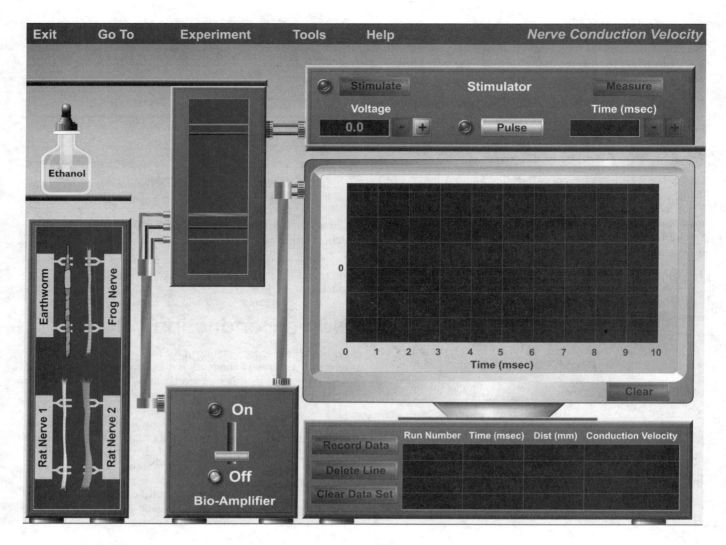

FIGURE 3.5 Opening screen of the Nerve Conduction Velocity experiment.

In this experiment, we will determine and compare the conduction velocities of different types of nerves. We will examine four nerves: an earthworm nerve, a frog nerve, and two rat nerves. The earthworm nerve is the smallest of the four. The frog nerve is a medium-sized myelinated nerve. Rat nerve 1 is a medium-sized unmyelinated nerve. Rat nerve 2 is a large, myelinated nerve—the largest nerve in this group. We will observe the effects of size and myelination on nerve conductivity.

The basic layout of the materials is shown in Figure 18B.5. The two wires (red and black) from the stimulator connect with the top right side of the nerve chamber. Three recording wires (red, black, and a bare wire cable) are attached to connectors on the other end of the nerve chamber and go to the bio-amplifier. The bare cable serves as a ground reference for the electrical circuit and provides the reference for comparison of any change in membrane potential. The bio-amplifier is connected to the oscilloscope so that any amplified membrane changes can be observed. The

stimulator output, called the *pulse,* has been connected to the oscilloscope so that when the nerve is stimulated, the tracing will start across the oscilloscope screen. Thus, the time from the start of the trace on the left side of the screen (when the nerve was stimulated) to the actual nerve deflection (from the recording electrodes) can be accurately measured. This amount of time, usually in milliseconds, is critical for determining conduction velocity.

ACTIVITY 8

Measuring Nerve Conduction Velocity

1. On the stimulator, click the **Pulse** button.

2. Turn the bio-amplifier on by clicking the horizontal bar on the bio-amplifier and dragging it to the **On** setting.

On the left side of the screen are the four nerves that will be studied. The nerves included are the earthworm, a frog nerve, and two rat nerves of different sizes. The earthworm as a whole is used because it has a nerve running down its ventral surface. A frog nerve is used as the frog has long been the animal of choice in many physiology laboratories. The rat nerves are used so that you may compare (a) the conduction velocity of different sized nerves and (b) the conduction velocity of a myelinated versus unmyelinated nerve. Remember that the frog nerve is myelinated and that rat nerve 1 is the same size as the frog nerve but unmyelinated. Rat nerve 2, the largest nerve of the bunch, is myelinated.

3. Using the mouse, click and drag the dropper from the bottle of ethanol over the earthworm and release the mouse button to dispense drops of ethanol. This will narcotize the worm so it does not move around during the experiment but will not affect nerve conduction velocity. The alcohol is at a low enough percentage that the worm will be fine and back to normal within 15 minutes.

4. Click and drag the earthworm into the nerve chamber. Be sure the worm is over both of the stimulating electrodes and all three of the recording electrodes.

5. Using the (+) button next to the **Voltage** display, set the voltage to 1.0 V. Then click **Stimulate** to stimulate the nerve. Do you see an action potential? If not, increase the voltage by increments of 1.0 V until a trace is obtained.

At what threshold voltage do you first see an action potential

generated? _____ V

6. Next, click on the **Measure** button located on the stimulator. You will see a vertical yellow line appear on the far left edge of the oscilloscope screen. Now click the (+) button under the Measure button. This will move the yellow line to the right. This line lets you measure how much time has elapsed on the graph at the point that the line is crossing the graph. You will see the elapsed time appear on the **Time (msec)** display on the stimulator. Keep clicking (+) until the yellow line is exactly at the point in the graph where the graph ceases being a flat line and first starts to rise.

7. Once you have the yellow line positioned at the start of the graph's ascent, note the time elapsed at this point. Click **Record Data** to record the elapsed time on the data collection graph. PhysioEx will automatically compute the conduction velocity based on this data. Note that the data collection box includes a **Distance (mm)** column and that the distance is always 43 mm. This is the distance from the red stimulating wire to the red recording wire. In a wet lab, you would have to measure the distance yourself before you could proceed with calculating the conduction velocity.

It is important that you have the yellow vertical measuring line positioned at the start of the graph's rise before you click **Record Data**—otherwise, the conduction velocity calculated for the nerve will be inaccurate.

8. Fill in the data in the Earthworm column on Chart 1.

9. Click and drag the earthworm to its original place. Click **Clear** to clear the oscilloscope screen.

10. Repeat steps 4 through 9 for the remaining nerves. Remember to click **Record Data** after each experimental run and to fill in the chart for question 8.

11. Click **Tools** → **Print Data** to print your data.

CHART 1				
Nerve	Earthworm (small nerve)	Frog (medium nerve, myelinated)	Rat nerve 1 (medium nerve, unmyelinated)	Rat nerve 2 (large nerve, myelinated)
Threshold voltage				
Elapsed time from stimulation to action potential				
Conduction velocity				

Which nerve in the group has the slowest conduction velocity?

_____

_____

What was the speed of the nerve? _____

Which nerve in the group of four has the fastest conduction velocity?

_____

_____

What was the speed of the nerve? _____

What is the relationship between nerve size and conduction

velocity? _____

_____

_____

_____

Based on the results, what is your conclusion regarding conduction velocity and whether the nerve is myelinated or not?

_____

_____

_____

_____

What is the major reason for the differences seen in conduction velocity between the myelinated nerves and the

unmyelinated nerves? _____

_____

_____

_____

Histology Review Supplement

For a review of nervous tissue, go to **Exercise H: Histology Atlas and Review** on the **PhysioEx website** to print out the **Nervous Tissue Review** worksheet.

NAME _____

LAB TIME/DATE _____

Neurophysiology of Nerve Impulses

Eliciting (Generating) a Nerve Impulse

1. Why don't the terms *depolarization* and *action potential* mean the same thing?

   _____

   _____

   _____

2. What was the threshold voltage in Activity 1? _____

3. What was the effect of increasing the voltage? How does this change correlate to changes in the nerve?_____

   _____

   _____

4. How did the action potential generated with the unheated rod compare to that generated with the heated rod? _____

   _____

5. Describe the types of stimuli that generated an action potential._____

   _____

   _____

6. If you were to spend a lot of time studying nerve physiology in the laboratory, what type of stimulus would you use and why?

   _____

   _____

   _____

7. Why does the addition of sodium chloride elicit an action potential? Hint: Think about the sodium permeability of the neuron

   (Figure 3.2e)._____

   _____

   _____

Inhibiting a Nerve Impulse

8. What was the effect of ether on eliciting an action potential? _____

_____

9. Does the addition of ether to the nerve cause any permanent alteration in neural response?

_____

10. What was the effect of curare on eliciting an action potential?

_____

11. Explain the reason for your answer to question 10 above.

_____

12. What was the effect of lidocaine on eliciting an action potential?

_____

Nerve Conduction Velocity

13. What is the relationship between size of the nerve and conduction velocity? _____

_____

_____

14. Keeping your answer to question 13 in mind, how might you draw an analogy between the nerves in the human body and electrical wires?

_____

15. How does myelination affect nerve conduction velocity? Explain, using your data from Chart 1. _____

_____

_____

_____

16. If any of the nerves used were reversed in their placement on the stimulating and recording electrodes, would any differences be seen in conduction velocity? Explain.

_____

_____

_____

Endocrine System Physiology

The endocrine system exerts many complex and interrelated effects on the body as a whole, as well as on specific tissues and organs. Studying the effects of hormones on the body is difficult to do in a wet lab because experiments often take days, weeks, or even months to complete and are expensive. In addition, live animals may need to be sacrificed, and technically difficult surgical procedures are sometimes necessary. This computer simulation allows you to study the effects of given hormones on the body by using "virtual" animals rather than live ones. You can carry out delicate surgical techniques with the click of a button and complete experiments in a fraction of the time that it would take in an actual wet lab environment.

Hormones and Metabolism

Metabolism is the broad term used for all biochemical reactions occurring in the body. Metabolism involves *catabolism,* a process by which complex materials are broken down into simpler substances, usually with the aid of enzymes found in the body cells. Metabolism also involves *anabolism,* in which the smaller materials are built up by enzymes into larger, more complex molecules. When larger molecules are made, energy is stored in the various bonds formed. When bonds are broken in catabolism, energy that was stored in the bonds is released for use by the cell. Some of the energy liberated may go into the formation of ATP, the energy-rich material used by the body to run itself. However, not all of the energy liberated goes into this pathway; some is given off as body heat. Humans are *homeothermic* animals, meaning they have a fixed body temperature. Maintaining this temperature is important to maintaining the metabolic pathways found in the body.

The most important hormone in maintaining metabolism and body heat is *thyroxine,* the hormone of the thyroid gland, which is found in the neck. The thyroid gland secretes thyroxine, but the production of thyroxine is really controlled by the pituitary gland, which secretes *thyroid-stimulating hormone (TSH).* TSH is carried by the blood to the thyroid gland (its *target tissue*) and causes the thyroid to produce more thyroxine. So in an indirect way, an animal's metabolic rate is the result of pituitary hormones.

In the following experiments, you will investigate the effects of thyroxine and TSH on an animal's metabolic rate (see Figure 4.1b). To begin, select **Exercise 4: Endocrine System Physiology** from the drop-down menu and click **GO.** Before you perform the activities, watch the **BMR Measurement** video to see an

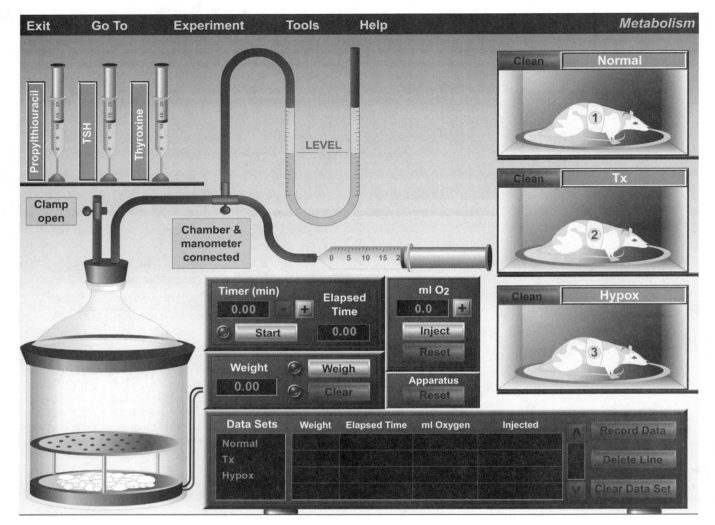

(a)

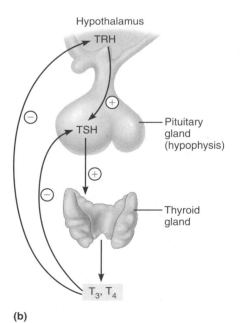

(b)

FIGURE 4.1 Metabolism and the thyroid gland. (**a**) Opening screen of the Metabolism experiment. (**b**) The regulation of thyroid secretion. + indicates stimulation of release, − indicates inhibition of release, T_3 = triiodothyronine, T_4 = thyroxine, TRH = thyrotropin-releasing hormone, TSH = thyroid-stimulating hormone.

experiment in which basal metabolic rate is measured. Then click **Metabolism.** The opening screen will appear in a few seconds (see Figure 4.1a). Select **Balloons On/Off** from the **Help** menu for help identifying the equipment on-screen (you will see labels appear as you roll the mouse over each piece of equipment). Select **Balloons On/Off** to turn this feature off before you begin the experiments.

Study the screen. You will see a jar-shaped chamber to the left, connected to a *respirometer-manometer apparatus* (consisting of a U-shaped tube, a syringe, and associated tubing). You will be placing animals—in this case, rats—in the chamber in order to gather information about how thyroxine and TSH affect their metabolic rates. Note that the chamber also includes a weight scale, and under the timer is a weight display. Next to the chamber is a timer for setting and timing the length of a given experiment.

Two tubes are connected to the top of the chamber. The left tube has a clamp on it that can be opened or closed. Leaving the clamp open allows outside air into the chamber; closing the clamp creates a closed, airtight system. The other tube leads to a *T-connector.* One branch of the T leads to a fluid-containing U-shaped tube, called a *manometer.* As an animal uses up the air in the closed system, this fluid will rise in the left side of the U-shaped tube and fall in the right.

The other branch of the T-connector leads to a syringe filled with air. Using the syringe to inject air into the tube, you will measure the amount of air that is needed to return the fluid columns to their original levels. This measurement will be equal to the amount of oxygen used by the animal during the elapsed time of the experiment. Soda lime, found at the bottom of the chamber, absorbs the carbon dioxide given off by the animal so that the amount of oxygen used can easily be measured. The amount of oxygen used by the animal, along with its weight, will be used to calculate the animal's metabolic rate.

Also on the screen are three white rats in their individual cages. These are the specimens you will use in the following experiments. One rat is *normal;* the second is *thyroidectomized* (abbreviated on the screen as *Tx*), meaning its thyroid has been removed; and the third is *hypophysectomized* (abbreviated on the screen as *Hypox*), meaning its pituitary gland has been removed. The pituitary gland is also known as the *hypophysis,* and removal of this organ is called a *hypophysectomy.*

To the top left of the screen are three syringes with various chemicals inside: propylthiouracil, thyroid-stimulating hormone (TSH), and thyroxine. TSH and thyroxine have been previously mentioned; propylthiouracil is a drug that inhibits the production of thyroxine. You will perform four experiments on each animal to: (1) determine its baseline metabolic rate, (2) determine its metabolic rate after it has been injected with thyroxine, (3) determine its metabolic rate after it has been injected with TSH, and (4) determine its metabolic rate after it has been injected with propylthiouracil.

You will be recording all of your data on Chart 1. You may also record your data on-screen by using the equipment in the lower part of the screen, called the *data collection unit.* This equipment records and displays data you accumulate during the experiments. Check that the data set for **Normal** is highlighted in the **Data Sets** window; you will be experimenting with the normal rat first. The **Record Data** button lets you record data after an experimental trial. Clicking the **Delete Line** or **Clear Data Set** button erases any data you want to delete.

Determining Baseline Metabolic Rates

First, you will determine the baseline metabolic rate for each rat.

1. Using the mouse, click and drag the **normal** rat into the chamber and place it on top of the scale. When the animal is in the chamber, release the mouse button.

2. Be sure the clamp on the left tube (on top of the chamber) is open, allowing air to enter the chamber. If the clamp is closed, click on it to open it.

3. Be sure the indicator next to the T-connector reads "Chamber and manometer connected." If not, click on the **T-connector knob.**

4. Click on the **Weigh** button in the box to the right of the chamber to weigh the rat. Record this weight in the Baseline section of Chart 1 in the row labeled "Weight."

5. Click the (+) button on the **Timer** so that the Timer display reads 1 minute.

6. Click on the clamp to close it. This will prevent any outside air from entering the chamber and ensure that the only oxygen the rat is breathing is the oxygen inside the closed system.

7. Click **Start** on the Timer display. You will see the elapsed time appear in the "Elapsed Time" display. Watch what happens to the water levels in the U-shaped tube.

8. At the end of the 1-minute period, the timer will automatically stop. When it stops, click on the **T-connector knob** so that the indicator reads "Manometer and syringe connected."

9. Click on the clamp to open it so that the rat can once again breathe outside air.

10. Look at the difference between the levels in the left and right arms of the U-shaped tube. To estimate the volume of O_2 that you need to inject to equalize the levels, count the divider lines on both sides. Then click the (+) button next to the **ml O_2** display until the display shows your estimate. Click **Inject** and watch what happens to the fluid in the two arms. When the volume is equalized, the word "Level" will appear between the arms and stay on the screen. If too little was injected, click (+) and then **Inject** until the arms are level. If too much was injected, the word "Level" will flash and then disappear. You will then have to click the **Reset** button and try a lower volume. (The total amount injected to equalize the arm levels is equivalent to the amount of oxygen that the rat used up during 1 minute in the closed chamber.) Record this measurement in the Baseline section of Chart 1 in the row labeled "ml O_2 used in 1 minute."

11. Determine the oxygen consumption per hour for the rat. Use the following formula:

$$\frac{\text{ml } O_2 \text{ consumed}}{1 \text{ minute}} \times \frac{60 \text{ minutes}}{1 \text{ hr}} = \text{ml } O_2/\text{hr}$$

Record this data in the Baseline section of Chart 1 in the row labeled "ml O_2 used per hour."

CHART 1   Effects of Hormones on Metabolic Rate

	Normal rat	Thyroidectomized rat	Hypophysectomized rat
Baseline			
Weight	_____ grams	_____ grams	_____ grams
ml O_2 used in 1 minute	_____ ml	_____ ml	_____ ml
ml O_2 used per hour	_____ ml	_____ ml	_____ ml
Metabolic rate	_____ ml O_2/kg/hr	_____ ml O_2/kg/hr	_____ ml O_2/kg/hr
With thyroxine			
Weight	_____ grams	_____ grams	_____ grams
ml O_2 used in 1 minute	_____ ml	_____ ml	_____ ml
ml O_2 used per hour	_____ ml	_____ ml	_____ ml
Metabolic rate	_____ ml O_2/kg/hr	_____ ml O_2/kg/hr	_____ ml O_2/kg/hr
With TSH			
Weight	_____ grams	_____ grams	_____ grams
ml O_2 used in 1 minute	_____ ml	_____ ml	_____ ml
ml O_2 used per hour	_____ ml	_____ ml	_____ ml
Metabolic rate	_____ ml O_2/kg/hr	_____ ml O_2/kg/hr	_____ ml O_2/kg/hr
With propylthiouracil			
Weight	_____ grams	_____ grams	_____ grams
ml O_2 used in 1 minute	_____ ml	_____ ml	_____ ml
ml O_2 used per hour	_____ ml	_____ ml	_____ ml
Metabolic rate	_____ ml O_2/kg/hr	_____ ml O_2/kg/hr	_____ ml O_2/kg/hr

12. Now that you have the amount of oxygen used per hour, determine the metabolic rate per kilogram of body weight by using the following formula. (Note that you will need to convert the weight data from g to kg before you can use the formula.)

$$\text{Metabolic rate} = \frac{\text{ml } O_2/\text{hr}}{\text{wt. in kg}} = \text{_____ ml } O_2/\text{kg/hr}$$

Record this data in the Baseline section of Chart 1 in the row labeled "Metabolic rate."

13. Click **Record Data.**

14. Click and drag the rat from the chamber back to its cage.

15. Click the **Reset** button in the box labeled Apparatus.

16. Now repeat steps 1–15 for the **thyroidectomized (Tx)** and **hypophysectomized (Hypox)** rats. Record your data in the Baseline section of Chart 1 in the appropriate column for each rat. Note that when you put the Tx vat in the chamber, the simulation highlights **Tx** under **Data Sets** (on the data collection box); likewise, it highlights **Hypox** when you move the hypophysectomized rat.

Which rat had the fastest baseline metabolic rate?

_____

_____

_____

Why did the metabolic rates differ?

_____

_____

_____ ▬

Determining the Effect of Thyroxine on Metabolic Rate

Next, you will investigate the effects of thyroxine injections on the metabolic rates of all three rats.

Note that in a wet lab environment, you would normally need to inject thyroxine (or any other hormone) into a rat *daily* for a minimum of 1–2 weeks in order for any response to be seen. However, in the following simulations, you will inject the rat only once and be able to witness the same results as if you had administered multiple injections over the course of several weeks. In addition, by clicking the **Clean** button while a rat is inside its cage, you can magically remove all residue of any previously injected hormone from the rat and perform a new experiment on the same rat. In a real wet lab environment, you would need to either wait weeks for hormonal residue to leave the rat's system or use a different rat.

1. Choose and click on a rat to test. You will eventually test all three, and it doesn't matter in what order you test them. Do not drag the rat to the chamber yet. Under **Data Sets,** the simulation will highlight **Normal, Tx,** or **Hypox** depending on which rat you use.

2. Click the **Reset** button in the box labeled Apparatus.

3. Click on the syringe labeled **thyroxine** and drag it over to the rat. Release the mouse button. This will cause thyroxine to be injected into the rat.

4. Click and drag the rat into the chamber. Perform steps 1–12 of Activity 1 again, except this time record your data in the With Thyroxine section of Chart 1.

5. Click **Record Data.**

6. Click and drag the rat from the chamber back to its cage, and click **Clean** to cleanse it of all traces of thyroxine.

7. Now repeat steps 1–6 for the remaining rats. Record your data in the With Thyroxine section of Chart 1 in the appropriate column for each rat.

What was the effect of thyroxine on the normal rat's metabolic rate? How does it compare to the normal rat's baseline metabolic rate?

_____

_____

Why was this effect seen? _____

_____

What was the effect of thyroxine on the thyroidectomized rat's metabolic rate? How does it compare to the thyroidectomized rat's baseline metabolic rate?

_____

_____

_____

Why was this effect seen? _____

_____

What was the effect of thyroxine on the hypophysectomized rat's metabolic rate? How does it compare to the hypophysectomized rat's baseline metabolic rate?

_____

_____

_____

Why was this effect seen? _____

_____ ▬

Determining the Effect of TSH on Metabolic Rate

Now you will investigate the effects of TSH injections on the metabolic rates of the three rats. Select a rat to experiment on first, and then proceed.

1. Under **Data Sets,** highlight **Normal, Tx,** or **Hypox,** depending on which rat you are using.

2. Click the **Reset** button in the box labeled Apparatus.

3. Click and drag the syringe labeled **TSH** over to the rat and release the mouse button, injecting the rat.

4. Click and drag the rat into the chamber. Perform steps 1–12 of Activity 1 again. Record your data in the With TSH section of Chart 1.

5. Click **Record Data.**

6. Click and drag the rat from the chamber back to its cage, and click **Clean** to cleanse it of all traces of TSH.

7. Now repeat this activity for the remaining rats. Record your data in the With TSH section of the chart in the appropriate column for each rat.

What was the effect of TSH on the normal rat's metabolic rate? How does it compare to the normal rat's baseline metabolic rate?

_____

_____

_____

Why was this effect seen? _____

_____

What was the effect of TSH on the thyroidectomized rat's metabolic rate? How does it compare to the thyroidectomized rat's baseline metabolic rate?

_____

_____

_____

Why was this effect seen? _____

_____

What was the effect of TSH on the hypophysectomized rat's metabolic rate? How does it compare to the hypophysectomized rat's baseline metabolic rate?

_____

_____

_____

Why was this effect seen? _____

_____ ▪

A C T I V I T Y   4

Determining the Effect of Propylthiouracil on Metabolic Rate

Next, you will investigate the effects of propylthiouracil injections on the metabolic rates of the three rats. Keep in mind that propylthiouracil is a drug that inhibits the production of thyroxine by blocking the attachment of iodine to the amino acid tyrosine and interfering with the conversion of thyroxine to triiodothyronine. Select a rat to experiment on first, and then proceed.

1. Under **Data Sets,** the simulation will highlight **Normal, Tx,** or **Hypox,** depending on which rat you are using.

2. Click the **Reset** button in the box labeled Apparatus.

3. Click and drag the syringe labeled **propylthiouracil** over to the rat and release the mouse button, injecting the rat.

4. Click and drag the rat into the chamber. Perform steps 1–12 of Activity 1 again, except this time record your data in the With Propylthiouracil section of Chart 1.

5. Click **Record Data.**

6. Click and drag the rat from the chamber back to its cage, and click **Clean** to cleanse the rat of all traces of propylthiouracil.

7. Now repeat this activity for the remaining rats. Record your data in the With Propylthiouracil section of Chart 1 in the appropriate column for each rat.

What was the effect of propylthiouracil on the normal rat's metabolic rate? How does it compare to the normal rat's baseline metabolic rate?

_____

_____

_____

Why was this effect seen? _____

_____

What was the effect of propylthiouracil on the thyroidectomized rat's metabolic rate? How does it compare to the thyroidectomized rat's baseline metabolic rate?

_____

_____

_____

Why was this effect seen? _____

_____

What was the effect of propylthiouracil on the hypophysectomized rat's metabolic rate? How does it compare to the hypophysectomized rat's baseline metabolic rate?

_____

_____

_____

Why was this effect seen? _____

_____

8. If you wish, click **Tools → Print Data** to print all of your recorded data for this experiment. ▪

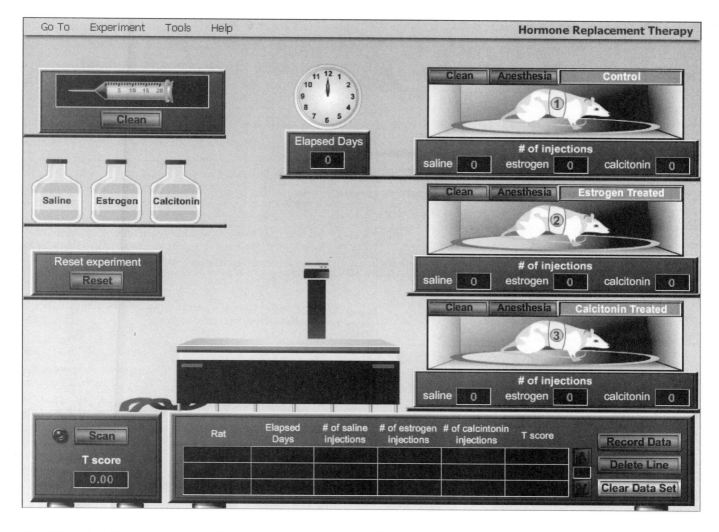

FIGURE 4.2 Opening screen of the Hormone Replacement Therapy experiment.

Hormone Replacement Therapy

Follicle-stimulating hormone (FSH) stimulates ovarian follicle growth. While the follicles are developing, they produce the hormone *estrogen.* As the female enters menopause, the ovaries stop producing estrogen. One of the symptoms of menopause is loss of bone density, which can result in osteoporosis and bone fractures. Postmenopausal treatments to prevent osteoporosis include the administration of estrogen to increase bone density. Calcitonin is a hormone that inhibits osteoclast activity and stimulates calcium uptake for deposit in bone.

In this experiment we will use three ovariectomized rats because they are no longer producing estrogen due to the removal of their ovaries. The three rats were chosen because each has a baseline T score of −2.6, indicating osteoporosis. T scores are interpreted as follows: normal = +1 to −0.99; osteopenia (bone thinning) = −1.0 to −2.49; osteoporosis = −2.5 and below. You will administer either estrogen therapy or calcitonin therapy, two types of **hormone replacement therapy.** The third rat will serve as an untreated control and receive daily injections of saline. The vertebral bone

density (VBD) of each rat will be measured with dual X-ray absorptiometry (DXA) to obtain the T score.

Start by selecting **Hormone Replacement Therapy** from the **Experiment** menu. A new screen will appear (Figure 4.2) with three ovariectomized rats in cages. (Note that if this were a wet lab, the ovariectomies would have been performed on the rats a month prior to the rest of the experiment in order to ensure that no residual hormones remained in the rats' systems.) Also on screen are a bottle of saline, a bottle of estrogen, a bottle of calcitonin, a clock, and a dual X-ray absorptiometry bone density scanner.

Hormone Replacement Therapy

1. Click on the syringe, drag it to the bottle of **saline,** and release the mouse button. The syringe will automatically fill with 1 ml of saline.

2. Click and hold the syringe, drag it to the **control** rat, and place the tip of the needle in the rat's lower abdominal area. Injections into this area are considered *intraperitoneal* and will quickly be picked up by the abdominal blood vessels.

Release the mouse button—the syringe will empty into the rat and automatically return to its holder. Click **Clean** on the syringe holder to clean the syringe of all residue.

3. Click on the syringe again, this time dragging it to the bottle of **estrogen,** and release the mouse button. The syringe will automatically fill with 1 ml of estrogen.

4. Click and hold the syringe, drag it to the **estrogen-treated** rat, and place the tip of the needle in the rat's lower abdominal area. Release the mouse button—the syringe will empty into the rat and automatically return to its holder. Click **Clean** on the syringe holder to clean the syringe of all residue.

5. Click on the syringe again, this time dragging it to the bottle of **calcitonin,** and release the mouse button. The syringe will automatically fill with 1 ml of calcitonin.

6. Click and hold the syringe, drag it to the **calcitonin-treated** rat, and place the tip of the needle in the rat's lower abdominal area. Release the mouse button—the syringe will empty into the rat and automatically return to its holder. Click **Clean** on the syringe holder to clean the syringe of all residue.

7. Click on the **clock.** You will notice the hands sweep the clock face twice, indicating that 24 hours have passed.

8. Repeat steps 1–7 until each rat has received a total of 7 injections over the course of 7 days (1 injection per day). Note that the **# of injections** displayed below each rat cage records how many injections the rat has received. The control rat should receive 7 injections of saline, the estrogen-treated rat should receive 7 injections of estrogen, and the calcitonin-treated rat should receive 7 injections of calcitonin.

9. You are now ready to measure the effect of each of the solutions. First, predict the effect that each solution will have on the rat's vertebral bone density.

Saline injections _____

_____

Estrogen injections _____

_____

Calcitonin injections _____

_____

10. A gaseous anesthetic will be applied to immobilize the rats for imaging. Click on the **Anesthesia** button for the control rat to immobilize the rat.

11. Click on the **control** rat and drag it to the exam table. Release the mouse to release the rat.

12. Click the **Scan** button to activate the scanner. Record the T score:

T score (control): _____

13. Click **Record Data.**

14. Click and drag the rat to return it to its cage.

15. Repeat steps 10–14 for the **estrogen-treated** rat.

T score (estrogen): _____

16. Repeat steps 10–14 for the **calcitonin-treated** rat.

T score (calcitonin): _____

17. Click **Tools → Print Data** to print your recorded data for this experiment.

Recall that the baseline value for all three rats was -2.6. T scores are interpreted as follows: normal$_)$ = $+1$ to -0.99; osteopenia (bone thinning) = -1.0 to -2.49; osteoporosis = -2.5 and below.

What effect did the administration of estrogen injections have on the estrogen-treated rat?

_____

_____

What effect did the administration of calcitonin injections have

on the calcitonin-treated rat? _____

_____

How did these results compare with your predictions?

_____

_____

_____ ▬

Insulin and Diabetes

Insulin is produced by the beta cells of the endocrine portion of the pancreas. It is vital to the regulation of blood glucose levels because it enables the body's cells to absorb glucose from the bloodstream (see Figure 4.4b). When insulin is not produced by the pancreas, **type 1 diabetes mellitus** results. When insulin is produced by the pancreas but the body fails to respond to it, **type 2 diabetes mellitus** results. In either case, glucose remains in the bloodstream, unable to be taken up by the body's cells to serve as the primary fuel for metabolism.

The following experiment is divided into two parts. In Part I, you will obtain a *glucose standard curve,* which will be explained shortly. In Part II, you will use the standard

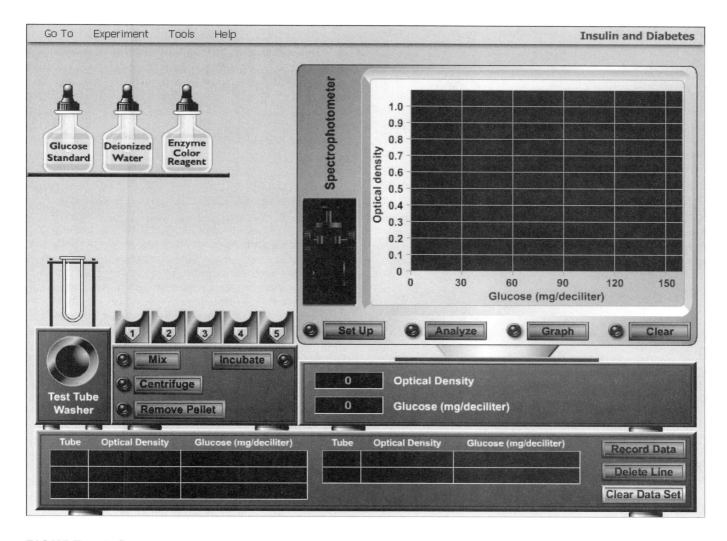

FIGURE 4.3 Opening screen of the Insulin and Diabetes experiment, Part I.

curve to measure fasting plasma glucose levels in patients to diagnose diabetes mellitus.

Part I

Obtaining a Glucose Standard Curve

To begin, select **Insulin and Diabetes-Part 1** from the **Experiment** menu (see Figure 4.3).

Select **Balloons On/Off** from the **Help** menu for help identifying the equipment on-screen. (You will see labels appear as you roll the mouse over each piece of equipment.) Select **Balloons On/Off** to turn this feature off before you begin the experiments.

On the right side of the opening screen is a special spectrophotometer. The **spectrophotometer** is one of the most widely used research instruments in biology. It is used to measure the amounts of light of different wavelengths absorbed and transmitted by a pigmented solution. Inside the spectrophotometer is a source for white light, which is separated into various wavelengths (or colors) by a prism. The user selects a wave-

length (color), and light of this color is passed through a special tube, or *cuvette*, containing the sample being tested. (For this experiment, the spectrophotometer light source will be preset for a wavelength of 450 nanometers, or nm.) The light transmitted by the sample then passes onto a photoelectric tube, which converts the light energy into an electrical current. This current is measured by a meter. Alternatively, the light may be measured before the sample is put into the light path, and the amount of light absorbed—called **optical density**—is measured. Using either method, the change in light transmitted or light absorbed can be used to measure the amount of a given substance in the sample being tested.

In Part II, you will use the spectrophotometer to determine how much glucose is present in blood samples taken from two rats. Before using the spectrophotometer, you must obtain a **glucose standard curve** so that you have a point of reference for converting optical density readings into glucose readings, which will be measured in mg/deciliter (mg/dl). To do this, you will prepare five test tubes that contain known amounts of glucose: 30 mg/dl, 60 mg/dl, 90 mg/dl, 120 mg/dl, and 150 mg/dl, respectively. You will then use the spectrophotometer to determine the corresponding optical density readings for each of these known amounts of glucose. Information obtained in Part I will be used to perform Part II.

Also on the screen are three dropper bottles, a test tube washer, a test tube dispenser (on top of the washer), and a test tube incubation unit with numbered cradles that you will need to prepare the samples for analysis.

1. Click and drag the test tube (on top of the test tube washer) into slot 1 of the incubation unit. You will see another test tube pop up from the dispenser. Click and drag this second test tube into slot 2 of the incubation unit. Repeat until you have dragged a total of five test tubes into the five slots in the incubation unit.

2. Click and hold the mouse button on the dropper cap of the **glucose standard** bottle. Drag the dropper cap over to tube 1. Release the mouse button to dispense the glucose. You will see that one drop of glucose solution is dropped into the tube.

3. The dropper will automatically slide over to each of the remaining samples. Notice that each subsequent tube will automatically receive one additional drop of glucose standard (i.e., tube 2 will receive two drops, tube 3 will receive three drops, tube 4 will receive four drops, and tube 5 will receive five drops).

4. Click and hold the mouse button on the dropper cap of the **deionized water** bottle. Drag the dropper cap over to tube 1. Release the mouse button to dispense the water. Notice that four drops of water are automatically added to the first tube.

5. The dropper will automatically slide over to each of the remaining samples. Notice that each subsequent tube will receive one *less* drop of water than the previous tube (i.e., tube 2 will receive three drops, tube 3 will receive two drops, tube 4 will receive one drop, and tube 5 will receive *no* drops of water).

6. Click on the **Mix** button of the incubator to mix the contents of the tubes.

7. Click on the **Centrifuge** button. The tubes will descend into the incubator and be centrifuged.

8. When the tubes resurface, click on the **Remove Pellet** button. Any pellets from the centrifuging process will be removed from the test tubes.

9. Click and hold the mouse button on the dropper cap of the **enzyme color reagent** bottle. Still holding the mouse button down, drag the dropper cap over to tube 1. When you release the mouse, you will note that five drops of reagent are added to the tube.

10. The dropper will automatically slide over to each of the remaining samples.

11. Now click **Incubate**. The tubes will descend into the incubator, incubate, and then resurface.

12. Using the mouse, click on **Set Up** on the spectrophotometer. This will warm up the instrument and get it ready for your readings.

13. Click and drag tube 1 into the spectrophotometer (above the **Set Up** button) and release the mouse button. The tube will lock into place.

14. Click **Analyze.** You will see a spot appear on the screen and values appear in the **Optical Density** and **Glucose** displays.

15. Click **Record Data** on the data collection unit.

16. Click and drag the tube into the test tube washer.

17. Repeat steps 13–16 for the remaining test tubes.

18. When all five tubes have been analyzed, click on the **Graph** button. This is the glucose standard graph, which you will use in Part II of the experiment. Click **Tools → Print Data** to print your recorded data. ▪▪▪▪

Part II

ACTIVITY 7

Measuring Fasting Plasma Glucose

Select **Insulin and Diabetes-Part 2** from the **Experiment** menu.

A new screen will appear (Figure 4.4a). Four reagents and five patient samples are present. To undergo the fasting plasma glucose (FPG) test, patients must fast for a minimum of 8 hours prior to the blood draw. Plasma samples will be measured in the spectrophotometer, and the glucose standard curve generated in Part I will be used to determine fasting plasma glucose levels in the five patient samples. A patient with two separate FPG tests greater than or equal to 126 mg/dl is diagnosed with diabetes. FPG values between 110 and 126 mg/dl are indicative of impairment or borderline impairment of glucose uptake by cells. FPG values less than 110 mg/dl are normal.

If the FPG is borderline, another test, the oral glucose tolerance test (OGTT), is performed. In this test, the patient also fasts for 8 hours. The patient then ingests a concentrated glucose solution, and blood is drawn and tested at periodic intervals. Glucose and sometimes insulin levels are measured. The 2-hour glucose level should be below 140 mg/dl. A 2-hour OGTT level between 140 and 200 mg/dl indicates impaired glucose tolerance, and a level above 200 mg/dl confirms the diabetes diagnosis. Individuals with impaired fasting glucose values and impaired glucose tolerance are at a higher risk of developing type 2 diabetes. If a patient is pregnant, an FPG value greater than 110 mg/dl could indicate gestational diabetes and a strict diet should be followed for the remainder of the pregnancy.

1. Click and drag a test tube (on top of the test tube washer) into slot 1 of the incubation unit. You will see another test tube pop up from the dispenser. Click and drag the second test tube into slot 2 of the incubation unit. Repeat until you have dragged a total of five test tubes into the five slots in the incubation unit.

2. Click and hold the mouse button on the dropper cap of **Sample 1** and then drag the dropper to the first test tube. The dropper will automatically dispense 3 drops of blood into the test tube and automatically return to the vial.

3. Repeat step 2 for the remaining patient samples.

4. Click and hold the mouse button on the dropper cap of the **deionized water** bottle. Drag the dropper cap over to test tube 1. Release the mouse to dispense the water. Five drops of water will be dispensed into the tube.

5. The dropper will automatically slide over to the remaining tubes and will add five drops to each tube. The dropper

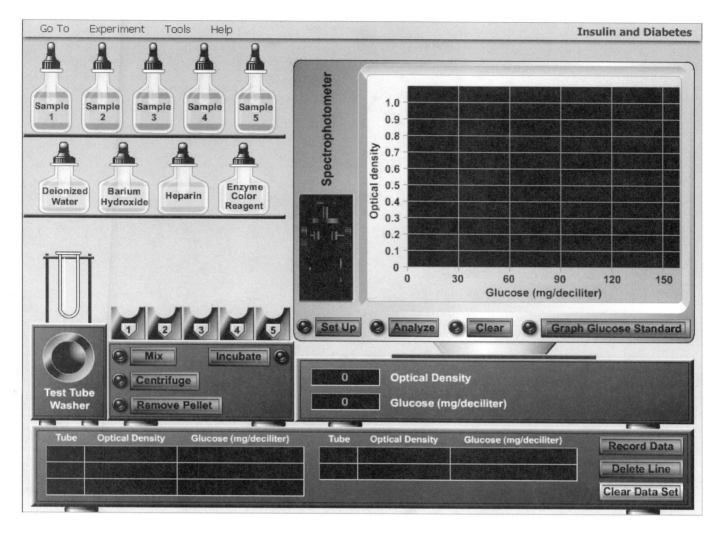

FIGURE 4.4 Insulin and diabetes. (a) Opening screen of the Insulin and Diabetes experiment, Part II.

will automatically return to the vial when the dispensing is complete.

6. Click and hold the mouse button on the dropper of **barium hydroxide.** Drag the dropper cap over to test tube 1. Release the mouse button to dispense the barium hydroxide. Five drops of the solution will be dispensed.

7. The dropper will automatically slide over to the remaining tubes and will add five drops to each tube. The dropper will automatically return to the vial when the dispensing is complete. (Barium hydroxide is used for clearing proteins and cells so that clear glucose readings may be obtained.)

8. Click and hold the mouse button on the dropper of the **heparin** bottle. Drag the dropper cap over to tube 1. Release the mouse button to dispense the heparin.

9. The dropper will automatically slide over to the remaining tubes and will add one drop to each tube. The dropper will automatically return to the vial when the dispensing is complete. (Heparin is an anticoagulant that prevents blood clotting.)

10. Click on the **Mix** button of the incubator to mix the contents of the tubes.

11. Click on the **Centrifuge** button. The tubes will descend into the incubator, be centrifuged, and then resurface.

12. Click on the **Remove Pellet** button to remove any pellets from the centrifugation process.

13. Click and hold the mouse button on the dropper of the **enzyme color reagent** bottle. Drag the dropper cap to test tube 1. Release the mouse to dispense the reagent.

14. The dropper will automatically slide over to the remaining tubes and will add five drops to each tube. The dropper will automatically return to the vial when the dispensing is complete.

15. Click **Incubate.** The tubes will descend into the incubator, incubate, and then resurface.

16. Click **Set Up** on the spectrophotometer to warm up the instrument and get it ready for your readings.

17. Click **Graph Glucose Standard.** The graph from Part I of the experiment will appear on the monitor.

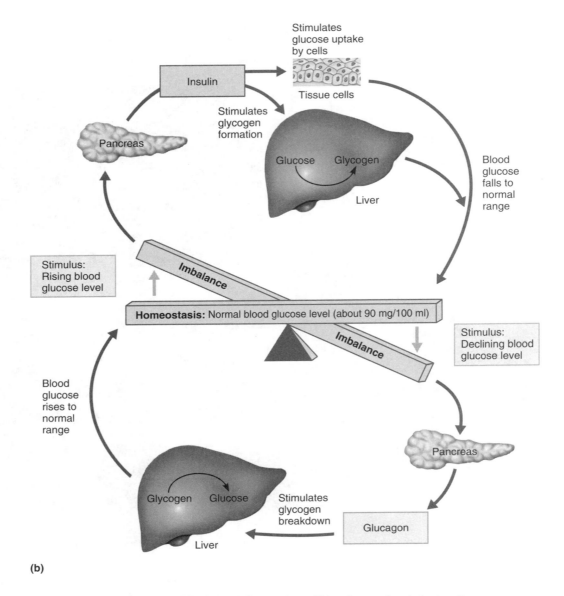

(b)

FIGURE 4.4 (*continued*) **Insulin and diabetes. (b)** Regulation of blood sugar levels by insulin and glucagon.

18. Click and drag tube 1 to the spectrophotometer and release the mouse button. The tube will lock into place.

19. Click **Analyze.** You will see a horizontal line appear on the screen and a value appear in the **Optical Density** display.

20. Drag the movable ruler (the vertical line on the far right of the spectrophotometer monitor) over to where the horizontal line (from step 19) crosses the glucose standard line. Watch what happens to the **Glucose** display as you move the movable ruler to the left.

What is the glucose reading where the horizontal line crosses the glucose standard line?

Sample 1: glucose concentration of _____ mg/deciliter

This is your glucose reading for the patient being tested.

21. Click **Record Data** on the data collection unit.

22. Click and drag the test tube from the spectrophotometer into the test tube washer, then click **Clear** under the display.

23. Repeat steps 17–22 for the remaining test tubes. Record your glucose readings for each test tube here:

Sample 2: glucose concentration of _____ mg/deciliter

Sample 3: glucose concentration of _____ mg/deciliter

Sample 4: glucose concentration of _____ mg/deciliter

Sample 5: glucose concentration of _____ mg/deciliter

For which patient(s) were the glucose reading(s) in the normal range? _____

_____

For which patient(s) were the fasting plasma glucose reading(s)

in the diabetic range? _____

_____

For which patient(s) were the fasting plasma glucose reading(s) in the impaired range?

_____

_____

What recommendations would you make to a patient with an impaired FPG value who also tested in the impaired range with the oral glucose tolerance test?

_____

_____

Patient 3 is pregnant; how might this change the diagnosis? What recommendations would you make to this patient?

_____

_____

_____ ▬

Measuring Cortisol and Adrenocorticotropic Hormone

Cortisol, a hormone secreted by the adrenal cortex, is key to the long-term regulation of stress. Cortisol release is stimulated by adrenocorticotropic hormone (ACTH), a hormone released by the anterior pituitary. ACTH release is stimulated by a hypothalamic hormone, corticotropin-releasing hormone (CRH). Increased levels of cortisol negatively feed back to inhibit the release of both ACTH and CRH. See Figure 4.5b for the regulation of cortisol secretion.

Increased cortisol in the blood, or hypercortisolism, is referred to as Cushing's syndrome if it is due to an adrenal tumor. Hypercortisolism caused by a pituitary tumor also causes levels of ACTH to increase and is referred to as Cushing's disease. Cushing's syndrome can also be iatrogenic; that is, physician induced. This occurs when glucocorticoid hormones such as prednisone are administered for the treatment of rheumatoid arthritis, asthma, or lupus and is often referred to as "steroid diabetes" because it results in hyperglycemia.

Hypocortisolism can occur due to adrenal insufficiency. In primary adrenal insufficiency, also known as Addison's disease, the low cortisol is directly due to gradual destruction of the adrenal cortex, and ACTH levels are typically elevated as a compensatory effect. Secondary adrenal insufficiency also results in low levels of cortisol, usually

TABLE 4.1	Cortisol and ACTH Disorders	
	Cortisol level	ACTH level
Cushing's syndrome (primary hypercortisolism)	High	Low
Cushing's disease (secondary hypercortisolism)	High	High
Iatrogenic Cushing's syndrome	High	Low
Addison's disease (primary adrenal insufficiency)	Low	High
Secondary adrenal insufficiency (hypopituitarism)	Low	Low

due to damage to the pituitary gland. Levels of ACTH are also low in secondary adrenal insufficiency.

A variety of endocrine disorders are related to both high and low levels of cortisol and adrenocorticotropic hormone. Table 4.1 summarizes these endocrine disorders.

Start by selecting **Measuring Cortisol and Adrenocorticotropic Hormone** from the **Experiment** menu. A new screen will appear (Figure 4.5a) with five patient plasma samples and an HPLC (high-performance liquid chromatography) column that will be used to simulate the measurement of cortisol and adrenocorticotropic hormone (ACTH). There is a syringe that will be used to inject the samples into the HPLC injector for analysis. The **Cortisol** and **ACTH** buttons are used to prepare the column with solvents used to separate the two different hormones. The detector will measure the amount of the hormone and convert it into a concentration value.

1.   Start the experiment by clicking on the **Cortisol** button. This will prepare the column for the separation and measurement of cortisol.

2.   Click and hold the syringe and drag it over to the first patient sample. Then release the mouse. The syringe will fill with plasma.

3.   Click and hold the syringe again and drag it over to the **HPLC injector.** Then release the mouse. The sample will enter the tubing and flow through the column. The detector will display the concentration of cortisol in the first patient sample.

4.   Click **Record Data.**

5.   Click the **Clean** button under the syringe to prepare it for the next sample.

6.   Click the **Clean Column** button near the top of the screen to remove residual cortisol from the column.

7.   Repeat steps 2–6 for the remaining four patient samples.

8.   Next, prepare the column for ACTH separation and measurement by clicking on the **ACTH** button.

9.   Click and hold the syringe and drag it over to the first patient sample. Then release the mouse. The syringe will fill with plasma.

10.   Click and hold the syringe again and drag it over to the HPLC injector. Then release the mouse. The sample will enter the tubing and flow through the column. The detector will display the concentration of ACTH in the first patient sample.

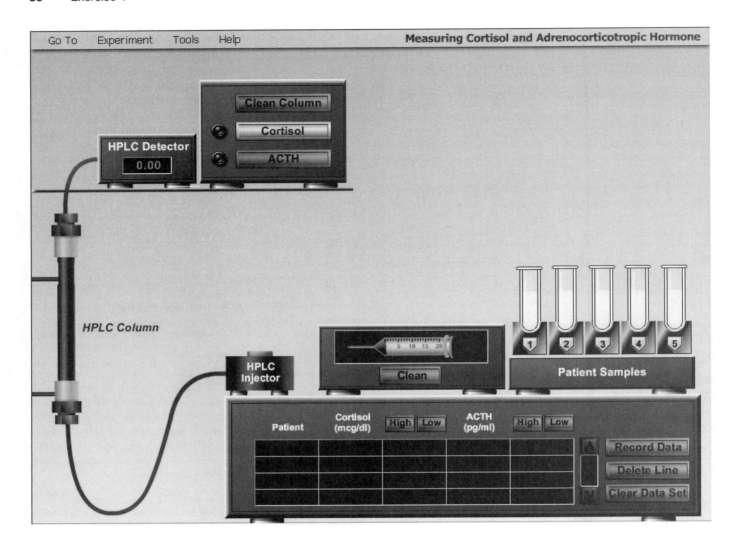

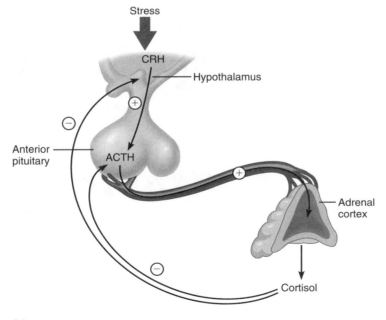

(b)

FIGURE 4.5 Following the cortisol release pathway. (a) Opening screen of the Measuring Cortisol and ACTH experiment. (b) The regulation of cortisol secretion. + indicates stimulation of release, − indicates inhibition of release, CRH = corticotropin-releasing hormone, ACTH = adrenocorticotropic hormone.

TABLE 4.2	Abnormal Morning Cortisol, ACTH Levels	
	High	Low
Cortisol	≥23 mcg/dl	<5 mcg/dl
ACTH	≥80 pg/ml	<20 pg/ml

Note: 1 mcg = 1μg = 1 microgram

11. Click **Record Data.**

12. Click the **Clean** button under the syringe to prepare it for the next sample.

13. Click the **Clean Column** button near the top of the screen.

14. Repeat steps 9–13 for the remaining four patient samples.

15. Select a row in the Data Set and choose **High** or **Low** based on the breakpoints shown in Table 4.2 for cortisol and ACTH in plasma from a morning blood draw.

16. Click **Tools → Print Data** to print your recorded data for this experiment.

17. Record your results for each patient here and circle High or Low:

Patient 1: Cortisol _____ mcg/dl   High/Low

ACTH _____ pg/ml   High/Low

Patient 2: Cortisol _____ mcg/dl   High/Low

ACTH _____ pg/ml   High/Low

Patient 3: Cortisol _____ mcg/dl   High/Low

ACTH _____ pg/ml   High/Low

Patient 4: Cortisol _____ mcg/dl   High/Low

ACTH _____ pg/ml   High/Low

Patient 5: Cortisol _____ mcg/dl   High/Low

ACTH _____ pg/ml   High/Low

NAME _____

LAB TIME/DATE _____

Endocrine System Physiology

Metabolism

The following questions refer to Activity 1: Determining Baseline Metabolic Rates.

1. Which rat had the fastest baseline metabolic rate? _____

_____

2. Compare the baseline metabolic rates for the thyroidectomized rat and the normal rat and explain your results. _____

_____

3. Compare the baseline metabolic rates for the hypophysectomized rat and the normal rat and explain your results. _____

_____

The following questions refer to Activity 2: Determining the Effect of Thyroxine on Metabolic Rate.

4. What effect did administering thyroxine have on each of the rats? _____

_____

_____

_____

5. Explain why thyroxine had these effects. _____

_____

_____

The following questions refer to Activity 3: Determining the Effect of TSH on Metabolic Rate.

6. Was there a change in the metabolic rate of the thyroidectomized rat with the administration of TSH? Explain your results. _____

_____

_____

7. Did the results for the thyroidectomized rat indicate hyperthyroidism or hypothyroidism? _____

_____

The following questions refer to Activity 4: Determining the Effect of Propylthiouracil on Metabolic Rate.

8. Describe the effect of administering propylthiouracil on each of the rats, and explain why it had this effect. _____

_____

_____

9. Do you think the drug propylthiouracil is used to treat hypothyroidism or hyperthyroidism? Explain your answer. _____

_____

Hormone Replacement Therapy

The following questions refer to Activity 5: Hormone Replacement Therapy.

10. Explain why ovariectomized rats were used in this experiment and correlate this to their baseline T score._____

_____

_____

11. Recap your predictions regarding the effects of calcitonin and estrogen on bone density and explain why you made those

    predictions. _____

_____

_____

12. Why was one of the ovariectomized rats injected with saline? _____

_____

13. What effect did the administration of estrogen injections have on the estrogen-treated rat? _____

_____

14. What effect did the administration of calcitonin injections have on the calcitonin-treated rat? _____

_____

15. How did your results compare to your predictions? _____

_____

_____

Insulin and Diabetes

The following question refers to Activity 6: Obtaining a Glucose Standard Curve.

16. What is a glucose standard curve, and how can you use this tool to determine a concentration of glucose? _____

_____

The following questions refer to Activity 7: Measuring Fasting Plasma Glucose.

17. Which patient(s) had glucose reading(s) in the normal range? _____

_____

18. Which patient(s) had glucose reading(s) in the diabetic range? _____

_____

19. Which patient(s) had glucose reading(s) in the impaired range? _____

_____

20. Describe the diagnosis for Patient 3. _____

_____

The following questions refer to Activity 8: Measuring Cortisol and Adrenocorticotropic Hormone.

21. Which patient would most likely be diagnosed with Cushing's disease? Why?

_____

_____

22. Which two patients have hormone levels characteristic of Cushing's syndrome?

_____

23. Patient 2 is being treated for rheumatoid arthritis with prednisone. How does this change the diagnosis? _____

_____

24. Which patient would most likely be diagnosed with Addison's disease? Why?

_____

_____

Cardiovascular Dynamics

The physiology of human blood circulation can be divided into two distinct but remarkably harmonized processes: (1) the pumping of blood by the heart, and (2) the transport of blood to all body tissues via the vasculature, or blood vessels. Blood supplies all body tissues with the substances needed for survival, so it is vital that blood delivery is ample for tissue demands.

The Mechanics of Circulation

To understand how blood is transported throughout the body, let's examine three important factors influencing how blood circulates through the cardiovascular system: blood flow, blood pressure, and peripheral resistance.

Blood flow is the amount of blood moving through a body area or the entire cardiovascular system in a given amount of time. Total blood flow is determined by cardiac output (the amount of blood the heart is able to pump per minute); however, blood flow to specific body areas can vary dramatically in a given time period. Organs differ in their requirements from moment to moment, and blood vessels constrict or dilate to regulate local blood flow to various areas in response to the tissues' immediate needs. Consequently, blood flow can increase to some regions and decrease to other areas at the same time.

Blood pressure is the force blood exerts against the wall of a blood vessel. Owing to cardiac activity, pressure is highest at the heart end of any artery. Because of the effect of peripheral resistance, which will be discussed shortly, pressure within the arteries (or any blood vessel) drops as the distance (vessel length) from the heart increases. This pressure gradient causes blood to move from and then back to the heart, always moving from high- to low-pressure areas.

Peripheral resistance is the opposition to blood flow resulting from the friction developed as blood streams through blood vessels. Three factors affect vessel resistance: blood viscosity, vessel radius, and vessel length.

Blood viscosity is a measure of the "thickness" of the blood, and is caused by the presence of proteins and formed elements in the plasma (the fluid part of the blood). As the viscosity of a fluid increases, its flow rate through a tube decreases.

Blood viscosity in healthy people normally does not change, but certain conditions such as too many or too few blood cells may modify it.

Controlling *blood vessel radius* (one-half of the diameter) is the principal method of blood flow control. This is accomplished by contracting or relaxing the smooth muscle within the blood vessel walls. To see why radius has such a pronounced effect on blood flow, consider the physical relationship between blood and the vessel wall. Blood in direct contact with the vessel wall flows relatively slowly because of the friction, or drag, between the blood and the lining of the vessel. In contrast, fluid in the center of the vessel flows more freely because it is not rubbing against the vessel wall. Now picture a large- and a small-radius vessel: proportionately more blood is in contact with the wall of the small vessel; hence blood flow is notably impeded as vessel radius decreases.

Although *vessel length* does not ordinarily change in a healthy person, any increase in vessel length causes a corresponding flow decrease. This effect is principally caused by friction between blood and the vessel wall. Consequently, given two blood vessels of the same diameter, the longer vessel will have more resistance, and thus a reduced blood flow.

The Effect of Blood Pressure and Vessel Resistance on Blood Flow

Blood flow is directly proportional to blood pressure because the pressure difference (Δ pressure) between the two ends of a vessel is the driving force for blood flow. Peripheral resistance is the force that opposes blood flow. This relationship is represented in the following equation:

$$\text{Blood flow (ml/min)} = \frac{\Delta \text{ pressure}}{\text{peripheral resistance}}$$

Three factors contribute to peripheral resistance: viscosity (V), blood vessel length (L), and the radius of the blood vessel (r). These relationships are expressed in the following equation:

$$\text{Peripheral resistance} = \frac{8(V)(L)}{\pi r^4}$$

From this equation, we can see that the viscosity of the blood and the length of the blood vessel are directly proportional to peripheral resistance. The peripheral resistance is inversely proportional to the fourth power of the vessel radius.

If we combine the two equations, we get the following result:

$$\text{Blood flow (ml/min)} = \frac{\Delta \text{ pressure } \pi r^4}{8(V)(L)}$$

From this combination, we can see that blood flow is directly proportional to the fourth power of vessel radius, which means that small changes in vessel radius result in dramatic changes in blood flow.

Vessel Resistance

Imagine for a moment that you are one of the first cardiovascular researchers interested in the physics of blood flow. Your first task as the principal investigator for this project is to plan an effective experimental design simulating a simple fluid pumping system that can be related to the mechanics of the cardiovascular system. The initial phenomenon you study is how fluids, including blood, flow through tubes or blood vessels. Questions you might ask include:

1. What role does pressure play in the flow of fluid?

2. How does peripheral resistance affect fluid flow?

The equipment required to solve these and other questions has already been designed for you in the form of a computerized simulation, which frees you to focus on the logic of the experiment. The first part of the computer simulation indirectly investigates the effects of pressure, vessel radius, viscosity, and vessel length on fluid flow. The second part of the experiment will explore the effects of several variables on the output of a single-chamber pump. Follow the specific guidelines in the exercise for collecting data. As you do so, also try to imagine alternate methods of achieving the same experimental goal.

Choose **Exercise 5: Cardiovascular Dynamics** from the drop-down menu and click **GO**. Then click **Vessel Resistance.** The opening screen will appear in a few seconds (Figure 5.1). Select **Balloons-On/Off** from the **Help** menu for help identifying the equipment on-screen (you will see labels appear as you roll the mouse over each piece of equipment). Select **Balloons On/Off** to turn this feature off before you begin the experiments.

The primary features on the screen when the program starts are a pair of glass beakers perched atop a simulated electronic device called the *equipment control unit,* which is used to set experimental parameters and to operate the equipment. When the **Start** button (beneath the left beaker) is clicked, the simulated blood flows from the left beaker (source) to the right beaker (destination) through the connecting tube. To relate this to the human body, think of the left beaker as the left side of your heart, the tube as your aorta, and the right beaker as any organ to which blood is flowing.

Clicking the **Refill** button refills the source beaker after an experimental trial. Experimental parameters can be adjusted by clicking the plus (+) or minus (−) buttons to the right of each display window.

The equipment in the lower part of the screen is called the *data collection unit.* This equipment records and displays data you accumulate during the experiments. The data set for the first experiment (Radius) is highlighted in the **Data Sets** window. You can add or delete a data set by clicking the appropriate button to the right of the **Data Sets** window. The **Record Data** button in the lower right part of the screen activates automatically after an experimental trial. Clicking the **Delete Line** or **Clear Data Set** buttons erases any data you want to delete.

You will record the data you accumulate in the experimental values grid in the lower middle part of the screen.

A C T I V I T Y   1

Studying the Effect of Flow Tube Radius on Fluid Flow

Our initial study will examine the effect of flow tube radius on fluid flow.

1. Open the **Vessel Resistance** window if it isn't already open.

The Radius line in the data collection unit should be highlighted in bright blue. If it is not, choose it by clicking the

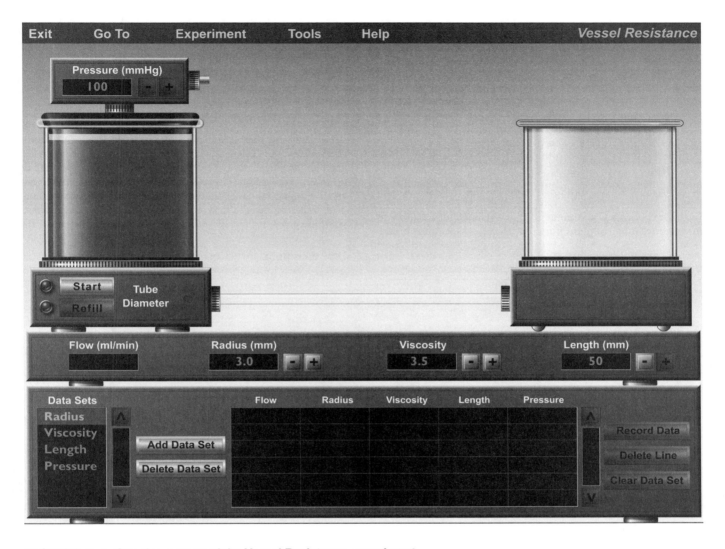

FIGURE 5.1 Opening screen of the Vessel Resistance experiment.

Radius line. The data collection unit will now record flow variations due to changing flow tube radius.

If the data grid is not empty, click **Clear Data Set** to discard all previous values.

If the left beaker is not full, click **Refill.**

2.   Adjust the flow tube radius to 1.5 mm and the viscosity to 1.0 by clicking the appropriate (+) or (−) button. During the course of this part of the experiment, maintain the other experiment conditions at:

100 mm Hg driving pressure (top left)

50-mm flow tube length (middle right)

3.   Click **Start,** and watch the fluid move into the right beaker. (Fluid moves slowly under some conditions—be patient!) Pressure (currently set to 100 mm Hg) propels fluid from the left beaker to the right beaker through the flow tube. The flow rate is displayed in the Flow window when the left beaker has finished draining. Now click **Record Data** to display the flow rate and experimental parameters in the experimental values grid

(and retain the data in the computer's memory for printing and saving). Click **Refill** to replenish the left beaker.

4.   Increase the radius in 0.5-mm increments, and repeat step 3 until the maximum radius (6.0 mm) is achieved. Be sure to click **Record Data** after each fluid transfer. If you make an error and want to delete a data value, click the data line in the experimental values grid and then click **Delete Line.**

5.   View your data graphically by choosing **Plot Data** from the **Tools** menu. Choose **Radius** as the data set to be graphed, and then use the slider bars to select the radius data to be plotted on the X-axis and the flow data to be plotted on the Y-axis. You can highlight individual data points by clicking a line in the data grid. When you are finished, click the close box at the top of the plot window.

What happened to the fluid flow rate as the radius of the flow tube was increased?

_____

_____

_____

Circle the correct term within the parentheses: Because fluid flow is proportional to the fourth power of the radius, (increases / decreases) in tube radius cause (increases / decreases) in fluid flow.

Is the relationship between the fluid flow rate and the flow

tube radius linear or exponential? _____

In this experiment, a simulated motor changes the diameter of the flow tube. Explain how our blood vessels alter blood flow.

_____

_____

_____

_____

After a heavy meal when we are relatively inactive, we might expect blood vessels in the skeletal muscles to be somewhat

_____, whereas blood vessels in the digestive

organs are probably _____. ▆

ACTIVITY 2

Studying the Effect of Viscosity on Fluid Flow

With a viscosity of 3 to 4, blood is much more viscous than water (1.0 viscosity). Although viscosity is altered by factors such as dehydration and altered blood cell numbers, a body in homeostatic balance has a relatively stable blood consistency. Nonetheless it is useful to examine the effects of viscosity changes on fluid flow because we can then predict what might occur in the human cardiovascular system during certain homeostatic imbalances.

1. Set the starting conditions as follows:
- 100 mm Hg driving pressure
- 5.0-mm flow tube radius
- 1.0 viscosity
- 50-mm flow tube length

2. Click the **Viscosity** data set in the data collection unit. (This action prepares the experimental values grid to record the viscosity data.)

3. **Refill** the left beaker if you have not already done so.

4. Click **Start** to begin the experiment. After all the fluid has drained into the right beaker, click **Record Data** to record this data point, and then click **Refill** to replenish the left beaker.

5. In 1.0-unit increments, increase the fluid viscosity by clicking (+) next to the **Viscosity** window, and repeat step 4 until the maximum viscosity (10.0) is reached.

6. View your data graphically by choosing **Plot Data** from the **Tools** menu. Choose **Viscosity** as the data set to be graphed, and then use the slider bars to have the viscosity data be plotted on the X-axis and the flow data be plotted on the Y-axis. You can highlight individual data points by clicking a line in the data grid. When finished, click the close box at the top of the plot window.

How does fluid flow change as viscosity is modified?

_____

_____

_____

Is fluid flow versus viscosity an inverse or direct relationship?

_____

Is the effect of viscosity greater or less than the effect of radius on fluid flow?

_____

_____

Predict the effect of anemia (e.g., fewer red blood cells than normal) on blood flow.

_____

_____

What might happen to blood flow if we increased the number of blood cells?

_____

_____

_____

Blood viscosity would _____ in conditions of

dehydration, resulting in _____ blood flow. ▆

Studying the Effect of Flow Tube Length on Fluid Flow

With the exception of the normal growth that occurs until the body reaches full maturity, blood vessel length does not significantly change. In this activity you will investigate the physical relationship between vessel length and blood movement; specifically, how blood flow changes in flow tubes (vessels) of constant radius but of different lengths.

1. Set the starting conditions as follows:
- 100 mm Hg driving pressure
- 5.0-mm flow tube radius
- 3.5 viscosity
- 10-mm flow tube length

2. Click the **Length** data set in the data collection unit. (This action prepares the experimental values grid to display the length data.)

3. **Refill** the left beaker if you have not already done so.

4. Click **Start** to begin the experiment. After all the fluid has drained into the right beaker, click **Record Data** to record this data point, and then click **Refill** to refill the left beaker.

5. In 5-mm increments, increase the flow tube length by clicking (+) next to the **Length** window, and repeat step 4 until the maximum length (50 mm) has been reached.

6. View your data graphically by choosing **Plot Data** from the **Tools** menu. Choose **Length** as the data set to be graphed, and then use the slider bars to select the length data to be plotted on the X-axis and the flow data to be plotted on the Y-axis. You can highlight individual data points by clicking a line in the grid. When finished, click the close box at the top of the plot window.

How does flow tube length affect fluid flow?

_____

_____

_____

What effect do you think obesity would have on blood flow? Hint: Relate obesity to changes in blood vessel length.

_____

_____

_____

_____

Studying the Effect of Pressure on Fluid Flow

The pressure difference between the two ends of a blood vessel is the driving force behind blood flow. In comparison, our experimental setup pressurizes the left beaker, thereby providing the driving force that propels fluid through the flow tube to the right beaker. You will examine the effect of pressure on fluid flow in this part of the experiment.

1. Set the starting conditions as follows:
- 25 mm Hg driving pressure
- 5.0-mm flow tube radius
- 3.5 viscosity
- 50-mm flow tube length

2. Click the **Pressure** data set in the data collection unit. (This action prepares the experimental values grid for the pressure data.)

3. **Refill** the left beaker if you have not already done so.

4. Click **Start** to begin the experiment. After all the fluid has moved into the right beaker, click **Record Data** to record this data point. Click **Refill** to refill the left beaker.

5. In increments of 25 mm Hg, increase the driving pressure by clicking (+) next to the **Pressure** window, and repeat step 4 until the maximum pressure (225 mm Hg) has been reached.

6. View your data graphically by choosing **Plot Data** from the **Tools** menu. Choose **Pressure** as the data set to be graphed, and then use the slider bars to have the pressure data be plotted on the X-axis and the flow data be plotted on the Y-axis. You can highlight individual data points by clicking a line in the data grid. When finished, click the close box at the top of the plot window.

How does driving pressure affect fluid flow?

_____

_____

_____

How does this plot differ from the plots for tube radius, viscosity, and tube length?

_____

_____

_____

Although changing pressure could be used as a means of blood flow control, explain why this approach would not be as effective as altering blood vessel radius.

_____

_____

_____

7. Click **Tools** → **Print Data** to print your recorded data for this experiment. ▬▬

Pump Mechanics

In the human body, the heart beats approximately 70 strokes each minute. Each heartbeat consists of a filling interval, during which blood moves into the chambers of the heart, and an ejection period when blood is actively pumped into the great arteries. The pumping activity of the heart can be described in terms of the phases of the cardiac cycle. Heart chambers fill during **diastole** (relaxation of the heart) and pump blood out during **systole** (contraction of the heart). As you can imagine, the length of time the heart is relaxed is one factor that determines the amount of blood within the heart at the end of the filling interval. Up to a point, increasing ventricular filling time results in a corresponding increase in ventricular volume. The volume in the ventricles at the end of diastole, just before cardiac contraction, is called the **end diastolic volume,** or **EDV.**

Blood moves from the heart into the arterial system when systolic pressure increases above the residual pressure (from the previous systole) in the great arteries leaving the heart. Although ventricular contraction causes blood ejection, the heart does not empty completely; a small quantity of blood—the **end systolic volume,** or **ESV**—remains in the ventricles at the end of systole.

Because the oxygen requirements of body tissue change depending on activity levels, we would expect the **cardiac output** (amount of blood pumped by each ventricle per minute) to vary correspondingly. We can calculate the **stroke volume** (**SV,** the amount of blood pumped per contraction of each ventricle) by subtracting the end systolic volume from the end diastolic volume (SV = EDV – ESV). We then compute cardiac output by multiplying the stroke volume by heart rate.

The human heart is a complex four-chambered organ, consisting of two individual pumps (the right and left sides) connected together in series. The right heart pumps blood through the lungs into the left heart, which in turn delivers blood to the systems of the body. Blood then returns to the right heart to complete the circuit.

Using the Pump Mechanics part of the PhysioEx program you will explore the operation of a simple one-chambered pump and apply the physical concepts in the simulation to the operation of either of the two pumps composing the human heart.

In this experiment you can vary the starting and ending volumes of the pump (analogous to EDV and ESV, respectively), driving and resistance pressures, and the diameters of the flow tubes leading to and from the pump chamber. As you proceed through the exercise, try to apply the ideas of ESV, EDV, cardiac output, stroke volume, and blood flow to the on-screen simulated pump system. For example, imagine that the flow tube leading to the pump from the left represents the pulmonary veins, and the flow tube exiting the pump to the right represents the aorta. The pump would then represent the left side of the heart.

Select **Pump Mechanics** from the **Experiment** menu. The equipment for the Pump Mechanics experiment appears. Figure 5.2 shows the opening screen with labels added.

As in the previous experiment, there are two simulated electronic control units on the computer's screen. The upper apparatus is the *equipment control unit,* which is used to adjust experiment parameters and to operate the equipment. The lower apparatus is the *data collection unit,* in which you will record the data you accumulate.

This equipment differs slightly from that used in the Vessel Resistance experiment. There are still two beakers: the *source* beaker on the left and the *destination* beaker on the right. Now the pressure in each beaker is individually controlled by the small pressure units on top of the beakers. Between the two beakers is a simple pump, which can be thought of as one side of the heart, or even as a single ventricle (e.g., left ventricle). The left beaker and flow tube are analogous to the venous side of human blood flow, and arterial circulation is simulated by the right flow tube and beaker. One-way valves in the flow tubes supplying the pump ensure fluid movement in one direction—from the left beaker into the pump, and then into the right beaker. If you imagine that the pump represents the left ventricle, then think of the valve to the left of the pump as the bicuspid valve and the valve to the right of the pump as the aortic semilunar valve. The pump is driven by a pressure unit mounted on its cap. An important distinction between the pump's pressure unit and the pressure units atop the beakers is that the pump delivers pressure only during its downward stroke. Upward pump strokes are driven by pressure from the left beaker (the pump does not exert any resistance to flow from the left beaker during pump filling). In contrast, pressure in the right beaker works against the pump pressure, which means that the net pressure driving the fluid into the right beaker is calculated (automatically) by subtracting the right beaker pressure from the pump pressure. The resulting pressure difference between the pump and the right beaker is displayed in the experimental values grid in the data collection unit as **Press.Dif.R.**

Clicking the **Auto Pump** button will cycle the pump through the number of strokes indicated in the Max. strokes window. Clicking the **Single** button cycles the pump through one stroke. During the experiment, the pump and flow rates are automatically displayed when the number of pump strokes is five or greater. The radius of each flow tube is individually controlled by clicking the appropriate button. Click (+) to increase flow tube radius or (−) to decrease flow tube radius.

The pump's stroke volume (the amount of fluid ejected in one stroke) is automatically computed by subtracting its ending volume from the starting volume. You can adjust starting and ending volumes, and thereby stroke volume, by clicking the appropriate (+) or (−) button in the equipment control unit.

The data collection unit records and displays data you accumulate during the experiments. The data set for the first experiment (**Rad.R.,** which represents right flow tube radius)

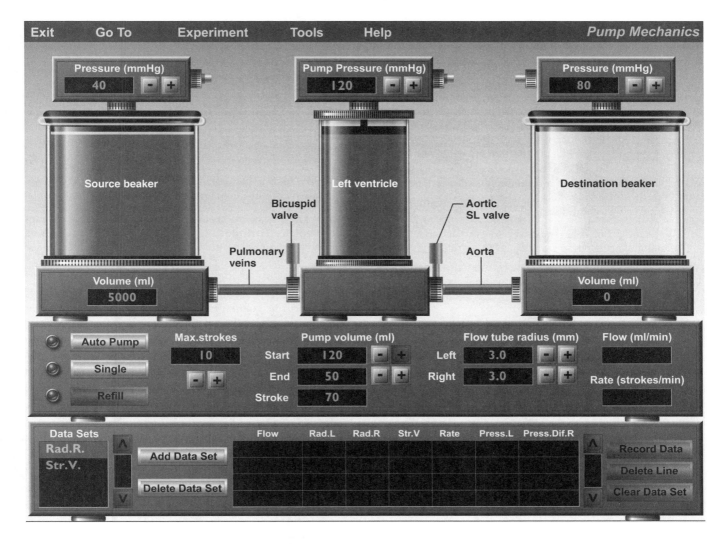

FIGURE 5.2 Opening screen of the Pump Mechanics experiment with labels added.

is highlighted in the **Data Sets** window. You can add or delete a data set by clicking the appropriate button to the right of the **Data Sets** window. Clicking **Delete Data Set** will erase the data set itself, including all the data it contained. The **Record Data** button at the right edge of the screen activates automatically after an experimental trial. When clicked, the **Record Data** button displays the flow rate data in the experimental values grid and saves it in the computer's memory. Clicking the **Delete Line** or **Clear Data Set** button erases any data you want to delete.

Studying the Effect of Radius on Pump Activity

Although you will be manipulating the radius of only the right flow tube in this part of the exercise, try to predict the consequence of altering the left flow tube radius as you collect the experimental data. (Remember that the left flow tube simulates the pulmonary veins and the right flow tube simulates the aorta, as labeled in Figure 5.2.)

1. Open the **Pump Mechanics** window if it isn't already open.

Click the **Rad.R.** data set to activate it. The data collection unit is now ready to record flow variations due to changing flow tube radius.

If the experimental values grid is not empty, click **Clear Data Set** to discard all previous values.

If the left beaker is not full, click **Refill.**

2. Adjust the **right** flow tube radius to 2.5 mm, and the **left** flow tube radius to 3.0 mm by clicking and holding the appropriate button. During the entire radius part of the experiment, maintain the other experiment conditions at:

- 40 mm Hg for left beaker pressure (this pressure drives fluid into the pump, which offers no resistance to filling)
- 120 mm Hg for pump pressure (pump pressure is the driving force that propels fluid into the right beaker)

- 80 mm Hg for right beaker pressure (this pressure is the resistance to the pump's pressure)
- 120-ml Start volume in pump (analogous to EDV)
- 50-ml End volume in pump (analogous to ESV)
- 10 strokes in the Max. strokes window

Notice that the displayed 70-ml stroke volume is automatically calculated. Before starting, click the **Single** button one or two times and watch the pump action.

To be sure you understand how this simple mechanical pump can be thought of as a simulation of the human heart, complete the following statements by circling the correct term within the parentheses:

a. When the piston is at the bottom of its travel, the volume remaining in the pump is analogous to the (EDV / ESV) of the heart.

b. The amount of fluid ejected into the right beaker by a single pump cycle is analogous to (stroke volume / cardiac output) of the heart.

c. The volume of blood in the heart just before systole is called the (EDV / ESV) and is analogous to the volume of fluid present in the simulated pump when it is at the (top / bottom) of its stroke.

3. Click the **Auto Pump** button in the equipment control unit to start the pump. After the 10 stroke volumes have been delivered, the Flow and Rate windows will automatically display the experimental results. Now click **Record Data** to display the figures you just collected in the experimental values grid. Click **Refill** to replenish the left beaker.

4. Increase the *right* flow tube radius in 0.5-mm increments, and repeat step 3 above until the maximum radius (6.0 mm) is achieved. Be sure to click **Record Data** after each trial.

5. When you have completed the experiment, view your data graphically by choosing **Plot Data** from the **Tools** menu. Choose **Rad.R.** as the data set to be graphed, and then use the slider bars to have the Rad.R. data be plotted on the X-axis and the flow data be plotted on the Y-axis. You can highlight individual data points by clicking a line in the data grid.

The total flow rates you just determined depend on the flow rate into the pump from the left and on the flow rate out of the pump toward the right. Consequently, the shape of the plot is different from what you might predict after viewing the vessel resistance radius graph.

Try to explain why this graph differs from the radius plot in the Vessel Resistance experiment. Remember that the flow rate into the pump did not change, whereas the flow rate out of the pump varied according to your radius manipulations.

_____

_____

_____

When you have finished, click the close box at the top of the plot window.

Complete the following statements by circling the correct term within the parentheses.

a. As the right flow tube radius is increased, fluid flow rate (increases / decreases). This is analogous to (dilation / constriction) of blood vessels in the human body.

b. Even though the pump pressure remains constant, the pump rate (increases / decreases) as the radius of the right flow tube is increased. This happens because the resistance to fluid flow is (increased / decreased).

Apply your observations of the simulated mechanical pump to complete the following statements about human heart function. If you are not sure how to formulate your response, use the simulation to arrive at an answer. Circle the correct term within the parentheses.

c. The heart must contract (more / less) forcefully to maintain cardiac output if the resistance to blood flow in the vessels exiting the heart is increased.

d. Increasing the resistance of (that is, constricting) the blood vessels entering the heart would (increase / decrease) the time needed to fill the heart chambers.

What do you think would happen to the flow rate and the pump rate if the left flow tube radius is changed (either increased or decreased)?

_____

_____

_____ ▬

Studying the Effect of Stroke Volume on Pump Activity

The heart of a person at rest pumps about 60% of the blood in its chambers, and the other 40% remains in the chambers after systole. The 60% of blood ejected by the heart is called the stroke volume and is the difference between EDV and ESV. Even though our simple pump in this experiment does not work exactly like the human heart, you can apply the concepts to basic cardiac function. In this experiment, you will examine how the activity of the simple pump is affected by changing the pump's starting and ending volumes.

1. Click the **Str.V.** (stroke volume) data set to activate it. If the experimental values grid is not empty, click **Clear Data Set** to discard all previous values. If the left beaker is not full, click **Refill.**

2. Adjust the stroke volume to 10 ml by setting the **Start** volume (EDV) to 120 ml and the **End** volume (ESV) to 110 ml (stroke volume = start volume – end volume). During the entire stroke volume part of the experiment, keep the other experimental conditions at:

- 40 mm Hg for left beaker pressure
- 120 mm Hg for pump pressure

- 80 mm Hg for right beaker pressure
- 3.0 mm for flow tube radius, both left and right
- 10 strokes in the Max. strokes window

3.   Click the **Auto Pump** button to start the experiment. After 10 stroke volumes have been delivered, the Flow and Rate windows will display the experimental results given the current parameters. Click **Record Data** to display the figures you just collected in the experimental values grid. Click **Refill** to replenish the left beaker.

4.   Increase the stroke volume in 10-ml increments (by decreasing the End volume) and repeat step 3 until the maximum stroke volume (120 ml) is achieved. Be sure to click the **Record Data** button after each trial. Watch the pump action during each stroke to see how you can apply the concepts of starting and ending pump volumes to EDV and ESV of the heart.

5.   View your data graphically by choosing **Plot Data** from the **Tools** menu. Choose **Str.V.** as the data set to be graphed, and then use the slider bars to have the Str.V. data be plotted on the X-axis and the pump rate data be plotted on the Y-axis. Answer the following questions. When you have finished, click the close box at the top of the plot window.

What happened to the pump's rate as its stroke volume was increased?

_____

_____

_____

Using your simulation results as a basis for your answer, explain why an athlete's resting heart rate might be lower than that of the average person.

_____

_____

_____

Applying the simulation outcomes to the human heart, predict the effect of increasing the stroke volume on cardiac output (at any given rate).

_____

_____

_____ ▬

Studying Combined Effects

In this section, you will set up your own experimental conditions to answer the following questions. Carefully examine each question and decide how to set experimental parameters

to arrive at an answer. You can examine your previously collected data if you need additional information. Record several data points for each question as evidence for your answer (unless the question calls for a single pump stroke).

Click the **Add Data Set** button in the data collection unit. Next, create a new data set called Combined. Your newly created data set will be displayed beneath Str.V. Now click the **Combined** line to activate the data set. As you collect the supporting data for the following questions, be sure to click **Record Data** each time you have a data point you wish to keep for your records.

How is the flow rate affected when the right flow tube radius is kept constant (at 3.0 mm) and the left flow tube radius is modified (either up or down)?

_____

_____

_____

_____

How does decreasing left flow tube radius affect pump chamber filling time? Does it affect the ability of the pump to empty?

_____

_____

_____

_____

You have already examined the effect of changing the pump's end volume as a way of manipulating stroke volume. What effect will decreasing stroke volume have on the pump rate?

_____

_____

_____

_____

Try manipulating the pressure delivered to the left beaker. How does changing the left beaker pressure affect flow rate? (This change would be similar to changing pulmonary vein pressure.)

_____

_____

If the left beaker pressure is decreased to 10 mm Hg, how is pump-filling time affected?

_____

_____

_____

What happens to the pump rate if the filling time is shortened?

_____

_____

What happens to fluid flow when the right beaker pressure equals the pump pressure?

_____

_____

_____ ▬

Studying Compensation

In this activity you will explore the concept of cardiovascular compensation. Click the **Add Data Set** button in the data collection unit. Next, create a new data set called **Comp.** Your newly created data set will be displayed beneath Combined. Now click the **Comp.** line to activate the data set. As you collect the supporting data for the following questions, be sure to click **Record Data** each time you have a data point you wish to keep for your records.

Adjust the experimental conditions to the following:

* 40 mm Hg for left beaker pressure
* 120 mm Hg for pump pressure
* 80 mm Hg for right beaker pressure
* 3.0 mm for left and right flow tube radius
* 10 strokes in the Max. strokes window
* 120-ml Start volume in pump
* 50-ml End volume in pump

Click **Auto Pump,** and then record your flow rate data. Let's declare the value you just obtained to be the "normal" flow rate for the purpose of this exercise.

Now decrease the right flow tube radius to 2.5 mm, and run another trial. How does this flow rate compare with "normal"?

_____

_____

Leave the right flow tube radius at 2.5 mm radius, and try to adjust one or more other conditions to return flow to "normal."

Think logically about what condition(s) might compensate for a decrease in flow tube radius. How were you able to accomplish this? (Hint: There are several ways.)

_____

_____

_____

Circle the correct term within the parentheses: Decreasing the right flow tube radius is similar to a partial (leakage / blockage) of the aortic valve or (increased / decreased) resistance in the arterial system.

Explain how the human heart might compensate for such a condition.

_____

_____

_____

_____

To increase (or decrease) blood flow to only one particular body system (e.g., digestive), would it be better to adjust heart rate or blood vessel diameter? Explain.

_____

_____

_____

_____

Complete the following statements by circling the correct response. (If necessary, use the pump simulation to help you with your answers.)

a. If we decreased overall peripheral resistance in the human body (as in an athlete), the heart would need to generate (more / less) pressure to deliver an adequate amount of blood flow, and arterial pressure would be (higher / lower).

b. If the diameter of the arteries of the body were partly filled with fatty deposits, the heart would need to generate (more / less) force to maintain blood flow, and pressure in the arterial system would be (higher / lower) than normal.

Click **Tools → Print Data** to print your recorded data for this experiment. ▬

Histology Review Supplement

For a review of cardiovascular tissue, go to **Exercise H: Histology Atlas and Review** on the **PhysioEx website** to print out the **Cardiovascular Tissue Review** worksheet.

NAME _____

LAB TIME/DATE _____

Cardiovascular Dynamics

Vessel Resistance

The following questions refer to Activity 1: Studying the Effect of Flow Tube Radius on Fluid Flow.

1. At which radius was the fluid flow rate the highest? _____

2. What was the flow rate at this radius? _____

3. Describe the relationship between flow rate and radius size. _____

_____

4. What happens to blood vessels in the body if increased blood flow is needed?

_____

The following questions refer to Activity 2: Studying the Effect of Viscosity on Fluid Flow.

5. At what viscosity level was the fluid flow rate the highest? _____

6. Describe the relationship between flow rate and viscosity. _____

_____

7. Was the effect of viscosity greater or less than the effect of radius on fluid flow? Why? _____

_____

8. What effect would anemia have on blood flow? Why? _____

_____

The following questions refer to Activity 3: Studying the Effect of Flow Tube Length on Fluid Flow.

9. At what flow tube length was the flow rate the highest? _____

10. Describe the relationship between flow tube length and fluid flow rate. _____

_____

11. What effect do you think obesity would have on blood flow? Why? _____

_____

_____

The following questions refer to Activity 4: Studying the Effect of Pressure on Fluid Flow.

12. What effect did increased pressure have on the fluid flow rate? _____

_____

13. In the body, where does the driving pressure for fluid flow come from? _____

_____

_____

Pump Mechanics

The following questions refer to Activity 5: Studying the Effect of Radius on Pump Activity.

14. What happened to the flow rate as the right vessel radius was increased? _____

_____

15. What happened to the rate (strokes/min) as the right vessel radius was increased?

Why did this occur? _____

_____

The following questions refer to Activity 6: Studying the Effect of Stroke Volume on Pump Activity.

16. At what stroke volume tested was the pump rate the lowest? _____

17. Describe the relationship between stroke volume and pump rate. _____

_____

18. Use the relationship in question 17 to explain why an athlete's resting heart rate would be lower than that of a sedentary

individual. _____

_____

The following questions refer to Activity 7: Studying Combined Effects.

19. How did decreasing the left flow tube radius affect pump chamber filling time? Hint: Look at the change in flow rate and

relate this to filling time. _____

_____

20. When the left beaker pressure was decreased to 10 mm Hg, what happened to the filling time? _____

The following questions refer to Activity 8: Studying Compensation.

21. With the right flow tube radius decreased to 2.5 mm, what conditions did you change to bring the flow rate back to

    normal? _____

    _____

22. A decreased tube radius is analogous to atherosclerosis (plaque formation in vessels). Describe the effect this would have on

    resistance in the arterial system and how the human heart might compensate for this change. _____

    _____

Frog Cardiovascular Physiology

1. To list the properties of cardiac muscle as automaticity and rhythmicity, and to define each.

2. To explain the statement, "Cardiac muscle has an intrinsic ability to beat."

3. To compare the relative length of the refractory period of cardiac muscle with that of skeletal muscle, and to explain why it is not possible to tetanize cardiac muscle.

4. To define *extrasystole,* and to explain at what point in the cardiac cycle (and on an ECG tracing) an extrasystole can be induced.

5. To describe the effect of the following on heart rate: vagal stimulation, cold, heat, pilocarpine, atropine, epinephrine, digitalis, and potassium, sodium, and calcium ions.

6. To define *vagal escape* and discuss its value.

7. To define *ectopic pacemaker.*

Investigation of human cardiovascular physiology is very interesting, but many areas obviously do not lend themselves to experimentation. It would be tantamount to murder to inject a human subject with various drugs to observe their effects on heart activity or to expose the human heart in order to study the length of its refractory period. However, this type of investigation can be done on frogs or computer simulations and provides valuable data because the physiological mechanisms in these animals, or programmed into the computer simulation, are similar if not identical to those in humans.

In this exercise, you will conduct the cardiac investigations just mentioned.

Special Electrical Properties of Cardiac Muscle: Automaticity and Rhythmicity

Cardiac muscle differs from skeletal muscle both functionally and in its fine structure. Skeletal muscle must be electrically stimulated to contract. In contrast, heart muscle can and does depolarize spontaneously in the absence of external stimulation. This property, called **automaticity,** is due to plasma membranes that have reduced permeability to potassium ions but still allow sodium ions to slowly leak into the cells. This leakage causes the muscle cells to slowly depolarize until the action potential threshold is reached and *fast calcium channels* open, allowing Ca^{2+} entry from the extracellular fluid. Shortly thereafter, contraction occurs.

The spontaneous depolarization-repolarization events occur in a regular and continuous manner in cardiac muscle, a property referred to as **rhythmicity.**

In the following experiment, you will observe these properties of cardiac muscle in a computer simulation. Additionally, your instructor may demonstrate this procedure using a real frog.

Nervous Stimulation of the Heart

Both the parasympathetic and sympathetic nervous systems innervate the heart. Stimulation of the sympathetic nervous system increases the rate and force of contraction of the heart. Stimulation of the parasympathetic nervous system (vagal nerves) decreases the depolarization rhythm of the sinoatrial node and slows transmission of excitation through the atrio-ventricular node. If vagal stimulation is excessive, the heart will stop beating. After a short time, the ventricles will begin to beat again. This is referred to as **vagal escape** and may be the result of sympathetic reflexes or initiation of a rhythm by the Purkinje fibers.

Baseline Frog Heart Activity

The heart's effectiveness as a pump is dependent both on intrinsic (within the heart) and extrinsic (external to the heart) controls. In the first experimental series, Activities 1–3, you will investigate some of these factors.

The nodal system, in which the "pacemaker" imposes its depolarization rate on the rest of the heart, is one intrinsic factor that influences the heart's pumping action. If its impulses fail to reach the ventricles (as in heart block), the ventricles continue to beat but at their own inherent rate, which is much slower than that usually imposed on them. Although heart contraction does not depend on nerve impulses, its rate can be modified by extrinsic impulses reaching it through the autonomic nerves. Cardiac activity is also modified by various chemicals, hormones, ions, and metabolites. The effects of several of these chemical factors are examined in the next experimental series, Activities 4–9.

The frog heart has two atria and a single, incompletely divided ventricle. The pacemaker is located in the sinus venosus, an enlarged region between the venae cavae and the right atrium. The sinoatrial (SA) node of mammals may have evolved from the sinus venosus.

Choose **Exercise 6: Frog Cardiovascular Physiology** from the drop-down menu and click **GO.** Then click **Electrical Stimulation.** The opening screen will appear in a few seconds (Figure 6.1). When the program starts, you will see a tracing of the frog's heartbeat on the *oscilloscope display* in the upper right part of the screen. Because the simulation automatically adjusts itself to your computer's speed, you may not see the heart tracing appear in real time. If you want to increase the speed of the tracing (at the expense of tracing quality), click the **Tools** menu, choose **Modify Display,** and then select **Increase Speed.**

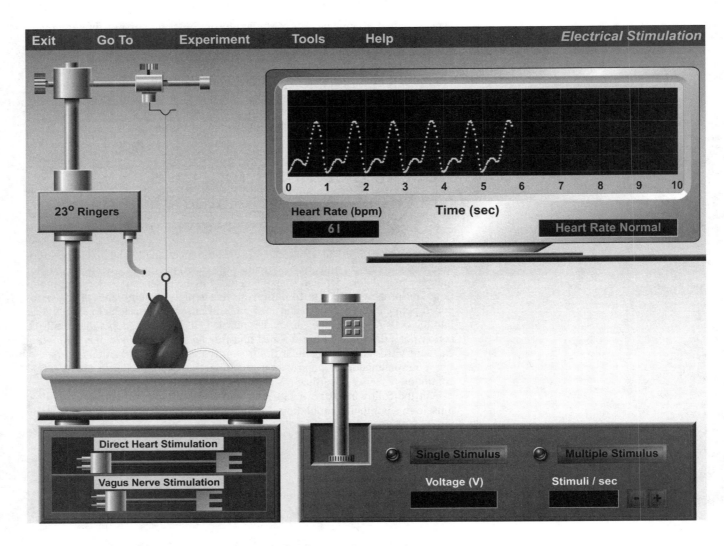

FIGURE 6.1 Opening screen of the Electrical Stimulation experiment.

To familiarize yourself with the equipment, choose **Balloons On/Off** from the **Help** menu. This feature allows you to scroll around the screen and view equipment labels. You can turn off this feature by returning to the **Help** menu and selecting **Balloons On/Off**.

The oscilloscope display shows the ventricular contraction rate in the Heart Rate window. The *heart activity window* to the right of the Heart Rate display provides the following messages:

- Heart Rate Normal—displayed when the heart is beating under resting conditions.

- Heart Rate Changing—displayed when the heart rate is increasing or decreasing.

- Heart Rate Stable—displayed when the heart rate is steady, but higher or lower than normal. For example, if you applied a chemical that increased heart rate to a stable but higher-than-normal rate, you would see this message.

The *electrical stimulator* is below the oscilloscope display. In the experiment, clicking **Single Stimulus** delivers a single electrical shock to the frog heart. Clicking **Multiple Stimulus** delivers repeated electrical shocks at the rate indicated in the Stimuli/sec window just below the Multiple Stimulus button. When the **Multiple Stimulus** button is clicked, it changes to a **Stop Stimulus** button that allows you to stop electrical stimulation as desired. Clicking the (+) or (−) buttons next to the Stimuli/sec window adjusts the stimulus rate. The voltage delivered when Single Stimulus or Multiple Stimulus is clicked is displayed in the **Voltage** window just below the Single Stimulus button. The simulation automatically adjusts the voltage for the experiment. The postlike apparatus extending upward from the electrical stimulator is the *electrode holder* into which you will drag-and-drop electrodes from the supply cabinet in the bottom left corner of the screen.

The left side of the screen contains the apparatus that sustains the frog heart. The heart has been lifted away from the body of the frog by a hook passed through the apex of the heart. Although the frog cannot be seen because it is in the dissection tray, its heart has not been removed from its circulatory system. A thin string connects the hook in the heart to the force transducer at the top of the support bracket. As the heart contracts, the string exerts tension on the force transducer, which converts the contraction into the oscilloscope tracing. The slender white strand extending from the heart toward the right side of the dissection tray is the vagus nerve. In the simulation, room-temperature (23°C) frog Ringer's solution continuously drips onto the heart to keep it moist and responsive so that a regular heart beat is maintained.

The two *electrodes* you will use during the experiment are located in the supply cabinet beneath the dissection tray. The **Direct Heart Stimulation** electrode is used to stimulate the ventricular muscle directly. The **Vagus Nerve Stimulation** electrode is used to stimulate the vagus nerve. To position either electrode, click and drag the electrode to the two-pronged plug in the electrode holder and then release the mouse button.

ACTIVITY 1

Recording Baseline Frog Heart Activity

1. Before beginning to stimulate the frog heart experimentally, watch several heartbeats. Be sure you can distinguish atrial and ventricular contraction (Figure 6.2a).

2. Record the number of ventricular contractions per minute displayed in the Heart Rate window under the oscilloscope.

_____ bpm (beats per minute) ▇

ACTIVITY 2

Investigating the Refractory Period of Cardiac Muscle

In Exercise 2 you saw that repeated rapid stimuli could cause skeletal muscle to remain in a contracted state. In other words, the muscle could be tetanized. This was possible because of the relatively short refractory period of skeletal muscle. In this experiment you will investigate the refractory period of cardiac muscle and its response to stimulation.

1. Click and hold the mouse button on the **Direct Heart Stimulation** electrode, and drag it to the electrode holder.

2. Release the mouse button to lock the electrode in place. The electrode will touch the ventricular muscle tissue.

3. Deliver single shocks in succession by clicking **Single Stimulus** rapidly. You may need to practice to acquire the correct technique.

Watch for **extrasystoles,** which are extra beats that show up riding on the ventricular contraction peak. Also note the compensatory pause, which allows the heart to get back on schedule after an extrasystole (Figure 6.2b).

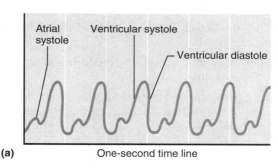

(a)   One-second time line

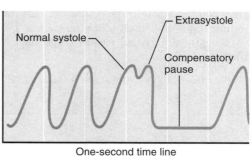

(b)   One-second time line

FIGURE 6.2 Recording of contractile activity of a frog heart. (a) Normal heartbeat. **(b)** Induction of an extrasystole.

On the basis of the recording, during which portion of the cardiac cycle was it possible to induce an extrasystole? Use Figures 6.2a and b to help you decide.

_____

_____

4. Attempt to tetanize the heart by clicking **Multiple Stimulus.** Electrical shocks will be delivered to the muscle at a rate of 20 stimuli/sec. What is the result?

_____

_____

Considering the function of the heart, why is it important that the heart muscle cannot be tetanized?

_____

_____

5. Click **Stop Stimulus** to stop the electrical stimulation. ▬▬

ACTIVITY 3

Examining the Effect of Vagus Nerve Stimulation

The vagus nerve carries parasympathetic impulses to the heart, which modify heart activity.

1. Click the **Direct Heart Stimulation** electrode to return it to the supply cabinet.

2. Click and drag the **Vagus Nerve Stimulation** electrode to the electrode holder.

3. Release the mouse button to lock the electrode in place. The vagus nerve will automatically be draped over the electrode contacts.

4. Adjust the stimulator to 50 stimuli/sec by clicking the (+) or (−) buttons.

5. Click **Multiple Stimulus.** Allow the vagal stimulation to continue until the heart stops momentarily and then begins to beat again (**vagal escape**), and then click **Stop Stimulus.**

What is the effect of vagal stimulation on heart rate?

_____

_____

_____

The phenomenon of vagal escape demonstrates that many factors are involved in heart regulation and that any deleterious factor (in this case, excessive vagal stimulation) will be overcome, if possible, by other physiological mechanisms such as activation of the sympathetic division of the autonomic nervous system (ANS). ▬▬

Assessing Physical and Chemical Modifiers of Heart Rate

Now that you have observed normal frog heart activity, you will have an opportunity to investigate the effects of various modifying factors on heart activity. After removing the agent in each activity, allow the heart to return to its normal rate before continuing with the testing.

Choose **Modifiers of Heart Rate** from the **Experiment** menu. The opening screen will appear in a few seconds (Figure 6.3). The appearance and functionality of the *oscilloscope display* is the same as it was in the Electrical Stimulation experiment. The *solutions shelf* above the oscilloscope display contains the chemicals you'll use to modify heart rate in the experiment. You can choose the temperature of the Ringer's solution dispensed by clicking the appropriate button in the Ringer's dispenser at the left part of the screen. The doors to the supply cabinet are closed during this experiment because the electrical stimulator is not used.

When you click **Record Data** in the *data control unit* below the oscilloscope, your data is stored in the computer's memory and is displayed in the data grid at the bottom of the screen; data displayed include the solution used and the resulting heart rate. If you are not satisfied with a trial, you can click **Delete Line.** Click **Clear Table** if you wish to repeat the entire experiment.

ACTIVITY 4

Assessing the Effect of Temperature

Predict what effect a decrease in temperature will have on heart rate and write your prediction below.

_____

1. Click the **5°C Ringer's** button to bathe the frog heart in cold Ringer's solution. Watch the recording for a change in cardiac activity.

2. When the heart activity window displays the message Heart Rate Stable, click **Record Data** to retain your data in the data grid.

What change occurred with the cold (5°C) Ringer's solution? Compare to the baseline value recorded in Activity 1.

_____

Did this change match your prediction? _____

3. Now click the **23°C Ringer's** button to flood the heart with fresh room-temperature Ringer's solution.

4. After you see the message Heart Rate Normal in the heart activity window, click the **32°C Ringer's** button.

5. When the heart activity window displays the message Heart Rate Stable, click **Record Data** to retain your data.

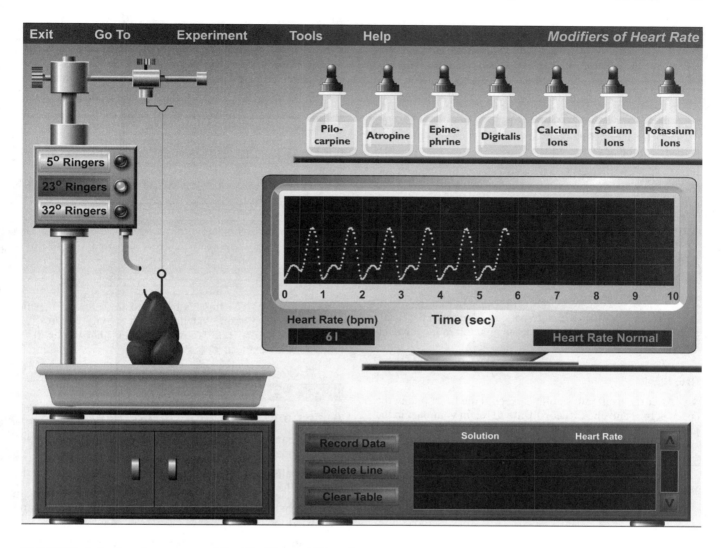

FIGURE 6.3 Opening screen of the Modifiers of Heart Rate experiment.

What change occurred with the warm (32°C) Ringer's solution?

_____

Record the heart rate at the two temperatures below.

_____ bpm at 5°C; _____ bpm at 32°C

What can you say about the effect of temperature on heart rate?

_____

_____

6.   Click the **23°C Ringer's** button to flush the heart with fresh Ringer's solution. Watch the heart activity window for the message Heart Rate Normal before beginning the next test. ▬

ACTIVITY 5

Assessing the Effect of Pilocarpine

1.   Click and hold the mouse on the **pilocarpine** dropper cap.

2.   Drag the dropper cap to a point about an inch above the heart, and release the mouse.

3.   Pilocarpine solution will be dispensed onto the heart, and the dropper cap will automatically return to the pilocarpine bottle.

4.   Watch the heart activity window for the message Heart Rate Stable, indicating that the heart rate has stabilized under the effects of pilocarpine.

5.   After the heart rate stabilizes, record the heart rate in the space provided below, and click **Record Data** to retain your data in the grid.

_____ bpm

What happened when the heart was bathed in the pilocarpine solution?

_____

_____

6. Click the **23°C Ringer's** button to flush the heart with fresh Ringer's solution. Watch the heart activity window for the message Heart Rate Normal, an indication that the heart is ready for the next test. ▬▬

Pilocarpine simulates the effect of parasympathetic nerve (hence, vagal) stimulation by enhancing acetylcholine release; such drugs are called parasympathomimetic drugs.

ACTIVITY 6

Assessing the Effect of Atropine

1. Drag-and-drop the **atropine** dropper cap to a point about an inch above the heart.

2. Atropine solution will automatically drip onto the heart, and the dropper cap will return to its position in the atropine bottle.

3. Watch the heart activity window for the message Heart Rate Stable.

4. After the heart rate stabilizes, record the heart rate in the space below, and click **Record Data** to retain your data in the grid.

_____ bpm

What is the effect of atropine on the heart?

_____

Atropine is a drug that blocks the effect of the neurotransmitter acetylcholine, liberated by the parasympathetic nerve endings. Do your results accurately reflect this effect of atropine?

_____

_____

Are pilocarpine and atropine agonists or antagonists with respect to each other in their effects on heart activity?

_____

_____

5. Click the **23°C Ringer's** button to flush the heart with fresh Ringer's solution. Watch the heart activity window for the message Heart Rate Normal before beginning the next test. ▬▬

ACTIVITY 7

Assessing the Effect of Epinephrine

1. Drag-and-drop the **epinephrine** dropper cap to a point about an inch above the heart.

2. Epinephrine solution will be dispensed onto the heart, and the dropper cap will return to the epinephrine bottle.

3. Watch the heart activity window for the message Heart Rate Stable.

4. After the heart rate stabilizes, record the heart rate in the space provided below, and click **Record Data** to retain your data in the grid.

_____ bpm

What happened when the heart was bathed in the epinephrine solution?

_____

Which division of the autonomic nervous system does its effect imitate?

_____

_____

5. Click the **23°C Ringer's** button to flush the heart with fresh Ringer's solution. Watch the heart activity window for the message Heart Rate Normal, meaning that the heart is ready for the next test. ▬▬

ACTIVITY 8

Assessing the Effect of Digitalis

1. Drag-and-drop the **digitalis** dropper cap to a point about an inch above the heart.

2. Digitalis solution will automatically drip onto the heart, and then the dropper will return to the digitalis bottle.

3. Watch the heart activity window to the right of the Heart Rate window for the message Heart Rate Stable.

4. After the heart rate stabilizes, record the heart rate in the space provided below, and click **Record Data** to retain your data in the grid.

_____ bpm

What is the effect of digitalis on the heart?

_____

5. Click the **23°C Ringer's** button to flush the heart with fresh Ringer's solution. Watch the heart activity window for the message Heart Rate Normal, then proceed to the next test. ▬▬

Digitalis (also known as digoxin and digitoxin) is a drug commonly prescribed for heart patients with congestive heart failure. It slows heart rate and strengthens the force of contraction of the heart, providing more time for venous return and decreasing the workload on the weakened heart. These effects are thought to be due to inhibition of the sodium-potassium pump and enhancement of Ca^{2+} entry into myocardial fibers.

Assessing the Effect of Various Ions

To test the effect of various ions on the heart, apply the desired solution using the following method.

1. Drag-and-drop the **calcium ions** dropper cap to a point about an inch above the heart.

2. Calcium ions will automatically be dripped onto the heart, and the dropper cap will return to the calcium ions bottle.

3. Watch the heart activity window for the message Heart Rate Stable.

4. When you see Heart Rate Stable on the screen, record the heart rate in the space provided below step 6, and click **Record Data** to retain your data in the grid.

5. Click the **23°C Ringer's** button to flush the heart with fresh Ringer's solution. Watch the heart activity window for the message Heart Rate Normal, which means that the heart is ready for the next test.

6. Repeat steps 1 through 5 for **sodium ions** and then **potassium ions.**

Effect of Ca^{2+}:

Does the heart rate stabilize and remain stable?

_____

Describe your observations of the rhythm of the heartbeat.

_____

_____

Effect of Na^{+}:

Does the heart rate stabilize and remain stable?

_____

Describe your observations of the rhythm of the heartbeat.

_____

_____

Effect of K^{+}:

Describe what happened to the recording.

_____

_____

Describe your observations of the rhythm of the heartbeat.

_____

_____

Potassium ion concentration is normally higher within cells than in the extracellular fluid. *Hyperkalemia* decreases the resting potential of plasma membranes, thus decreasing the force of heart contraction. In some cases, the conduction rate of the heart is so depressed that **ectopic pacemakers** (pacemakers appearing erratically and at abnormal sites in the heart muscle) appear in the ventricle, and fibrillation may occur.

Was there any evidence of premature beats in the recording of potassium ion effects?

_____

Was arrhythmia produced with any of the ions tested?

_____ If so, which? _____

7. Click **Tools → Print Data** to print your recorded data for this experiment. ▆▆

Histology Review Supplement

For a review of cardiovascular tissue, go to **Exercise H: Histology Atlas and Review** on the **PhysioEx website** to print out the **Cardiovascular Tissue Review** worksheet.

Frog Cardiovascular Physiology

NAME _____

LAB TIME/DATE _____

Baseline Frog Heart Activity

The following questions refer to Activity 1: Recording Baseline Frog Heart Activity.

1. What was the baseline heart rate for the frog? _____

2. Which wave is larger, the one for atrial contraction or the one for ventricular contraction?_____

   Why? _____

   _____

The following questions refer to Activity 2: Investigating the Refractory Period of Cardiac Muscle.

3. At what time during the contraction cycle was it possible to induce an extrasystole?

   _____

4. By clicking the Multiple Stimulus button and delivering 20 stimuli/sec, were you able to achieve tetanus? Why or why

   not? _____

   _____

The following questions refer to Activity 3: Examining the Effect of Vagus Nerve Stimulation.

5. What happens to the heart rate with vagal stimulation? _____

   _____

6. What happens during vagal escape? _____

   _____

Assessing Physical and Chemical Modifiers of Heart Rate

The following questions refer to Activity 4: Assessing the Effect of Temperature.

7. List the frog heart rate for the following conditions:

    _____ bpm with 5°C Ringer's solution

    _____ bpm with 32°C Ringer's solution

8. Describe the effect of temperature on heart rate. _____

    _____

9. Did this effect match your prediction? Explain. _____

    _____

The following questions refer to Activity 5: Assessing the Effect of Pilocarpine.

10. What was the heart rate after treatment with pilocarpine?

    _____ bpm with pilocarpine

11. Did this effect match your prediction? Explain. _____

    _____

The following questions refer to Activity 6: Assessing the Effect of Atropine.

12. What was the heart rate after treatment with atropine?

    _____ bpm with atropine

13. Are the effects of pilocarpine and atropine the same or opposite?

    _____

The following questions refer to Activity 7: Assessing the Effect of Epinephrine.

14. What was the heart rate after treatment with epinephrine?

    _____ bpm with epinephrine

15. Did this effect match your prediction? Explain. _____

    _____

16. What division of the autonomic nervous system does the addition of epinephrine imitate? _____

    _____

The following questions refer to Activity 8: Assessing the Effect of Digitalis.

17. What was the heart rate after treatment with digitalis?

    _____ bpm with digitalis

18. Describe the effect that digitalis had on the heart. _____

    _____

The following questions refer to Activity 9: Assessing the Effect of Various Ions.

19. Which ions resulted in arrhythmia of the frog heart? _____

    _____

20. Which ion had the greatest effect on the frog heart? Explain. _____

    _____

    _____

Respiratory System Mechanics

The two phases of **pulmonary ventilation** or **breathing** are **inspiration,** during which air is taken into the lungs, and **expiration,** during which air is expelled from the lungs. Inspiration occurs as the external intercostal muscles and the diaphragm contract. The diaphragm, normally a dome-shaped muscle, flattens as it moves inferiorly while the external intercostal muscles between the ribs lift the rib cage. These cooperative actions increase the thoracic volume. Because the increase in thoracic volume causes a partial vacuum, air rushes into the lungs. During normal expiration, the inspiratory muscles relax, causing the diaphragm to rise and the chest wall to move inward. The thorax returns to its normal shape due to the elastic properties of the lung and thoracic wall. Like a deflating balloon, the pressure in the lungs rises, which forces air out of the lungs and airways. Although expiration is normally a passive process, abdominal wall muscles and the internal intercostal muscles can contract to force air from the lungs. Blowing up a balloon is an example where such **forced expiration** would occur.

Simulating Spirometry: Measuring Respiratory Volumes and Capacities

This computerized simulation allows you to investigate the basic mechanical function of the respiratory system as you determine lung volumes and capacities. The concepts you will learn by studying this simulated mechanical lung can then be applied to help you understand the operation of the human respiratory system.

Normal quiet breathing moves about 500 ml (0.5 liter) of air (the tidal volume) in and out of the lungs with each breath, but this amount can vary due to a person's size, sex, age, physical condition, and immediate respiratory needs. The terms used for the normal respiratory volumes are defined next. The values are for the normal adult male and are approximate.

Normal Respiratory Volumes

Tidal volume (TV): Amount of air inhaled or exhaled with each breath under resting conditions (500 ml)

Expiratory reserve volume (ERV): Amount of air that can be forcefully exhaled after a normal tidal volume exhalation (1200 ml)

Inspiratory reserve volume (IRV): Amount of air that can be forcefully inhaled after a normal tidal volume inhalation (3100 ml)

Residual volume (RV): Amount of air remaining in the lungs after complete exhalation (1200 ml)

Vital capacity (VC): Maximum amount of air that can be exhaled after a normal maximal inspiration (4800 ml)

$$VC = TV + IRV + ERV$$

Total lung capacity (TLC): Sum of vital capacity and residual volume

Pulmonary Function Tests

Forced vital capacity (FVC): Amount of air that can be expelled when the subject takes the deepest possible breath and exhales as completely and rapidly as possible

Forced expiratory volume (FEV_1): Measures the percentage of the vital capacity that is exhaled during 1 second of the FVC test (normally 75% to 85% of the vital capacity)

Choose **Exercise 7: Respiratory System Mechanics** from the drop-down menu and click **GO.** Before you perform the activities, watch the **Water-Filled Spirometer** video to see the experiment performed with a human subject. Then click **Respiratory Volumes.** The opening screen for the Respiratory Volumes experiment will appear in a few seconds (Figure 7.1a). The main features on the screen when the program starts are a pair of *simulated lungs within a bell jar* at the left side of the screen, an *oscilloscope* in the upper right part of the screen, a *data display* area beneath the oscilloscope, and a *data control unit* at the bottom of the screen.

The black rubber "diaphragm" sealing the bottom of the glass bell jar is attached to a rod in the pump just below the jar. The rod moves the rubber diaphragm up and down to change the pressure within the bell jar (comparable to the intrapleural pressure in the body). As the diaphragm moves inferiorly, the resulting volume increase creates a partial vacuum in the bell jar because of lowered pressure. This partial vacuum causes air to be sucked into the tube at the top of the bell jar and then into the simulated lungs.

Conversely, as the diaphragm moves up, the rising pressure within the bell jar forces air out of the lungs. The partition between the two lungs compartmentalizes the bell jar into right and left sides. The lungs are connected to an airflow tube in which the diameter is adjustable by clicking the (+) and (−) buttons next to the Radius window in the equipment atop the bell jar. The volume of each breath that passes through the single airflow tube above the bell jar is displayed in the Flow window. Clicking **Start** below the bell jar begins a trial run in which the simulated lungs will "breathe" in normal tidal volumes and the oscilloscope will display the tidal tracing. When **ERV** is clicked, the program will simulate forced exhalation utilizing the contraction of the internal in-

tercostal muscles and abdominal wall muscles, and the expiratory reserve volume will be displayed in the Exp. Res. Vol. window below the oscilloscope. When **FVC** is clicked, the lungs will first inhale maximally and then exhale fully to demonstrate forced vital capacity. After ERV and FVC have been measured, the remaining lung values will be calculated and displayed in the small windows below the oscilloscope.

The data control equipment in the lower part of the screen records and displays data accumulated during the experiments. When you click **Record Data,** your data are recorded in the computer's memory and displayed in the data grid. Data displayed in the data grid include the Radius, Flow, TV (tidal volume), ERV (expiratory reserve volume), IRV (inspiratory reserve volume), RV (residual volume), VC (vital capacity), FEV_1 (forced expiratory volume—1 second), TLC (total lung capacity), and Pump Rate. Clicking **Delete Line** allows you to discard the data for a single run; clicking **Clear Table** erases the entire experiment to allow you to start over.

If you need help identifying any piece of equipment, choose **Balloons On/Off** from the **Help** menu, and move the mouse pointer onto any piece of equipment visible on the computer's screen. As the pointer touches the object, a pop-up window will identify the equipment. To close the pop-up window, move the mouse pointer away from the equipment. Choose **Balloons On/Off** to turn off this Help feature.

> **A C T I V I T Y   1**

Measuring Respiratory Volumes

Your first experiment will establish the baseline respiratory values.

1.   If the grid in the data control unit is not empty, click **Clear Table** to discard all previous data.

2.   Adjust the radius of the airways to 5.00 mm by clicking the appropriate button next to the Radius window.

3.   Click **Start,** and allow the tracing to complete. Watch the simulated lungs begin to breathe as a result of the "contraction and relaxation" of the diaphragm. Simultaneously, the oscilloscope will display a tracing of the tidal volume for each breath. The Flow window atop the bell jar indicates the tidal volume for each breath, and the Tidal Vol. window below the oscilloscope shows the average tidal volume. The Pump Rate window displays the number of breaths per minute.

4.   Click **Clear Tracings.**

5.   Now click **Start** again. After a second or two, click **ERV,** wait 2 seconds and then click **FVC** to complete the measurement of respiratory volumes. The expiratory reserve volume, inspiratory reserve volume, and residual volume will be automatically calculated and displayed from the tests you have performed so far. Also, the equipment calculates and displays the total lung capacity.

6.   Compute the **minute respiratory volume (MRV)** using the following formula:

$$MRV = TV \times BPM \text{ (breaths per minute)}$$

MRV _____ml/min

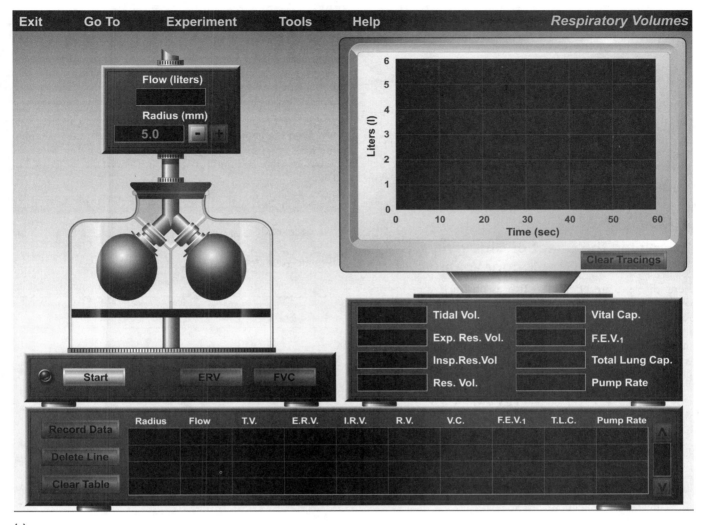

(a)

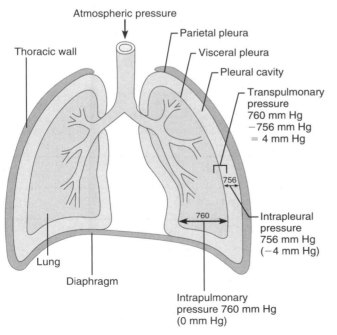

(b)

FIGURE 7.1 Respiratory Volumes. (a) Opening screen
of the Respiratory Volumes experiment.
(b) Intrapulmonary and intrapleural pressure relationships.

7.   Does expiratory reserve volume include tidal volume?

_____ Explain your answer. _____

_____

_____

8.   Now click **Record Data** to record the current experimental data in the data grid. Then click **Clear Tracings.**

9.   If you want to print a tracing at any time, click **Tools** and then **Print Graph.** ▬▬

Examining the Effect of Changing Airway Resistance on Respiratory Volumes

Lung diseases are often classified as obstructive or restrictive. With an **obstructive** problem, expiratory flow is affected, whereas a **restrictive** problem might indicate reduced inspiratory volume. Although they are not diagnostic, pulmonary function tests such as FEV_1 can help a clinician determine the difference between obstructive and restrictive problems. FEV_1 is the forced volume exhaled in 1 second. In obstructive disorders like chronic bronchitis and asthma, airway resistance is increased and FEV_1 will be low. Here you will explore what effect changing the diameter of the airway has on pulmonary function.

1.   Do *not* clear the data table from the previous experiment.

2.   Adjust the radius of the airways to 4.50 mm by clicking the ($-$) button next to the Radius window.

3.   Click **Start** to begin respirations.

4.   Click **FVC.** As you saw in the previous test, the simulated lungs will inhale maximally and then exhale as forcefully as possible. FEV_1 will be displayed in the FEV_1 window below the oscilloscope.

5.   When the lungs stop respiring, click **Record Data** to record the current data in the data grid.

6.   Decrease the radius of the airways in 0.50-mm decrements and repeat steps 4 and 5 until the minimum radius (3.00 mm) is achieved. Be sure to click **Record Data** after each trial. Click **Clear Tracings** between trials. If you make an error and want to delete a single value, click the data line in the data grid and then click **Delete Line.**

7.   A useful way to express FEV_1 is as a percentage of the forced vital capacity. Copy the FEV_1 and vital capacity values from the computer screen to Chart 1, and then calculate the FEV_1 (%) by dividing the FEV_1 volume by the vital capacity volume and multiply by 100. Record the FEV_1 (%) in Chart 1.

What happened to the FEV_1 (%) as the radius of the airways

was decreased? _____

Explain your answer. _____

_____

_____

8.   Click **Tools** → **Print Data** to print your data. ▬▬

Simulating Factors Affecting Respirations

This part of the computer simulation allows you to explore the action of surfactant on pulmonary function and the effect of changing the intrapleural pressure.

Choose **Factors Affecting Respirations** from the **Experiment** menu. The opening screen will appear in a few seconds (Figure 7.2). The basic features on the screen when the program starts are the same as in the Respiratory Volumes experiment screen. Additional equipment includes a surfactant dispenser atop the bell jar and valves on each side of the bell jar. Each time **Surfactant** is clicked, a measured amount of surfactant is sprayed into the lungs. Clicking **Flush** washes surfactant from the lungs to prepare for another run.

CHART 1	FEV₁ as % of VC		
Radius (mm)	FEV₁ (ml)	Vital Capacity (ml)	FEV₁ (%)
5.00			
4.50			
4.00			
3.50			
3.00			

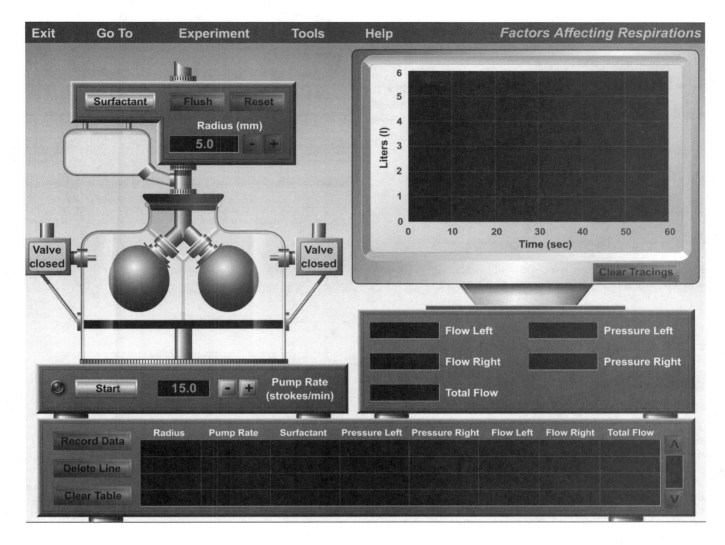

FIGURE 7.2 Opening screen of the Factors Affecting Respirations experiment.

Clicking the valve button (which currently reads **valve closed**) allows the pressure within that side of the bell jar to equalize with the atmospheric pressure. When **Reset** is clicked, the lungs are prepared for another run.

Data accumulated during a run are displayed in the windows below the scilloscope. When you click **Record Data,** that data are recorded in the computer's memory and displayed in the data grid. Data displayed in the data grid include the Radius, Pump Rate, the amount of Surfactant, Pressure Left (pressure in the left lung), Pressure Right (pressure in the right lung), Flow Left (airflow in the left lung), Flow Right (airflow in the right lung), and Total Flow. Clicking **Delete Line** allows you to discard data values for a single run, and clicking **Clear Table** erases the entire experiment to allow you to start over.

ACTIVITY 3

Examining the Effect of Surfactant

At any gas-liquid boundary, the molecules of the liquid are attracted more strongly to each other than they are to the air molecules. This unequal attraction produces tension at the liquid surface called *surface tension*. Because surface tension resists any force that tends to increase surface area, it acts to decrease the size of hollow spaces, such as the alveoli or microscopic air spaces within the lungs. If the film lining the air spaces in the lung were pure water, it would be very difficult, if not impossible, to inflate the lungs. However, the aqueous film covering the alveolar surfaces contains **surfactant,** a detergent-like lipoprotein that decreases surface tension by reducing the attraction of water molecules for each other. You will explore the action of surfactant in this experiment.

1. If the data grid is not empty, click **Clear Table** to discard all previous data values.

2. Adjust the airway radius to 5.00 mm by clicking the appropriate button next to the Radius window.

3. If necessary, click **Flush** to clear the simulated lungs of existing surfactant.

4. Click **Start,** and allow a baseline run without added surfactant to complete.

5. When the run completes, click **Record Data.**

6. Now click **Surfactant** twice.

7. Click **Start** to begin the surfactant run.

8. When the lungs stop respiring, click **Record Data** to display the data in the grid.

What happened to the FEV$_1$ (%) as the radius of the airways

was decreased? _____

_____

How has the airflow changed compared to the baseline run?

_____

_____

Premature infants often have difficulty breathing. Explain why this might be so. (Use your text as needed.)

_____

_____ ▬

ACTIVITY 4

Investigating Intrapleural Pressure

The pressure within the pleural cavity, **intrapleural pressure,** is less than the pressure within the alveoli. This negative pressure condition is caused by two forces, the tendency of the lung to recoil due to its elastic properties and the surface tension of the alveolar fluid. These two forces act to pull the lungs away from the thoracic wall, creating a partial vacuum in the pleural cavity (refer to Figure 7.1b). Because the pressure in the intrapleural space is lower than atmospheric pressure, any opening created in the thoracic wall equalizes the intrapleural pressure with the atmospheric pressure by allowing air to enter the pleural cavity, a condition called **pneumothorax.** Pneumothorax allows lung collapse, a condition called **atelectasis.**

In the simulated respiratory system on the computer screen, the intrapleural space is the space between the wall of the bell jar and the outer wall of the lung it contains. The pressure difference between inspiration and expiration for the left lung is displayed in the Pressure Left window below the oscilloscope; the Pressure Right window gives the data for the right lung.

1. Do *not* discard your previous data.

2. Click **Clear Tracings** to clean up the screen, and then click **Flush** to clear the lungs of surfactant from the previous run.

3. Adjust the radius of the airways to 5.00 mm by clicking the appropriate button next to the Radius window.

4. Click **Start,** and allow one screen of respirations to complete. Notice the negative pressure condition displayed below the oscilloscope when the lungs inflate.

5. When the lungs stop respiring, click **Record Data** to display the data in the grid.

6. Now click the valve button (which currently reads **Valve closed**) on the left side of the bell jar above the Start button to open the valve.

7. Click **Start** to begin the run.

8. When the run completes, click **Record Data** again.

What happened to the lung in the left side of the bell jar?

_____

_____

How did the pressure in the left lung differ from that in the right lung?

_____

Explain your reasoning. _____

_____

How did the total air flow in this trial compare with that in the previous trial in which the pleural cavities were intact?

_____

_____

What do you think would happen if the two lungs were in a single large cavity instead of separate cavities?

_____

_____

9. Now close the valve you opened earlier by clicking it again, and then click **Start** to begin a new trial.

10. When the run completes, click **Record Data** to display the data in the grid.

Did the deflated lung reinflate? _____

Explain your answer. _____

_____

_____

11. Click the **Reset** button atop the bell jar. This action draws the air out of the intrapleural space and returns it to normal resting condition.

12. Click **Start,** and allow the run to complete.

13. When the run completes, click **Record Data** to display the data in the grid.

14. Click **Tools** → **Print Data** to print data.

Why did lung function in the deflated (left) lung return to normal after you clicked Reset?

_____

_____ ▬

Simulating Variations in Breathing

This part of the computer simulation allows you to examine the effects of hyperventilation, rebreathing, and breath holding on CO_2 level in the blood.

Choose **Variations in Breathing** from the **Experiment** menu. The opening screen will appear in a few seconds (Figure 7.3). The basic features on the screen when the program starts are the same as in the lung volumes screen. The buttons beneath the oscilloscope control the various possi-

ble breathing patterns. Clicking **Hyperventilation** causes the lungs to breathe faster than normal. A small bag automatically covers the airway tube when **Rebreathing** is clicked. Clicking **Breath Holding** causes the lungs to stop respiring. Click **Normal Breathing** at any time to resume normal tidal cycles. The window next to the Start button displays the breathing pattern being performed by the simulated lungs.

The windows below the oscilloscope display the P_{CO_2} (partial pressure of CO_2) of the air in the lungs, Maximum P_{CO_2}, Minimum P_{CO_2}, and Pump Rate.

Data accumulated during a run are displayed in the windows below the oscilloscope. When you click **Record Data,** that data is recorded in the computer's memory and is displayed in the data grid. Data displayed in the data grid include the Condition, P_{CO_2}, Maximum P_{CO_2}, Minimum P_{CO_2}, Pump Rate, Radius, and Total Flow. Clicking **Delete Line** allows you to discard data values for a single run, and clicking **Clear Table** erases the entire experiment to allow you to start over.

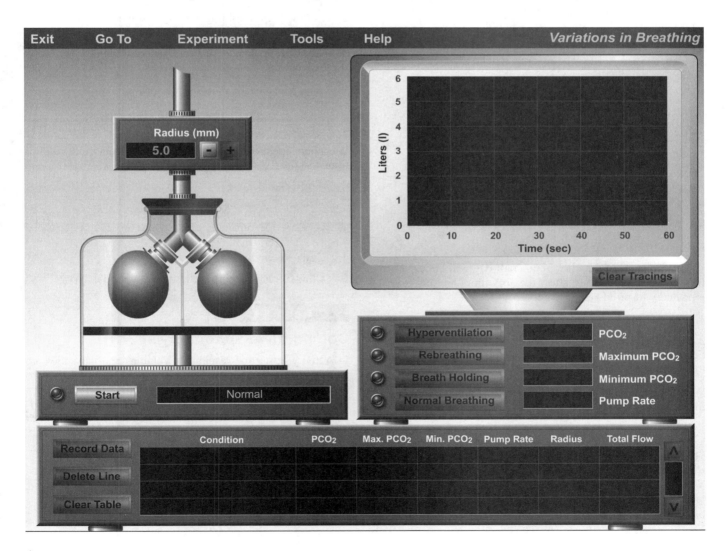

FIGURE 7.3 Opening screen of the Variations in Breathing experiment.

Exploring Various Breathing Patterns

You will establish the baseline respiratory values in the first part of this experiment.

1.   If the grid in the data control unit is not empty, click **Clear Table** to discard all previous data.

2.   Adjust the radius of the airways to 5.00 mm by clicking the appropriate button next to the Radius window. Now, read through steps 3–5 before attempting to execute them.

3.   Click **Start,** and notice that it changes to **Stop** to allow you to stop the respiration. Watch the simulated lungs begin to breathe as a result of the external mechanical forces supplied by the pump below the bell jar. Simultaneously, the oscilloscope will display a tracing of the tidal volume for each breath.

4.   After 2 seconds, click the **Hyperventilation** button and watch the P_{CO_2} displays. The breathing pattern will change to short, rapid breaths. The P_{CO_2} of the air in the lungs will be displayed in the small window to the right of the Hyperventilation button.

5.   Watch the oscilloscope display and the P_{CO_2} window, and click **Stop** before the tracing reaches the end of the screen.

What happens to P_{CO_2} during rapid breathing? Explain your answer.

_____

_____

6.   Click **Record Data.**

7.   Now click **Clear Tracings** to prepare for the next run.

Rebreathing

When **Rebreathing** is clicked, a small bag will appear over the end of the air tube to allow the air within the lungs to be repeatedly inspired and expired.

1.   Click **Start,** wait 2 seconds, and then click **Rebreathing.**

2.   Watch the breathing pattern on the oscilloscope, and notice the P_{CO_2} during the course of the run. Click **Stop** when the tracing reaches the right edge of the oscilloscope.

What happens to P_{CO_2} during the entire time of the rebreathing activity?

_____

_____

Did the depth of the breathing pattern change during rebreathing? (Carefully examine the tracing for rate and depth changes; the changes can be subtle.) Explain your observations.

_____

_____

_____

_____

3.   Click **Record Data,** and then click **Clear Tracings** to prepare for the next run.

Breath Holding

Breath holding can be considered an extreme form of rebreathing in which there is no gas exchange between the outside atmosphere and the air within the lungs.

1.   Click **Start,** wait a second or two, and then click **Breath Holding.**

2.   Let the breath-holding activity continue for about 5 seconds, and then click **Normal Breathing.**

3.   Click **Stop** when the tracing reaches the right edge of the oscilloscope.

What happened to the P_{CO_2} during breath holding?

_____

What happened to the breathing pattern when normal respirations resume?

_____

_____

4.   Click **Record Data.**

5.   Click **Tools → Print Data** to print your data. ■

Comparative Spirometry

In Activity 1, normal respiratory volumes and capacities are measured. In this activity, you will explore what happens to these values when pathophysiology develops or during episodes of aerobic exercise. Using a water-filled spirometer and knowledge of respiratory mechanics, changes to these values in each condition can be predicted, documented, and explained.

Normal Breathing

1.   Click the **Experiment** menu, and then click **Comparative Spirometry.** The opening screen will appear in a few seconds (see Figure 7.4).

2. For the patient's type of breathing, select the **Normal** option from the drop-down menu in the **Patient Type** box. These values will serve as a basis of comparison in the diseased conditions.

3. Select the patient's breathing pattern as **Unforced Breathing** from the **Breathing Pattern Option** box.

4. After these selections are made, click the **Start** button and watch as the drum starts turning and the spirogram develops on the paper rolling off the drum across the screen, left to right.

5. When half the screen is filled with unforced tidal volumes and the trace has paused, select the **Forced Vital Capacity** button in the Breathing Pattern Options box.

6. Click the **Start** button and the trace will continue with the FVC maneuver. The trace ends as the paper rolls to the right edge of the screen.

7. Now click on the individual measure buttons that appear in the data table above each data column to measure the lung volume and lung capacity data. Note that when a measure button is selected, two things happen simultaneously: (1) a bracket

appears on the spirogram to indicate where that measurement originates on the spirogram and (2) the value in milliliters appears in the data table. Also note that when the FEV_1 measure button is selected, the final column labeled FEV_1/FVC will be automatically calculated and appear in the data table. The calculation is $(FEV_1/FVC) \times 100\%$, and the result will appear as a percentage in the data table.

What do you think is the clinical importance of the FVC and FEV_1 values?

_____

Why do you think the ratio of these two values is important to

the clinician when diagnosing respiratory diseases? _____

_____

$FEV_1/FVC \times 100\% =$ _____

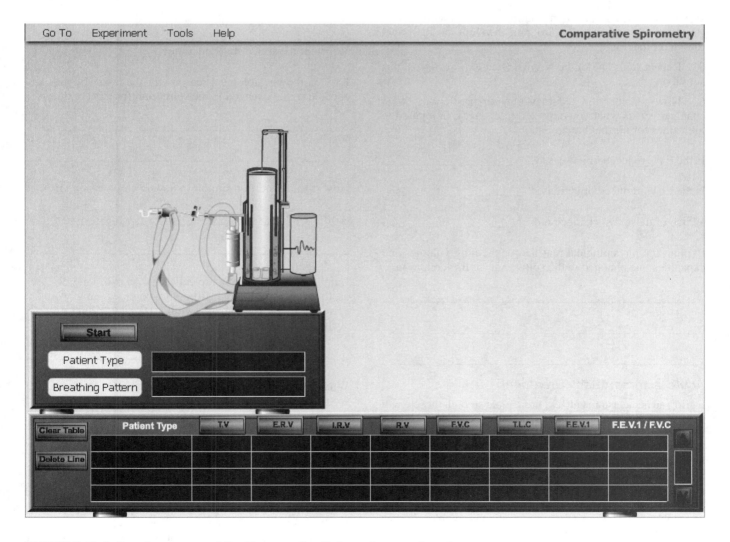

FIGURE 7.4 Opening screen of the Comparative Spirometry experiment.

Emphysema Breathing

In a person with emphysema, there is a significant loss of intrinsic elastic recoil in the lung tissue. This loss of elastic recoil occurs as the disease destroys the walls of the alveoli. Airway resistance is also increased as the lung tissue in general becomes more flimsy and exerts less mechanical tethering on the surrounding airways. Thus the lung becomes overly compliant and expands easily. Conversely, a great effort is required to exhale as the lungs can no longer passively recoil and deflate. A noticeable and exhausting muscular effort is required for each exhalation. Thus a person with emphysema exhales slowly.

1.   Using this information, predict what lung values will change in the spirogram when the patient with emphysema breathing is selected. Assume that significant disease has developed, and thus a loss of elastic recoil has occurred in this patient's lungs.

2.   Select **Emphysema** from the drop-down menu in the **Patient Type** box.

3.   Select the patient's breathing pattern as **Unforced Breathing** from the **Breathing Pattern** box.

4.   After these selections are made and the existing spirogram screen clears, click the **Start** button and watch as the drum starts turning and a new spirogram develops on the paper rolling off the drum.

5.   Repeat steps 5–7 of the Normal Breathing section in this activity.

6.   Now consider the accuracy of your predictions (what changed versus what you expected to change). Compared to the values for normal breathing:

Is the FVC reduced or increased? _____

Is the FEV_1 reduced or increased? _____

Which of these two changed more? _____

Explain the physiological reasons for the lung volumes and capacities that changed in the spirogram for this condition.

_____

_____

_____

Acute Asthma Attack Breathing

During an acute asthma attack, bronchiole smooth muscle will spasm and thus the airways become constricted (that is, they have a reduced diameter). They also become clogged with thick mucous secretions. These two facts lead to significantly increased airway resistance. Underlying these symptoms is an airway inflammatory response brought on by triggers such as allergens (e.g., dust and pollen), extreme temperature changes, and even exercise. Similar to emphysema, the airways collapse and pinch closed before a forced expiration is completed. Thus the volumes and peak flow rates are significantly reduced during an asthma attack. However, the elastic recoil is not diminished in an acute asthma attack.

1.   Using this information, predict what lung values will change in the spirogram when the patient who is having an acute asthma attack is selected. Assume that significantly decreased airway radius and increased airway resistance have developed in this patient's lungs.

2.   Select **Asthmatic** from the drop-down menu in the **Patient Type** box.

3.   Select the patient's breathing pattern as **Unforced Breathing** from the **Breathing Pattern** box.

4.   After these selections are made and the existing spirogram screen clears, click the **Start** button and watch as the drum starts turning, and a new spirogram develops as the paper rolls off the drum.

5.   Repeat steps 5–7 of the Normal Breathing section in this activity.

6.   Now consider the accuracy of your predictions (what changed versus what you expected to change). Compared to the values for normal breathing:

Is the FVC reduced or increased? _____

Is the FEV_1 reduced or increased? _____

Which of these two changed more? _____

Explain the physiological reasons for the lung volumes and capacities that changed in the spirogram for this condition.

_____

_____

How is this condition similar to having emphysema? How is

it different? _____

_____

Emphysema and asthma are called *obstructive* lung diseases as they limit expiratory flow and volume. How would a spirogram look for someone with a *restrictive* lung disease, such as pulmonary fibrosis?

_____

_____

What volumes and capacities would change in this case, and would these values be increased or decreased?

_____

_____

In an acute asthma attack, the compliance of the lung is decreased, not increased as it was for emphysema, and air flows freely through the bronchioles. Therefore, will the FEV_1/ FVC percentage be less than normal, equal to normal, or higher than normal? _____

Acute Asthma Attack Breathing with Inhaler Medication Applied

When an acute asthma attack occurs, many people seek relief from the symptoms by using an inhaler. This device atomizes the medication and allows for direct application onto the afflicted airways. Usually the medication includes a smooth muscle relaxant (e.g., a beta-2 agonist or an acetylcholine antagonist) that relieves the bronchospasms and induces bronchiole dilation. The medication may also contain an anti-inflammatory agent such as a corticosteroid that suppresses the inflammatory response. Airway resistance is reduced by the use of the inhaler.

1. Using this information, predict what lung values will change in the spirogram when the patient who is having an acute asthma attack applies the inhaler medication. By how much will the values change (will they return to normal)?

2. Select **Plus Inhaler** from the drop-down menu in the **Patient Type** box.

3. Select the patient's breathing pattern as **Unforced Breathing** from the **Breathing Pattern** box.

4. After these selections are made and the existing spirogram screen clears, click the **Start** button and watch as the drum starts turning, and a new spirogram develops as the paper rolls off the drum.

5. Repeat steps 5–7 of the Normal Breathing section.

6. Now consider the accuracy of your predictions (what changed versus what you expected to change). Compared to the values for the patient experiencing asthma symptoms:

Has the FVC reduced or increased? Is it "normal"? _____

Has the FEV$_1$ reduced or increased? Is it "normal"? _____

Which of these two changed more? _____

Explain the physiological reasons for the lung volumes and capacities that changed in the spirogram with the application

of the medication. _____

_____

How much of an increase in FEV$_1$ do you think is required for it to be considered significantly improved by the medication? _____

_____

Breathing During Exercise

During moderate aerobic exercise, the human body has an increased metabolic demand, which is met in part by changes in respiration. During heavy exercise, further changes in respiration are required to meet the extreme metabolic demands of the body.

a. In moderate aerobic exercise, which do you predict will

change more, the ERV or the IRV? _____

b. Do you predict that the respiratory rate will change

significantly in moderate exercise? _____

c. Comparing heavy exercise to moderate exercise, what values do you predict will change when the body's significantly increased metabolic demands are being met by the

respiratory system? _____

_____

d. During heavy exercise, what will happen to the lung volumes and capacities that have been considered thus far?

_____

e. Will the respiratory rate change? If so, how? _____

1. Select **Moderate Exercise** from the drop-down menu in the **Patient Type** box. The existing spirogram clears.

2. Click the **Start** button and watch as the drum starts turning and a new spirogram develops. Half of the screen will fill with breathing volumes and capacities for moderate exercise.

3. When the trace pauses, click on the individual measure buttons that appear in the data table above each data column to measure the lung volume and lung capacity data.

4. Select **Heavy Exercise** from the drop-down menu in the **Patient Type** box.

5. Click the **Start** button and the trace will continue with the breathing pattern for heavy exercise. The trace ends as the paper rolls to the right-hand edge of the screen.

6. Now click on the individual measure buttons that appear in the data table above each data column to measure the lung volume and lung capacity data.

7. Now consider the accuracy of your predictions (what changed versus what you expected to change).

Which volumes changed the most and when? _____

Compare the respiratory rate during moderate exercise with

that seen during heavy exercise. _____

_____

Histology Review Supplement

For a review of respiratory tissue, go to **Exercise H: Histology Atlas and Review** on the **PhysioEx website** to print out the **Respiratory Tissue Review** worksheet.

NAME _____

LAB TIME/DATE _____

Respiratory System Mechanics

Pulmonary Function Tests

The following questions refer to Activity 1: Measuring Respiratory Volumes.

1. What activity are you simulating when you click the ERV button? _____

   What additional muscles are used in this activity? _____

2. What was the MRV calculated in Activity 1? _____

3. What does the pump rate simulate? _____

   _____

The following questions refer to Activity 2: Examining the Effect of Changing Airway Resistance on Respiratory Volumes.

4. How did changing the radius effect FEV_1 (%)? _____

   _____

5. What was the FEV_1 at a radius of 5.00 mm? _____

6. Do the results suggest that there is an obstructive or restrictive problem? Explain.

   _____

Simulating Factors Affecting Respirations

The following questions refer to Activity 3: Examining the Effect of Surfactant.

7. What effect does the addition of surfactant have on the airflow? _____

   _____

8. Why does surfactant affect airflow? _____

   _____

9. Why do premature infants have difficulty breathing? _____

   _____

The following questions refer to Activity 4: Investigating Intrapleural Pressure.

10. What effect does opening the valve have on the left lung? Why does this happen?

_____

_____

11. What condition does opening the valve simulate? _____

_____

12. What is the value of the pressure in the left lung when the valve is opened? _____

_____

13. What happened to the total flow when the valve was opened? _____

_____

14. In the last part of this activity, when the reset button was clicked, what procedure would be used with real lungs? _____

Simulating Variations in Breathing

The following questions refer to Activity 5: Exploring Various Breathing Patterns.

15. What was the value of the P_{CO_2} with rapid breathing? _____

How does this compare to the value with normal breathing? Explain any differences.

_____

16. What was the value of the P_{CO_2} with rebreathing? _____

Explain any difference. _____

17. What happened to the rate of respirations with rebreathing? _____

_____

Why do you think this happened? (Hint: Think about the effects of chemoreceptors in the body). _____

18. What was the value of the P_{CO_2} with breath holding? Explain any difference.

_____

19. Was there a change in the rate of respirations when the breathing was resumed?

_____

The following questions refer to Activity 6: Comparative Spirometry.

20. What was the value obtained for the $(FEV_1/FVC) \times 100\%$ with "normal breathing"?

_____

21. What effect did "emphysema breathing" have on FVC and FEV_1?

_____

22. In "emphysema breathing" which of the two values, FVC and FEV_1 changed the most? _____

23. What effect did "acute asthma attack breathing" have on FVC and FEV_1?

_____

24. In "acute asthma attack breathing" which of the two values, FVC and FEV_1 changed the most? _____

25. Describe the effect that the inhaler medication had on the FVC and FEV_1.

_____

26. Did the values return to "normal"? Explain. _____

_____

27. During "moderate exercise breathing," which volumes changed the most?

_____

28. During "heavy exercise breathing," which volumes changed the most?

_____

Chemical and Physical Processes of Digestion

O B J E C T I V E S

1. To list the digestive system enzymes involved in the digestion of proteins, fats, and carbohydrates; to state their site of origin; and to summarize the environmental conditions promoting their optimal functioning.

2. To recognize the variation between different types of enzyme assays.

3. To name the end products of digestion of proteins, fats, and carbohydrates.

4. To perform the appropriate chemical tests to determine if digestion of a particular food has occurred.

5. To cite the function(s) of bile in the digestive process.

6. To discuss the possible role of temperature and pH in the regulation of enzyme activity.

7. To define enzyme, catalyst, hydrolase, substrate, and control.

8. To explain why swallowing is both a voluntary and a reflex activity.

9. To discuss the role of the tongue, larynx, and gastroesophageal sphincter in swallowing.

10. To compare and contrast segmentation and peristalsis as mechanisms of propulsion.

The digestive system is a physiological marvel, composed of finely orchestrated chemical and physical activities. The food we ingest must be broken down into smaller subunits for us to absorb the nutrients we need, and digestion involves a complex sequence of mechanical and chemical processes designed to achieve this goal as efficiently as possible. As food passes through the gastrointestinal tract, it is progressively broken down by the mechanical action of smooth muscle and the chemical action of enzymes until most nutrients have been extracted and absorbed into the blood.

Chemical Digestion of Foodstuffs: Enzymatic Action

Nutrients can only be absorbed when broken down into their monomer form, so food digestion is a prerequisite to food absorption.

Enzymes are large protein molecules produced by body cells. They are biological **catalysts** that increase the rate of a chemical reaction without becoming part of the product. The digestive enzymes are hydrolytic enzymes, or **hydrolases,** which break down organic food molecules, or **substrates,** by adding water to the molecular bonds, thus cleaving the bonds between the subunits or monomers.

A hydrolytic enzyme is highly specific in its action. Each enzyme hydrolyzes one or, at most, a small group of substrate molecules, and specific environmental conditions are necessary for an enzyme to function optimally. For example, in extreme environments such as high temperature, an enzyme can unravel or denature due to the effect that temperature has on the three-dimensional structure of the protein.

Because digestive enzymes actually function outside the body cells in the digestive tract lumen, their hydrolytic activity can also be studied in a test tube. See Figure 8.1b for an overview of chemical digestion sites in the body. Such in vitro studies provide a convenient laboratory environment for investigating the effect of various factors on enzymatic activity.

Carbohydrate Digestion

In this experiment you will investigate the hydrolysis of starch to maltose by salivary amylase, the enzyme produced by the salivary glands and secreted into the mouth. For you to be able to detect whether or not enzymatic action has occurred, you need to be able to identify the presence of these substances to determine to what extent hydrolysis has occurred. Thus, **controls** must be prepared to provide a known standard against which comparisons can be made. The controls will vary for each experiment and will be discussed in each enzyme section in this exercise.

Starch decreases and sugar increases as digestion proceeds according to the following equation:

$$\text{Starch} + \text{water} \xrightarrow{\text{amylase}} \text{X maltose}$$

Because the chemical changes that occur as starch is digested to maltose cannot be seen by the naked eye, you need to conduct an *enzyme assay,* the chemical method of detecting the presence of digested substances. You will perform two enzyme assays on each sample. The IKI assay detects the presence of starch and the Benedict's assay tests for the presence of reducing sugars, such as glucose or maltose, which are the digestion products of starch. Normally a caramel-colored solution, IKI turns blue-black in the presence of starch. Benedict's reagent is a bright blue solution that changes to green to orange to reddish-brown with increasing amounts of maltose. It is important to understand that enzyme assays only indicate the presence or absence of substances. It is up to you to analyze the results of the experiments to decide if enzymatic hydrolysis has occurred.

Choose **Exercise 8: Chemical and Physical Processes of Digestion** from the drop-down menu and click **GO**. Then click **Amylase**. The opening screen will appear in a few seconds (Figure 8.1). To familiarize yourself with the equipment, choose **Balloons On/Off** from the **Help** menu. This feature allows you to scroll around the screen and view equipment labels. You can turn off this feature by returning to the **Help**

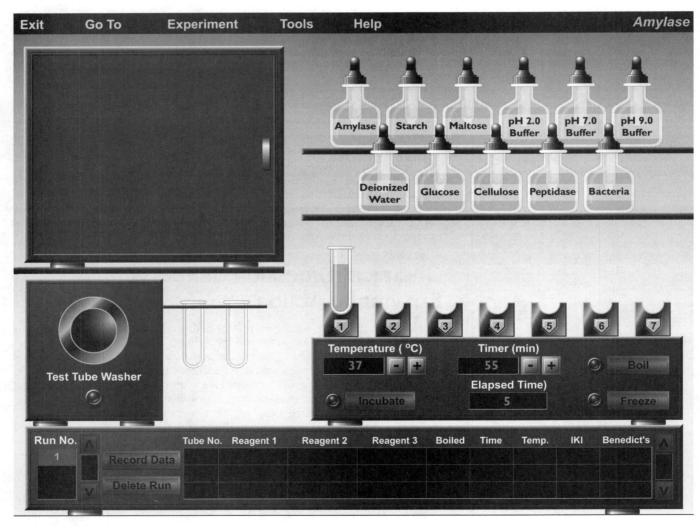

(a)

F I G U R E 8 . 1 Chemical digestion. (a) Opening screen of the Amylase experiment.

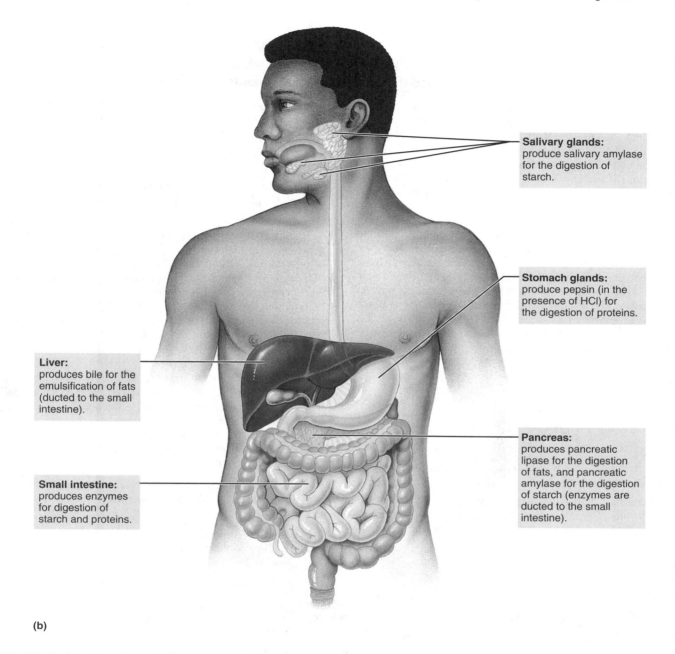

Salivary glands: produce salivary amylase for the digestion of starch.

Stomach glands: produce pepsin (in the presence of HCl) for the digestion of proteins.

Liver: produces bile for the emulsification of fats (ducted to the small intestine).

Pancreas: produces pancreatic lipase for the digestion of fats, and pancreatic amylase for the digestion of starch (enzymes are ducted to the small intestine).

Small intestine: produces enzymes for digestion of starch and proteins.

(b)

FIGURE 8.1 (*Continued*) **Chemical digestion. (b)** A few sites of chemical digestion and the organs that produce the enzymes of chemical digestion.

menu and selecting **Balloons On/Off**. The *solutions shelf* in the upper right part of the screen contains the substances to be used in the experiment. The *incubation unit* beneath the solutions shelf contains a rack of test tube holders and the apparatus needed to run the experiments. Test tubes from the *test tube washer* on the left part of the screen are loaded into the rack in the incubation unit by clicking and holding the mouse button on the first tube, and then releasing (dragging-and-dropping) it into any position in the rack. The substances in the dropper bottles on the solutions shelf are dispensed by dragging-and-dropping the dropper cap to a position over any test tube in the rack and then releasing it. During each dispensing event, five drops of solution drip into the test tube; then the dropper cap automatically returns to its position in the bottle.

Each test tube holder in the incubation unit not only supports but also allows you to boil the contents of a single test tube. Clicking the numbered button at the base of a test tube holder causes that single tube to descend into the incubation unit. To boil the contents of all tubes inside the incubation unit, click **Boil**. After they have been boiled, the tubes automatically rise. You can adjust the incubation temperature for the experiment by clicking the (+) or (−) buttons next to the Temperature window. Set the incubation time by clicking the (+) or (−) buttons next to the Timer window. Clicking the **Incubate** button starts the timer and causes the entire rack of tube holders to descend into the incubation unit where the tubes will be incubated at the temperature and the time indicated. While incubating, the tubes are automatically agitated to ensure that their contents are well mixed. During the experiment, elapsed time is displayed in the Elapsed Time window.

The cabinet doors in the *assay cabinet* above the test tube washer are closed at the beginning of the experiment, but they automatically open when the set time for incubation has elapsed. The assay cabinet contains the reagents and glassware needed to assay your experimental samples.

When you click the **Record Data** button in the *data control unit* at the bottom of the screen, your data is recorded in the computer's memory and displayed in the data grid at the bottom of the screen. Data displayed in the grid include the tube number, the three substances (additives) dispensed into each tube, whether or not a sample was boiled, the time and incubation temperature, and (+) or (−) marks indicating enzyme assay results. If you are not satisfied with a single run, you can click **Delete Run** to erase an experiment.

Once an experimental run is completed and you have recorded your data, discard the test tubes to prepare for a new run by dragging the used tubes to the large opening in the test tube washer. The test tubes will automatically be prepared for the next experiment.

The enzymes used in this simulation and their secreting organs are summarized in Figure 8.1b.

ACTIVITY 1

Assessing Starch Digestion by Salivary Amylase

Incubation

1. Individually drag seven test tubes to the test tube holders in the incubation unit.

2. Note that Chart 1 lists the substances and conditions for each test tube. Prepare tubes 1 through 7 with the substances indicated in Chart 1 below using the following approach.

- Click and hold the mouse button on the dropper cap of the desired substance on the solutions shelf.

- While still holding the mouse button down, drag the dropper cap to the top of the desired test tube.

- Release the mouse button to dispense the substance. The dropper cap automatically returns to its bottle.

3. When all tubes are prepared, click the number (**1**) under the first test tube. The tube will descend into the incubation unit. All other tubes should remain in the raised position.

4. Click **Boil** to boil tube 1. After boiling for a few moments, the tube will automatically rise.

5. Now adjust the incubation temperature to 37°C and the timer to 60 min (compressed time) by clicking the (+) or (−) buttons.

6. Click **Incubate** to start the run. The incubation unit will gently agitate the test tube rack, evenly mixing the contents of all test tubes throughout the incubation. Notice that the computer compresses the 60-minute time period into 60 seconds of real time, so what would be a 60-minute incubation in real life will take only 60 seconds in the simulation. When the incubation time elapses, the test tube rack will automatically rise, and the doors to the assay cabinet will open.

Assays

After the assay cabinet doors open, notice the two reagents in the assay cabinet. IKI tests for the presence of starch and Benedict's detects the presence of reducing sugars such as glucose or maltose, the digestion products of starch. Below the reagents are seven small assay tubes into which you will dispense a small amount of test solution from the incubated samples in the incubation unit, plus a drop of IKI.

1. Click and hold the mouse on the first tube in the incubation unit. Notice that the mouse pointer is now a miniature test tube tilted to the left.

2. While still holding the mouse button down, move the mouse pointer to the first small assay tube on the left side of

CHART 1	Salivary Amylase Digestion of Starch						
Tube no.	1	2	3	4	5	6	7
Additives	Amylase Starch pH 7.0 buffer	Amylase Starch pH 7.0 buffer	Amylase D.I. water pH 7.0 buffer	D.I. water Starch pH 7.0 buffer	D.I. water Maltose pH 7.0 buffer	Amylase Starch pH 2.0 buffer	Amylase Starch pH 9.0 buffer
Incubation condition	Boil first, then incubate at 37°C for 60 minutes	37°C	37°C	37°C	37°C	37°C	37°C
IKI test							
Benedict's test							

Note: D.I. water = deionized water

the assay cabinet. Release the mouse button. Watch the first test tube automatically decant approximately half of its contents into the first assay tube on the left.

3. Repeat steps 1 and 2 for the remaining tubes in the incubation unit, moving to a fresh assay tube each time.

4. Next, click and hold the mouse on the IKI dropper cap and drag it to the first assay tube. Release the mouse button to dispense a drop of IKI into the first assay tube on the left. You will see IKI drip into the tube, which may cause a color change in the solution. A blue-black color indicates a **positive starch test.** If starch is not present, the mixture will look like diluted IKI, a **negative starch test.** Intermediate starch amounts result in a pale gray color. The dropper will automatically move across and dispense IKI to the remaining tubes.

5. Record your results (+ for positive, − for negative) in Chart 1.

6. Dispense Benedict's reagent into the remaining mixture in each tube in the incubation unit by dragging-and-dropping the Benedict's dropper cap to the first tube. Repeat this for the remaining test tubes on top of the incubator.

7. After Benedict's reagent has been delivered to each tube in the incubation unit, click **Boil.** The entire tube rack will descend into the incubation unit and automatically boil the tube contents for a few moments.

8. When the rack of tubes rises, inspect the tubes for color change. A green-to-reddish color indicates that a reducing sugar is present; this is a **positive sugar test.** An orange-colored sample contains more sugar than a green sample. A reddish-brown color indicates even more sugar. A negative sugar test is indicated by no color change from the original bright blue. Record your results in Chart 1. Use a (+) for a green sample, a (+ +) for a reddish-brown sample, and a (−) for a blue sample.

9. Click **Record Data** to display your results in the grid and retain your data in the computer's memory for later analysis. To repeat the experiment, drag all test tubes to the test tube washer and start again.

10. Answer the following questions, referring to the chart (or the data grid in the simulation) as necessary. Hint: Closely examine the IKI and Benedict's results for each tube.

What do tubes 2, 6, and 7 reveal about pH and amylase activity? Hint: What variable was changed in the procedure?

_____

_____

Which pH buffer allowed the highest amylase activity?

_____

Which tube indicates that the amylase was not contaminated

with maltose? _____

Which tubes indicate that the deionized water did not contain

contaminating starch or maltose? _____

If we left out control tubes 3, 4, or 5, what objections could be raised to the statement: "Amylase digests starch to maltose"? (Hint: Think about the purity of the chemical solutions.)

_____

_____

Would the amylase present in saliva be active in the stomach? Explain your answer.

_____

_____

What effect does boiling have on enzyme activity?

_____

_____ ▬

Assessing Cellulose Digestion

If any test tubes are still in the incubator, click and drag them to the test tube washer before beginning this activity. In this activity, we will test to see whether amylase digests *cellulose.*

Incubation

1. Individually drag seven test tubes to the test tube holders in the incubation unit.

2. Prepare tubes 1 through 7 with the substances indicated in Chart 2 on the next page using the following approach:

- Click and hold the mouse button on the dropper cap of the desired substance on the solutions shelf.

- While holding the mouse button down, drag the dropper cap to the top of the desired test tube.

- Release the mouse button to dispense the substance. The dropper cap automatically returns to its bottle.

3. When all tubes are prepared, click the number (**1**) under the first test tube. The tube will descend into the incubation unit.

4. Click **Freeze.** The tube's contents will be subjected to a temperature of −25°C. The tube will then automatically rise, with the contents of the tube frozen.

5. Adjust the incubation temperature to 37°C and the timer to 60 minutes by clicking the appropriate (+) or (−) buttons.

6. Click **Incubate** to start the run. The incubation unit will gently agitate the tubes as they incubate to thoroughly mix the tubes' contents. At the end of the incubation period, the tubes will ascend to their original positions on top of the incubator, and the doors to the assay cabinet will open.

Assays

When the assay cabinet opens, notice the two reagents in the cabinet. They are the same ones as in the previous activity: IKI will test for the presence of starch, and Benedict's solution will test for the presence of maltose. IKI turns blue-black in the presence of cellulose as well as starch. On the floor of the cabinet are seven small tubes that you will use to test the results of your experiment. The procedure will be identical to the one from the previous activity:

1.   Click and hold the mouse on the first tube in the incubation unit. Notice that the mouse pointer is now a miniature test tube tilted to the left.

2.   While still holding the mouse button down, move the mouse pointer to the first small assay tube on the left side of the assay cabinet. Release the mouse button.

3.   Repeat steps 1 and 2 for the remaining tubes in the incubation unit, moving to a fresh assay tube each time.

4.   Next, click and hold the mouse on the IKI dropper cap, and drag it to the first assay tube. Release the mouse button to dispense a drop of IKI into the first assay tube on the left. You will see IKI drip into the tube, which may cause a color change in the solution. A blue-black color indicates the presence of starch. If there is only a small amount of starch, you may see a pale gray color. If starch is not present, the mixture will look like diluted IKI. The dropper will automatically move across and dispense IKI to the remaining tubes.

5.   Note the color of each tube. Record your results in Chart 2.

6.   Dispense Benedict's reagent into the remaining mixture in each tube in the incubation unit by dragging-and-dropping the Benedict's dropper cap to the first tube. Repeat this for the remaining test tubes on top of the incubator.

7.   After Benedict's reagent has been delivered to each tube in the incubation unit, click **Boil.** The entire tube rack will descend into the incubation unit and automatically boil the tube contents for a few moments.

8.   When the rack of tubes rises, inspect the tubes for color change. A green to reddish color indicates that a reducing sugar is present for a positive sugar test. An orange sample indicates more sugar than the green color, and a reddish-brown indicates the highest amounts of sugar. If there has been no color change from the original blue, no sugar is present in the tube. Record your results in Chart 2. Use a (+) for a green sample, a (++) for a reddish-brown sample, and a (−) for a blue sample.

9.   Click **Record Data** to display your results in the grid and retain your data in the computer's memory for later analysis. To repeat the experiment, drag all test tubes to the test tube washer and start again.

10.   Answer the following questions, referring to the chart.

Which tubes showed that starch or cellulose was still present?

_____

Which tubes tested positive for the presence of reducing sugars?

_____

What was the effect of freezing tube 1?

_____

How does the effect of freezing differ from the effect of boiling?

_____

_____

CHART 2	Enzyme Digestion of Starch and Cellulose						
Tube no.	1	2	3	4	5	6	7
Additives	Amylase Starch pH 7.0 buffer	Amylase Starch pH 7.0 buffer	Amylase Glucose pH 7.0 buffer	Amylase Cellulose pH 7.0 buffer	Amylase Cellulose D.I. water	Peptidase Starch pH 7.0 buffer	Bacteria Cellulose pH 7.0 buffer
Incubation condition	Freeze first, then incubate at 37°C for 60 minutes	37°C 60 min	37°C 60 min	37°C 60 min	37°C 60 min	37°C 60 min	37°C 60 min
IKI test							
Benedict's test							

Note: D.I. water = deionized water

Does amylase use cellulose as a substrate? Hint: Look at the results for tube 4.

_____

_____

What effect did the addition of bacteria have on the digestion of cellulose?

_____

_____

What was the effect of the different enzyme, peptidase, used in tube 6? Explain your answer, based on what you know about the substrate of peptidase.

_____

_____

11. Click **Tools** → **Print Data** to print your recorded data. ▆▆

Protein Digestion by Pepsin

The chief cells of the stomach glands produce pepsin, a protein-digesting enzyme. Pepsin hydrolyzes proteins to small fragments (polypeptides and a few free amino acids). In this experiment, you will use BAPNA, a synthetic "protein" that is transparent and colorless when in solution. However, if an active, protein-digesting enzyme such as pepsin is present, the solution will become yellow. You can use this characteristic to detect pepsin activity: the solution turns yellow if the enzyme digests the BAPNA substrate; it remains colorless if pepsin is not active or not present. One advantage of using a synthetic substrate is that you do not need any additional indicator reagents to see enzyme activity.

Choose **Pepsin** from the **Experiment** menu. The opening screen will appear in a few seconds (Figure 8.2). The solutions shelf, test tube washer, and incubation equipment are the same as in the amylase experiment; only the solutions have changed.

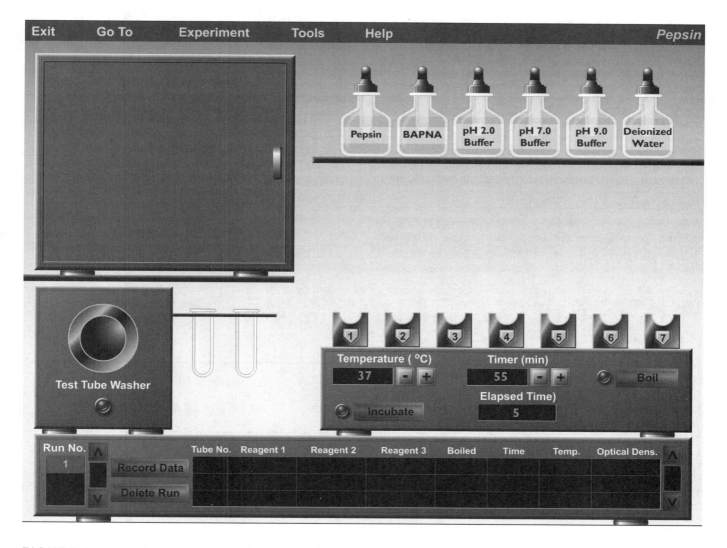

FIGURE 8.2 Opening screen of the Pepsin experiment.

Data displayed in the grid include the tube number, the three substances dispensed into each tube, a (+) or (−) mark indicating whether or not a sample was boiled, the time and temperature of the incubation, and the optical density measurement indicating enzyme assay results.

Assessing Protein Digestion by Pepsin

Pepsin Incubation

1. Individually drag six test tubes to the test tube holders in the incubation unit.

2. Prepare the tubes with the substances indicated in Chart 3 below using the following method.

• Click and hold the mouse button on the dropper cap of the desired substance and drag the dropper cap to the top of the desired test tube.

• Release the mouse button to dispense the substance.

3. Once all tubes are prepared, click the number (1) under the first test tube. The tube will descend into the incubation unit. All other tubes should remain in the raised position.

4. Click **Boil** to boil tube 1. After boiling for a few moments, the tube will automatically rise.

5. Adjust the incubation temperature to 37°C and the timer to 60 minutes (compressed time) by clicking the (+) or (−) button.

6. Click **Incubate** to start the run. The incubation unit will gently agitate the test tube rack, evenly mixing the contents of all test tubes throughout the incubation. The computer is compressing the 60-minute time period into 60 seconds of real time. When the incubation time elapses, the test tube rack will automatically rise, and the doors to the assay cabinet will open.

Pepsin Assay

After the assay cabinet doors open, you will see an instrument called a spectrophotometer, which you will use to measure how much yellow dye was liberated by pepsin digestion of BAPNA. When a test tube is dragged to the holder in the spectrophotometer and the **Analyze** button is clicked, the instrument will shine a light through a specimen to measure the amount of light absorbed by the sample within the tube. The measure of the amount of light absorbed by the solution is known as its *optical density.* A colorless solution does not absorb light, whereas a colored solution has a relatively high light absorbance. For example, a colorless solution has an optical density of 0.0. A colored solution, however, absorbs some of the light emitted by the spectrophotometer, resulting in an optical density reading greater than zero.

In this experiment a yellow-colored solution is a direct indication of the amount of BAPNA digested by pepsin. Although you can visually estimate the yellow color produced by pepsin digestion of BAPNA, the spectrophotometer precisely measures how much BAPNA digestion occurred in the experiment.

1. Click and hold the mouse on the first tube in the incubation unit and drag it to the holder in the spectrophotometer.

2. Release the mouse button to drop the tube into the holder.

3. Click **Analyze.** You will see light shining through the solution in the test tube as the spectrophotometer measures its optical density. The optical density of the sample will be displayed in the optical density window below the Analyze button.

4. Record the optical density in Chart 3.

5. Drag the tube to its original position in the incubation unit and release the mouse button.

6. Repeat steps 1 through 5 for the remaining test tubes in the incubation unit.

7. Click **Record Data** to display your results in the grid and retain your data in the computer's memory for later analysis. To repeat the experiment, you must drag all test tubes to the test tube washer and start again.

8. Answer the following questions, referring to Chart 3 (or the data grid in the simulation) as necessary.

Which pH provided the highest pepsin activity? _____

CHART 3	Pepsin Digestion of Protein					
Tube no.	1	2	3	4	5	6
Additives	Pepsin BAPNA pH 2.0 buffer	Pepsin BAPNA pH 2.0 buffer	Pepsin D.I. water pH 2.0 buffer	D.I. water BAPNA pH 2.0 buffer	Pepsin BAPNA pH 7.0 buffer	Pepsin BAPNA pH 9.0 buffer
Incubation condition	Boil first, then incubate at 37°C for 60 minutes	37°C 60 min	37°C 60 min	37°C 60 min	37°C 60 min	37°C 60 min
Optical density	>					

Note: D.I. water = deionized water

Would pepsin be active in the mouth? Explain your answer.

_____

_____

How did the results of tube 1 compare with those of tube 2?

_____

_____

Tubes 1 and 2 contained the same substances. Explain why their optical density measurements were different.

_____

_____

_____

Did the pepsin or deionized water contain any contaminating digested BAPNA? Which tubes confirm this?

_____

_____

_____

What do you think would happen if you reduced the incubation time to 30 minutes? Use the simulation to help you answer this question if you are not sure.

_____

_____

_____

What do you think would happen if you decreased the temperature of incubation to 10°C? Use the simulation to help you answer this question if you are not sure.

_____

_____

_____

9.   Click **Tools** → **Print Data** to print your recorded data. ▬

Fat Digestion by Pancreatic Lipase and the Action of Bile

The treatment that fats and oils undergo during digestion in the small intestine is a bit more complicated than that of carbohydrates or proteins. Fats and oils require pretreatment with bile to physically emulsify the fats. As a result, two sets of reactions must occur. First:

$$\text{Fats/oils} \xrightarrow[\text{(emulsification)}]{\text{bile}} \text{minute fat/oil droplets}$$

Then:

$$\text{Fat/oil droplets} \xrightarrow{\text{lipase}} \text{monoglycerides and fatty acids}$$

Lipase hydrolyzes fats and oils to their component monoglycerides and two fatty acids. Occasionally lipase hydrolyzes fats and oils to glycerol and three fatty acids.

The fact that some of the end products of fat digestion (fatty acids) are organic acids that decrease the pH provides an easy way to recognize that digestion is ongoing or completed. You will be using a pH meter in the assay cabinet to record the drop in pH as the test tube contents become acid.

Choose **Lipase** from the **Experiment** menu. The opening screen will appear in a few seconds (Figure 8.3). The solutions shelf, test tube washer, and incubation equipment are the same as in the previous two experiments; only the solutions have changed.

Data displayed in the grid include the tube number, the four reagents dispensed into each tube, a (+) or (−) mark indicating whether or not a sample was boiled, the time and temperature of the incubation, and the pH measurement indicating enzyme assay results.

ACTIVITY 4

Assessing Fat Digestion by Pancreatic Lipase and the Action of Bile

Lipase Incubation

1.   Individually drag 6 test tubes to the test tube holders in the incubation unit.

2.   Prepare the tubes with the solutions indicated in Chart 4 on page 111 by using the following method.

•   Click and hold the mouse button on the dropper cap of the desired substance.

•   While holding the mouse button down, drag the dropper cap to the top of the desired test tube.

•   Release the mouse button to dispense the substance.

3.   Adjust the incubation temperature to 37°C and the timer to 60 minutes (compressed time) by clicking the (+) or (−) button.

4.   Click **Incubate** to start the run. The incubation unit will gently agitate the test tube rack, evenly mixing the contents of all test tubes throughout the incubation. The computer is compressing the 60-minute time period into 60 seconds of real time. When the incubation time elapses, the test tube rack automatically rises, and the doors to the assay cabinet open.

Lipase Assay

After the assay cabinet doors open, you will see a pH meter that you will use to measure the relative acidity of your test solutions. When a test tube is dragged to the holder in the pH meter and the Measure pH button is clicked, a probe will descend into the sample, take a pH reading, and then retract. The pH of the sample will be displayed in the pH window below the Measure pH button. A solution containing fatty acids liberated from fat by the action of lipase will exhibit a lower pH than one without fatty acids.

1.   Click and hold the mouse on the first tube in the incubation unit, and drag it to the holder in the pH meter. Release the mouse button to drop the tube into the holder.

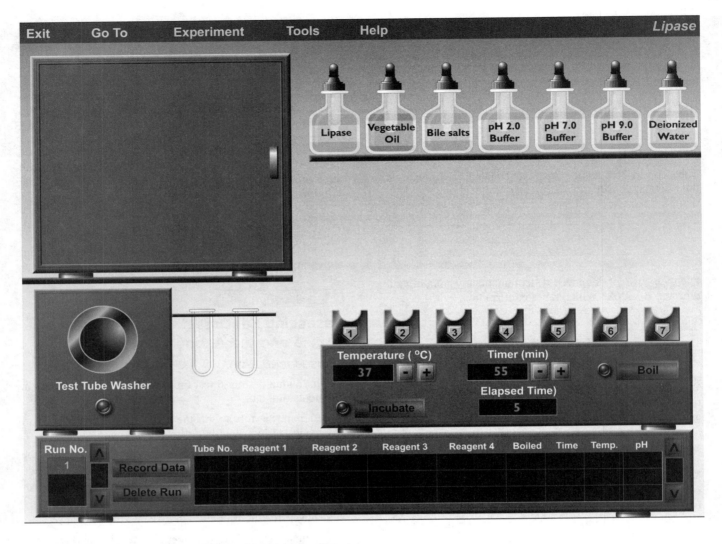

FIGURE 8.3 Opening screen of the Lipase experiment.

2.   Click **Measure pH.**

3.   In Chart 4, record the pH displayed in the pH window.

4.   Drag the test tube in the pH meter to its original position in the incubation unit, and release the mouse button.

5.   Repeat steps 1 through 4 for the remaining test tubes in the incubation unit.

6.   Click **Record Data** to display your results in the grid and retain your data in the computer's memory for later analysis. To repeat the experiment, you must drag all test tubes to the test tube washer and begin again.

7.   Answer the following questions, referring to chart 4 (or the data grid in the simulation) as necessary.

Explain the difference in activity between tubes 1 and 2.

_____

_____

Can we determine if fat hydrolysis has occurred in tube 6?

_____ Explain your answer. _____

_____

Which pH resulted in maximum lipase activity? _____

Can we determine if fat hydrolysis has occurred in tube 5?

_____

In theory, would lipase be active in the mouth? _____

Would it be active in the stomach? _____

Explain your answers. _____

_____

CHART 4	Pancreatic Lipase Digestion of Fats and the Action of Bile					
Tube no.	1	2	3	4	5	6
Additives	Lipase Vegetable oil Bile salts pH 7.0 buffer	Lipase Vegetable oil D.I. water pH 7.0 buffer	Lipase D.I. water Bile salts pH 9.0 buffer	D.I. water Vegetable oil Bile salts pH 7.0 buffer	Lipase Vegetable oil Bile salts pH 2.0 buffer	Lipase Vegetable oil Bile salts pH 9.0 buffer
Incubation condition	37°C 60 min	37°C 60 min	37°C 60 min	37°C 60 min	37°C 60 min	37°C 60 min
pH						

What is the substrate, and what subunit is formed in this experiment? _____

_____

8.   Click **Tools → Print Data** to print your recorded data. ▬

Physical Processes: Mechanisms of Food Propulsion and Mixing

Although enzyme activity is an essential part of the overall digestion process, food must also be processed physically by churning and chewing and moved by mechanical means along the tract if digestion and absorption are to be completed. Just about any time organs exhibit mobility, muscles are involved, and movements of and in the gastrointestinal tract are no exception. Although we tend to think only of smooth muscles for visceral activities, both skeletal and smooth muscles are necessary in digestion. This fact is demonstrated by the simple trials in the next activity. Obtain the following materials:

* Water pitcher
* Paper cups
* Stethoscope
* Alcohol swabs
* Disposable autoclave bag

ACTIVITY 5

Studying Mechanisms of Food Propulsion and Mixing: Deglutition (Swallowing)

Swallowing, or *deglutition,* which is largely the result of skeletal muscle activity, occurs in two phases: *buccal* (mouth) and *pharyngeal-esophageal.* The initial phase—the buccal—is voluntarily controlled and initiated by the tongue. Once begun, the process continues involuntarily in the pharynx and esophagus, through peristalsis, resulting in the delivery of the swallowed contents to the stomach.

1.   While swallowing a mouthful of water from a paper cup, consciously note the movement of your tongue during the process. Record your observations.

_____

_____

_____

2.   Repeat the swallowing process while your laboratory partner watches the externally visible movements of your larynx. This movement is more obvious in a male, who has a larger Adam's apple. Record your observations.

_____

_____

What do these movements accomplish? _____

_____

_____

3.   Your lab partner should clean the ear pieces of a stethoscope with an alcohol swab and don the stethoscope. Then your lab partner should place the diaphragm of the stethoscope on your abdominal wall, approximately 1 inch below the xiphoid process and slightly to the left, to listen for sounds as you again take two or three swallows of water. There should be two audible sounds. The first sound occurs when the water splashes against the gastroesophageal sphincter. The second occurs when the peristaltic wave of the esophagus arrives at the sphincter and the sphincter opens, allowing water to gurgle into the stomach. Determine, as accurately as possible, the time interval between these two sounds and record it below.

Interval between arrival of water at the sphincter and the opening of the sphincter:

_____ sec

This interval gives a fair indication of the time it takes for the peristaltic wave to travel down the 10-inch-long esophagus. Actually the time interval is slightly less than it seems because pressure causes the sphincter to relax before the peristaltic wave reaches it.

Dispose of the used paper cup in the autoclave bag. ▬

Segmentation and Peristalsis

Although several types of movement occur in the digestive tract organs, segmentation and peristalsis are most important as mixing and propulsive mechanisms.

Segmental movements are local constrictions of the organ wall that occur rhythmically. They serve mainly to mix the foodstuffs with digestive juices and to increase the rate of absorption by continually moving different portions of the chyme over adjacent regions of the intestinal wall. However, segmentation is an important means of food propulsion in the small intestine, and slow segmenting movements called haustral contractions are common in the large intestine.

Peristaltic movements are the major means of propelling food through most of the digestive viscera. Essentially they are waves of contraction followed by waves of relaxation that squeeze foodstuffs through the alimentary canal, and they are superimposed on segmental movements.

Histology Review Supplement

For a review of digestive tissue, go to **Exercise H: Histology Atlas and Review** on the **PhysioEx website** to print out the **Digestive Tissue Review** worksheet.

NAME _____

LAB TIME/DATE _____

Chemical and Physical Processes of Digestion

Carbohydrate Digestion

The following questions refer to Activity 1: Assessing Starch Digestion by Salivary Amylase.

1. At what pH did you see the highest activity of salivary amylase? _____ Why?

   _____

2. How do you know that the amylase did not have any contaminating maltose?

   _____

   _____

3. What effect did boiling have on enzyme activity? Why? _____

   _____

   _____

4. Describe the substrate and the subunit product of amylase. _____

   _____

The following questions refer to Activity 2: Assessing Cellulose Digestion.

5. Does amylase use cellulose as a substrate? Explain. _____

   _____

6. Did freezing have an effect on the activity of amylase? Explain. _____

   _____

7. Do you think that the bacterial suspension contained the enzyme cellulase (an enzyme that digests cellulose)? Why or why not?

   _____

   _____

8. What is the substrate of peptidase? Explain, based upon your results. _____

   _____

Protein Digestion by Pepsin

The following questions refer to Activity 3: Assessing Protein Digestion by Pepsin.

9. At which pH did you see the highest activity of pepsin? _____ How does this correlate to the location of pepsin in the

   body? _____

   _____

10. What effect did boiling have on pepsin? _____

    _____

11. Was there any digested BAPNA contaminating the pepsin or deionized (DI) water? _____

    How can you tell? _____

    _____

12. What is the substrate in this experiment? _____

    What is the usual substrate for pepsin, and what subunits are formed with pepsin activity?

    _____

    _____

13. What was the effect of decreasing the incubation time on the optical density results?

    _____

14. What effect would decreased incubation temperature have on pepsin activity? Why?

    _____

    _____

15. What was the significance of using 37°C for the incubation? _____

    _____

Fat Digestion by Pancreatic Lipase and the Action of Bile

The following questions refer to Activity 4: Assessing Fat Digestion by Pancreatic Lipase and the Action of Bile.

16. Describe the activity of lipase with and without the addition of bile salts. Refer to Chart 4 for pH values. _____

    _____

17. Is the activity of bile a chemical or a physical process? Explain. _____

    _____

18. What pH resulted in the maximum pancreatic lipase activity? _____

How does this optimal pH correlate to the enzyme's location in the body? _____

_____

19. Explain whether or not we can determine fat hydrolysis in tube 5. Why or why not?

_____

_____

20. What is the substrate in this experiment? _____

What subunits does lipase form? _____

Physical Process: Mechanisms of Food Propulsion and Mixing

The following questions refer to Activity 5: Studying Mechanisms of Food Propulsion and Mixing: Deglutition (Swallowing).

21. Explain the significance of the movement of the tongue during swallowing. _____

_____

22. Describe three events that occur during the pharyngeal-esophageal phase of deglutition. _____

_____

_____

23. What was the time interval that you recorded between the first and second sound?

_____

Renal System Physiology

OBJECTIVES

1. To define the following terms:

   glomerulus, glomerular capsule, renal corpuscle, renal tubule, nephron, proximal convoluted tubule, loop of Henle, and *distal convoluted tubule.*

2. To describe the blood supply to each nephron.

3. To identify the regions of the nephron involved in glomerular filtration and tubular reabsorption.

4. To study the factors affecting glomerular filtration.

5. To explore the concept of carrier transport maximum.

6. To understand how the hormones aldosterone and ADH affect the function of the kidney.

7. To describe how the kidneys can produce urine that is four times more concentrated than the blood.

Metabolism produces wastes that must be eliminated from the body. This excretory function is the job of the renal system, most importantly the paired kidneys. Each kidney consists of about one million nephrons that carry out two crucial services, blood filtration and fluid processing.

Microscopic Structure and Function of the Kidney

Each of the million or so **nephrons** in each kidney is a microscopic tubule consisting of two major parts: a glomerulus and a renal tubule. The **glomerulus** is a tangled capillary knot that filters fluid from the blood into the lumen of the renal tubule. The function of the **renal tubule** is to process that fluid, also called the **filtrate.** The beginning of the renal tubule is an enlarged end called the **glomerular capsule,** which surrounds the glomerulus and serves to funnel the filtrate into the rest of the renal tubule. Collectively, the glomerulus and the glomerular capsule are called the **renal corpuscle.**

As the rest of the renal tubule extends from the glomerular capsule, it becomes twisted and convoluted, then dips sharply down to form a hairpin loop, and then coils again before entering a collecting duct. Starting at the glomerular capsule, the anatomical parts of the renal tubule are as follows: the **proximal convoluted tubule,** the **loop of Henle** (nephron loop), and the **distal convoluted tubule.**

Two arterioles supply each glomerulus: an afferent arteriole feeds the glomerular capillary bed and an efferent arteriole drains it. These arterioles are responsible for blood flow through the glomerulus. Constricting the afferent arteriole lowers the downstream pressure in the glomerulus, whereas constricting the efferent arteriole will increase the pressure in the glomerulus. In addition, the diameter of the efferent arteriole is smaller than the diameter of the afferent arteriole, restricting blood flow out of the glomerulus. Consequently, the pressure in the glomerulus forces fluid through the endothelium of the glomerulus into the lumen of the surrounding glomerular capsule. In essence, everything in the blood except the cells and proteins are filtered through the glomerular wall. From the capsule, the filtrate moves into the rest of the renal tubule for processing. The job of the tubule is to reabsorb all the beneficial substances from its lumen while allowing the wastes to travel down the tubule for elimination from the body.

The nephron performs three important functions to process the filtrate into urine: glomerular filtration, tubular reabsorption, and tubular secretion. **Glomerular filtration** is a passive process in which fluid passes from the lumen of the glomerular capillary into the glomerular capsule of the renal tubule. **Tubular reabsorption** moves most of the filtrate back into the blood, leaving principally salt water plus the wastes in the lumen of the tubule. Some of the desirable or needed solutes are actively reabsorbed, and others move passively from the lumen of the tubule into the interstitial spaces. **Tubular secretion** is essentially the reverse of tubular reabsorption and is a process by which the kidneys can rid the blood of additional unwanted substances such as creatinine and ammonia.

The reabsorbed solutes and water that move into the interstitial space between the nephrons need to be returned to the blood, or the kidneys will rapidly swell like balloons. The peritubular capillaries surrounding the renal tubule reclaim the reabsorbed substances and return them to general circulation. Peritubular capillaries arise from the efferent arteriole exiting the glomerulus and empty into the veins leaving the kidney.

Simulating Glomerular Filtration

This computerized simulation allows you to explore one function of a single simulated nephron, glomerular filtration. The concepts you will learn by studying a single nephron can then be applied to understand the function of the kidney as a whole.

Choose **Exercise 9: Renal System Physiology** from the drop-down menu and click **GO.** Then click **Simulating Glomerular Filtration.** The opening screen for the Simulating Glomerular Filtration experiment will appear in a few seconds (Figure 9.1). The main features on the screen when the program starts are a *simulated blood supply* at the left side of the screen, a *simulated nephron* within a supporting tank on the right side, and a *data control unit* at the bottom of the display.

The left beaker is the "blood" source representing the general circulation supplying the nephron. The "blood pressure" in the beaker is adjustable by clicking the (+) and (−) buttons on top of the beaker. A tube with an adjustable radius called the *afferent flow* tube connects the left beaker to the simulated glomerulus. Another adjustable tube called the *efferent flow*

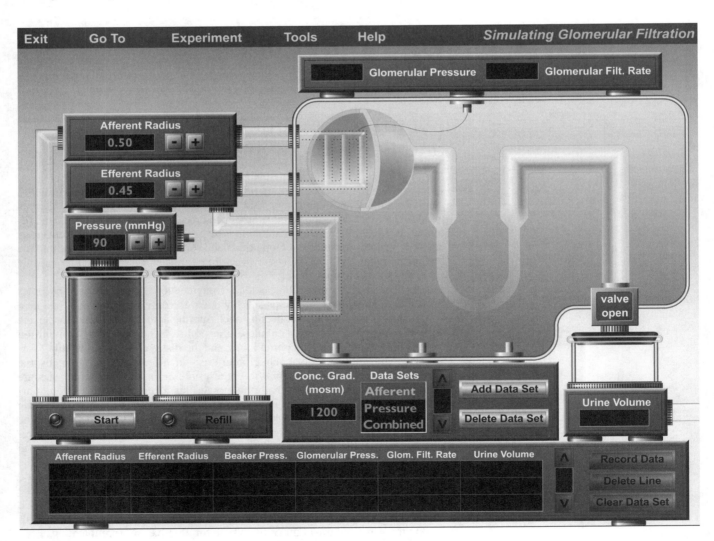

FIGURE 9.1 Opening screen of the Simulating Glomerular Filtration experiment.

tube drains the glomerulus. The afferent flow tube represents the afferent arteriole feeding the glomerulus of each nephron, and the efferent flow tube represents the efferent arteriole draining the glomerulus. The outflow of the nephron empties into a collecting duct, which in turn drains into another small beaker at the bottom right part of the screen. Clicking the valve at the end of the collecting duct (which currently reads **valve open**) stops the flow of fluid through the nephron and collecting duct.

The **Glomerular Pressure** window on top of the nephron tank displays the pressure within the glomerulus. The **Glomerular Filt. Rate** window indicates the flow rate of the fluid moving from the lumen of the glomerulus into the lumen of the renal tubule.

The concentration gradient bathing the nephron is fixed at 1200 milliosmoles (mosm). Clicking **Start** begins the experiment. Clicking **Refill** resets the equipment to begin another run.

The equipment in the lower part of the screen is called the *data control unit*. This equipment records and displays data you accumulate during the experiments. The data set for the first experiment (Afferent) is highlighted in the **Data Sets** window. You can add or delete a data set by clicking the appropriate button to the right of the Data Sets window. When you click **Record Data,** your data is recorded in the computer's memory and is displayed in the data grid. Data displayed in the data grid include the afferent radius, efferent radius, beaker pressure, glomerular pressure, glomerular filtration rate, and urine volume. Clicking **Delete Line** allows you to discard data values for a single run, and clicking **Clear Data Set** erases the entire experiment to allow you to start over.

If you need help identifying any piece of equipment, choose **Balloons On/Off** from the **Help** menu and move the mouse pointer onto any piece of equipment visible on the computer's screen. As the pointer touches the object, a pop-up window appears identifying the equipment. To close the pop-up window, move the mouse pointer away from the equipment. Choose **Balloons On/Off** to turn off this Help feature.

ACTIVITY 1

Investigating the Effect of Flow Tube Radius on Glomerular Filtration

Your first experiment will examine the effects of flow tube radii and pressures on the rate of glomerular filtration. Click **Start** to see the on-screen action. Continue when you understand how the simulation operates. Click **Refill** to reset the experiment.

1. The **Afferent** line in the **Data Sets** window of the data control unit should be highlighted in bright blue. If it is not, choose it by clicking the **Afferent** line. The data control unit will now record filtration rate variations due to changing afferent flow tube radius.

2. If the data grid is not empty, click **Clear Data Set** to discard all previous data.

3. Adjust the afferent radius to 0.35 mm and the efferent radius to 0.40 mm by clicking the appropriate (+) or (−) buttons.

4. If the left beaker is not full, click **Refill.**

5. Keep the beaker pressure at 90 mm Hg during this part of the experiment.

6. Click **Start,** and watch the blood flow. Simultaneously, filtered fluid will be moving through the nephron and into the collecting duct. The Glomerular Filtration Rate window will display the fluid flow rate into the renal tubule when the left beaker has finished draining.

7. Now click **Record Data** to record the current experiment data in the data grid. Click **Refill** to replenish the left beaker and prepare the nephron for the next run.

8. Increase the afferent radius in 0.05-mm increments and repeat steps 6 and 7 until the maximum radius (0.60 mm) is achieved. Be sure to click **Record Data** after each trial. If you make an error and want to delete a single value, click the data line in the data grid and then click **Delete Line.**

What happens to the glomerular filtration rate as the afferent radius is increased?

_____

_____

What happens to the glomerular pressure as the afferent radius is increased?

_____

_____

Predict what effect increasing or decreasing the efferent radius will have on glomerular filtration rate. Use the simulation to check your prediction and record your results.

_____

_____ ▬

ACTIVITY 2

Studying the Effect of Pressure on Glomerular Filtration

Both the blood pressure supplying the glomerulus and the pressure in the renal tubule have a significant impact on the glomerular filtration rate. In this activity, the data control unit will record filtration rate variations due to changing pressure.

1. Click the **Pressure** line in the **Data Sets** window of the data control unit.

2. If the data grid is not empty, click **Clear Data Set** to discard all previous data.

3. If the left beaker is not full, click **Refill.**

4. Adjust the pressure in the left beaker to 70 mm Hg by clicking the appropriate (+) or (−) button.

5. During this part of the experiment, maintain the afferent flow tube radius at 0.55 mm and the efferent flow tube radius at 0.45 mm.

6. Click **Start,** and watch the blood flow. Filtrate will move through the nephron into the collecting duct. At the end of the run, the Glomerular Filtration Rate window will display the filtrate flow rate into the renal tubule.

7. Now click **Record Data** to record the current experiment data in the data grid. Click **Refill** to replenish the left beaker.

8. Increase the pressure in the left beaker in increments of 10 mm Hg and repeat steps 6 and 7 until the maximum pressure (100 mm Hg) is achieved. Be sure to click **Record Data** after each trial. If you make an error and want to delete a single value, click the data line in the data grid and then click **Delete Line.**

What happened to the glomerular filtration rate as the beaker pressure was increased?

_____

_____

What was the effect on glomerular pressure as beaker pressure increased?

_____

_____ ▬

ACTIVITY 3

Exploring Intrinsic Controls: Renal Autoregulation

So far, you have examined the effects of flow tube radius and pressure on glomerular filtration rate. In this experiment you will be altering both variables to explore the combined effects on glomerular filtration rate and to see how one can compensate for the other to maintain an adequate glomerular filtration rate.

1. Click **Combined** in the **Data Sets** window of the data control unit.

2. If the data grid is not empty, click **Clear Data Set** to discard all previous data.

3. If the left beaker is not full, click **Refill.**

4. Set the starting conditions at:
- 100 mm Hg beaker pressure
- 0.55 mm afferent radius
- 0.45 mm efferent radius

5. Click **Start.**

6. Now click **Record Data** to record the current baseline data in the data grid.

7. Click **Refill.**

8. Set the starting conditions at:
- 80 mm Hg beaker pressure
- 0.55 mm afferent radius
- 0.45 mm efferent radius

9. Record the glomerular filtration rate at a beaker pressure

of 80 mm Hg: _____

10. If the left beaker is not full, click **Refill.**

11. Adjust the pressure in the left beaker to 85 mm Hg by clicking the appropriate (+) or (−) button.

12. Maintain the starting conditions for the afferent flow tube radius and the efferent flow tube radius.

13. Record the glomerular filtration rate at a beaker pressure

of 85 mm Hg: _____

14. What variables other than beaker pressure could you change to return the glomerular filtration rate to "normal" (the value when beaker pressure is 80 mm Hg)? Circle the correct change in each set of parentheses: (increase / decrease) in the afferent radius, (increase / decrease) in the efferent radius.

15. Test your predictions. Hint: Try small changes of each variable one at a time.

16. List the value of each variable that results in a glomerular filtration rate approximately the same as its starting value when beaker pressure is 85 mm Hg.

Afferent radius _____ mm

Efferent radius _____ mm

17. Click **Tools → Print Data** to print your recorded data. ▬

Simulating Urine Formation

This part of the computer simulation allows you to explore some aspects of urine formation by manipulating the interstitial solute concentration. Other activities include investigating the effects of aldosterone and ADH (antidiuretic hormone) and the role that glucose carrier proteins play in renal function.

Choose **Simulating Urine Formation** from the **Experiment** menu. The opening screen will appear in a few seconds (Figure 9.2). The basic features on the screen when the program starts are similar to the glomerular filtration screen. Most of the vascular controls have been moved off-screen to the left because they will not be needed in this set of experiments. Additional equipment includes *supply shelves* at the right side of the screen, a *glucose carrier control* located at the top of the nephron tank, and a *concentration probe* at the bottom left part of the screen.

The maximum concentration of the interstitial gradient to be dispensed into the tank surrounding the nephron is adjusted by clicking the (+) and (−) buttons next to the Conc. Grad. window. Click **Dispense** to fill the tank through the jets at the bottom of the tank with the chosen solute gradient. Click **Start** to begin a run. While the experiment is running, the concentration probe can be clicked and dragged over the nephron to display the solute concentration within.

Hormone is dispensed by dragging a hormone dropper cap to the gray cap button in the nephron tank at the top of the collecting duct and then letting go of the mouse button.

The (+) and (−) buttons in the glucose carrier control are used to adjust the number of glucose carriers that will be inserted into the simulated proximal convoluted tubule when the **Add Carriers** button is clicked.

Data displayed in the data grid will depend on which experiment is being conducted. Clicking **Delete Line** allows you to discard data values for a single run, and clicking **Clear Data Set** erases the entire experiment to allow you to start over.

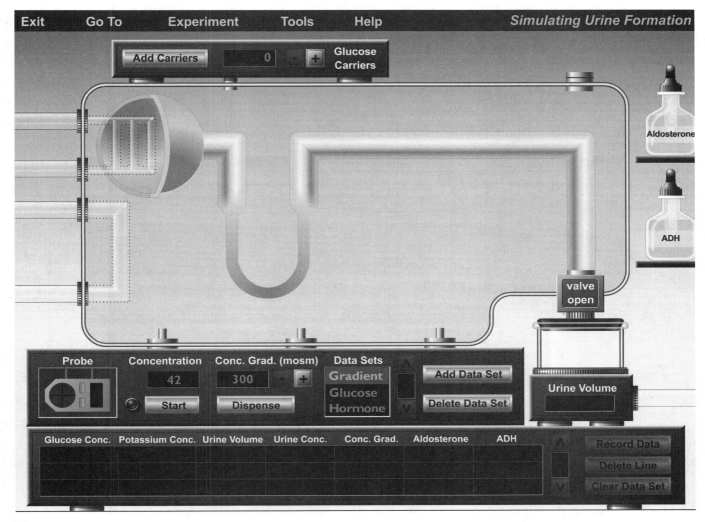

(a)

FIGURE 9.2 Urine formation. (a) Opening screen of the Simulating Urine Formation experiment.

ACTIVITY 4

Exploring the Role of the Solute Gradient on Maximum Urine Concentration Achievable

In the process of urine formation, solutes and water move from the lumen of the nephron into the interstitial spaces. The passive movement of solutes and water from the lumen of the renal tubule into the interstitial spaces relies in part on the total solute gradient surrounding the nephron. When the nephron is permeable to solutes or water, an equilibrium will be reached between the interstitial fluid and the contents of the nephron. Antidiuretic hormone (ADH) increases the water permeability of the distal convoluted tubule and the collecting duct, allowing water to flow to areas of higher solute concentration, usually from the lumen of the nephron into the surrounding interstitial area. You will explore the process of passive reabsorption in this experiment. While doing this part of the simulation, assume that when ADH is present the conditions favor the formation of the most concentrated urine possible. (Figure 9.2b and c).

1. **Gradient** in the **Data Sets** window of the data control unit should be highlighted in bright blue. If it is not, then click **Gradient.**

2. If the data grid is not empty, click **Clear Data Set** to discard all previous data.

3. Click and hold the mouse button on the **ADH** bottle cap and drag it to the gray cap at the top right side of the nephron tank. Release the mouse button to dispense ADH onto the collecting duct.

4. Adjust the maximum total solute concentration of the gradient (**Conc. Grad.**) to 300 mosm by clicking the appropriate (**+**) or (**−**) button. Because the blood solute concentration is also 300 mosm, there is no osmotic difference between the lumen of the nephron and the surrounding interstitial fluid.

5. Click **Dispense.**

6. Click **Start** to begin the experiment. Filtrate will move through the nephron and then drain into the beaker below the collecting duct.

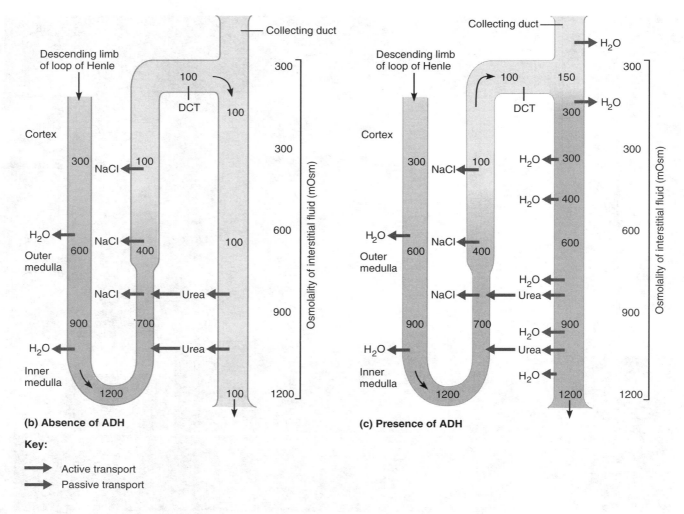

FIGURE 9.2 (*continued*) **Urine formation.** (**b**) Mechanisms for forming dilute urine (**c**) and concentrated urine.

7. While the experiment is running, watch the **Probe.** When it turns red, click and hold the mouse on it, and drag it to the urine beaker. Observe the total solute concentration in the **Concentration** window.

8. Now click **Record Data** to record the current experiment data in the data grid.

9. Increase the maximum concentration of the gradient in 300-mosm increments, and repeat steps 3 through 8 until 1200 mosm is achieved. Be sure to click **Record Data** after each trial. If you make an error and want to delete a single value, click the data line in the data grid and then click **Delete Line.**

What happened to the urine concentration as the gradient concentration was increased?

_____

_____

What happened to the volume of urine?

_____

What factor limits the maximum possible urine concentration?

_____

_____

_____

Was equilibrium achieved?

_____

_____

_____

ACTIVITY 5

Studying the Effect of Glucose Carrier Proteins on Glucose Reabsorption

Because carrier proteins are needed to move glucose from the lumen of the nephron into the interstitial spaces, there is a limit to the amount of glucose that can be reabsorbed. When all glucose carriers are bound with the glucose they are transporting, excess glucose is eliminated in urine. In this experiment, you will examine the effect of varying the number of glucose transport proteins in the proximal convoluted tubule.

1. Click **Glucose** in the **Data Sets** window of the data control unit.

2. If the data grid is not empty, click **Clear Data Set** to discard all previous data.

3. Set the concentration gradient (**Conc. Grad.**) to 1200 mosm.

4. Click **Dispense.**

5. Adjust the number of glucose carriers to 100 (an arbitrary figure) by clicking the appropriate (**+**) or (**−**) button.

6. Click **Add Carriers.** This action inserts the specified number of glucose carrier proteins per unit area into the membrane of the proximal convoluted tubule.

7. Click **Start** to begin the run after the carriers have been added.

8. Click **Record Data** to record the current experimental data in the data grid. Glucose presence in the urine will be displayed in the data grid.

9. Now increase the number of glucose carrier proteins in the proximal convoluted tubule in increments of 100 glucose carriers, and repeat steps 6 through 8 until the maximum number of glucose carrier proteins (500) is achieved. Remember to click **Add Carriers** each time. Be sure to click **Record Data** after each trial. If you make an error and want to delete a single value, click the data line in the data grid and then click **Delete Line.**

What happened to the amount of glucose present in the urine as the number of glucose carriers was increased?

_____

_____

The amount of glucose present in normal urine is minimal because there are normally enough glucose carriers present to handle the "traffic." Predict the consequence in the urine if there was more glucose than could be transported by the available number of glucose carrier proteins.

_____

_____

Explain why we would expect to find glucose in the urine of a diabetic person.

_____

_____

ACTIVITY 6

Testing the Effect of Hormones on Urine Formation

The concentration of the urine excreted by our kidneys changes depending on our immediate needs. For example, if a person consumes a large quantity of water, the excess water will be eliminated, producing dilute urine. On the other hand, under conditions of dehydration, there is a clear benefit in being able to produce urine as concentrated as possible, thereby retaining precious water. Although the medullary gradient makes it possible to excrete concentrated urine, urine dilution or concentration is ultimately under hormonal control. In this experiment, you will investigate the effects of two different hormones on renal function, aldosterone produced by the adrenal gland and ADH manufactured by the hypothalamus and stored in the posterior pituitary gland. Aldosterone works to reabsorb sodium ions (and thereby water) at the expense of losing potassium ions; its site of action is the distal convoluted tubule. ADH makes the distal tubule and collecting duct more permeable to water, thereby allowing the body to reabsorb more water from the filtrate when it is present.

1. Click **Hormone** in the **Data Sets** window of the data control unit.

2. If the data grid is not empty, click **Clear Data Set** to discard all previous data.

3. During this part of the experiment, keep the concentration gradient at 1200 mosm.

4. Click **Dispense** to add the gradient, and then click **Start** to begin the experiment.

5. Now click **Record Data** to record the current experiment data in the data grid.

You will use this baseline data to compare with the conditions of the filtrate under the control of the two hormones.

Baseline urine volume _____

6. Keeping all experiment conditions the same as before, do the following:

- Drag the **Aldosterone** dropper cap to the gray cap on the top right side of the nephron tank, and release the mouse to automatically dispense aldosterone into the tank surrounding the distal convoluted tubule and collecting duct.

- Click **Start,** and allow the run to complete.

- Click **Record Data.**

Urine volume with aldosterone present _____

In this run, how does the volume of urine differ from the previously measured baseline volume?

_____

_____

Explain the difference in the total amount of potassium in the urine between this run and the baseline run.

_____

_____

7. Drag the **ADH** bottle cap to the gray cap on the top right side of the nephron tank, and release it to dispense ADH.

• Click **Start,** and allow the run to complete.

• Click **Record Data.**

In this run, how does the volume of urine differ from the baseline measurement?

_____

_____

Is there a difference in the total amount of potassium in this run and the total amount of potassium in the baseline run? Explain your answer. (Hint: The urine volume with ADH present is about one-tenth the urine volume when it is not present.)

_____

_____

Are the effects of aldosterone and ADH similar or antag-

onistic? _____

Consider this situation: we want to reabsorb sodium ions but do not want to increase the volume of the blood by reabsorbing water from the filtrate. Assuming that aldosterone and ADH are both present, how would you adjust the hormones to accomplish the task?

_____

_____

_____

_____

8. Click **Tools → Print Data** to print your recorded data. ▨

Histology Review Supplement

For a review of renal tissue, go to **Exercise H: Histology Atlas and Review** on the **PhysioEx website** to print out the **Renal Tissue Review** worksheet.

Renal System Physiology

NAME _____

LAB TIME/DATE _____

Simulating Glomerular Filtration

The following questions refer to Activity 1: Investigating the Effect of Flow Tube Radius on Glomerular Filtration.

1. Describe the effect of increasing the afferent radius on glomerular filtration rate and glomerular pressure.

   _____

   _____

2. Describe the effect of decreasing the efferent radius on glomerular filtration rate and glomerular pressure.

   _____

   _____

3. Describe the effect of increasing the efferent radius on glomerular filtration rate and glomerular pressure.

   _____

   _____

The following questions refer to Activity 2: Studying the Effect of Pressure on Glomerular Filtration.

4. Describe the effect of increasing the beaker pressure on glomerular filtration rate.

   _____

5. Describe the effect of increasing the beaker pressure on glomerular pressure.

   _____

6. In the absence of any regulatory mechanisms, what effect do you think an increase in blood pressure would have on

   glomerular filtration rate? _____

   _____

The following questions refer to Activity 3: Exploring Intrinsic Controls: Renal Autoregulation.

7. What was the glomerular filtration rate at 80 mm Hg beaker pressure, 0.55 mm afferent radius, and 0.45 mm efferent radius?

_____

8. With the beaker pressure increased to 85 mm Hg, at what afferent radius was the glomerular filtration rate in question 7 restored? _____

9. With the beaker pressure increased to 85 mm Hg, at what efferent radius was the glomerular filtration rate in question 7 restored? _____

10. In the body, what mechanisms play a role in maintaining glomerular filtration rate with fluctuating blood pressure?

_____

_____

Simulating Urine Formation

The following questions refer to Activity 4: Exploring the Role of the Solute Gradient on Maximum Urine Concentration Achievable.

11. As you increased the concentration gradient of the interstitial fluid, what happened to the concentration of the urine?

_____

12. What happened to the volume of the urine as you increased the concentration gradient of the interstitial fluid?

_____

13. What effect does the concentration gradient of the interstitial fluid have on the maximum urine concentration?

_____

The following questions refer to Activity 5: Studying the Effect of Glucose Carrier Proteins on Glucose Reabsorption.

14. What happens to the concentration of glucose in the urine as the number of glucose carriers increases?

_____

15. Glucose can be elevated in the blood of a diabetic person. Relate this information to glucose in the urine and glucose carriers.

_____

_____

The following questions refer to Activity 6: Testing the Effects of Hormones on Urine Formation.

16. What was the volume of urine in the presence of aldosterone? ——————————————————————————

   How did aldosterone affect the urine volume? ——————————————————————————————

17. What happened to the concentration of potassium in the urine in the presence of aldosterone? ——————————————

18. What was the volume of the urine in the presence of ADH? ——————————————————————————

   How did ADH affect the urine volume? ——————————————————————————————————

19. Why did the concentration of potassium change in the presence of ADH without a change in the excretion of potassium?

   ——

   ——

20. Does ADH favor the formation of dilute or concentrated urine? Explain. ——————————————————————

   ——

   ——

Acid-Base Balance

OBJECTIVES

1. To define *pH,* and to identify the normal range of human blood pH levels.

2. To define *acid* and *base,* and to explain what characterizes each of the following: *strong acid, weak acid, strong base,* and *weak base.*

3. To explain how chemical and physiological buffering systems help regulate the body's pH levels.

4. To define the conditions of *acidosis* and *alkalosis.*

5. To explain the difference between *respiratory acidosis and alkalosis* and *metabolic acidosis and alkalosis.*

6. To understand the causes of respiratory acidosis and alkalosis.

7. To explain how the renal system compensates for respiratory acidosis and alkalosis.

8. To understand the causes of metabolic acidosis and alkalosis.

9. To explain how the respiratory system compensates for metabolic acidosis and alkalosis.

The term **pH** is used to denote the hydrogen ion concentration, $[H^+]$, in body fluids. The pH values are the reciprocal of $[H^+]$ and follow the formula

$$pH = \log(1/[H^+])$$

At a pH of 7.4, $[H^+]$ is about 40 nanomoles (nM) per liter. Because the relationship is reciprocal, $[H^+]$ is higher at *lower* pH values (indicating higher acid levels) and lower at *higher* pH values (indicating lower acid levels).

The pH of a body's fluids is also referred to as its **acid-base balance.** An **acid** is a substance that releases H^+ in solution (such as in body fluids). A **base,** often a hydroxyl ion (OH^-) or bicarbonate ion (HCO_3^-), is a substance that binds to H^+. A *strong acid* is one that completely dissociates in solution, releasing all of its hydrogen ions and thus lowering the solution's pH level. A *weak acid* dissociates incompletely and does not release all of its hydrogen ions in solution. A *strong base* has a strong tendency to bind to H^+, which has the effect of raising the pH value of the solution. A *weak base* binds less of the H^+, having a lesser effect on solution pH.

The body's pH levels are very tightly regulated. Blood and tissue fluids normally have pH values between 7.35 and 7.45. Under pathological conditions, blood pH values as low as 6.9 or as high as 7.8 have been recorded; however, values higher or lower than these cannot sustain human life. The narrow range of 7.35–7.45 is remarkable when one considers the vast number of biochemical reactions that take place in the body. The human body normally produces a large amount of H^+ as the result of metabolic processes, ingested acids, and the products of fat, sugar, and amino acid metabolism. The regulation of a relatively constant internal pH environment is one of the major physiological functions of the body's organ systems.

To maintain pH homeostasis, the body utilizes both *chemical* and *physiological* buffering sytems. Chemical buffers are composed of a mixture of weak acids and weak bases. They help regulate body pH levels by binding H^+ and removing it from solution as its concentration begins to rise or by releasing

H^+ into solution as its concentration begins to fall. The body's three major chemical buffering systems are the *bicarbonate, phosphate,* and *protein buffer systems.* We will not focus on chemical buffering systems in this lab, but keep in mind that chemical buffers are the fastest form of compensation and can return pH to normal levels within a fraction of a second.

The body's two major physiological buffering systems are the renal and respiratory systems. The renal system is the slower of the two, taking hours to days to do its work. The respiratory system usually works within minutes but cannot handle the amount of pH change that the renal system can. These physiological buffer systems help regulate body pH by controlling the output of acids, bases, or carbon dioxide (CO_2) from the body. For example, if there is too much acid in the body, the renal system may respond by excreting more H^+ from the body in urine. Similarly, if there is too much carbon dioxide in the blood, the respiratory system may respond by breathing faster to expel the excess carbon dioxide. Carbon dioxide levels have a direct effect on pH levels because the addition of carbon dioxide to the blood results in the generation of more H^+. The following reaction shows what happens in the respiratory system when carbon dioxide combines with water in the blood:

$$H_2O + CO_2 \rightleftharpoons \underset{\substack{\text{carbonic} \\ \text{acid}}}{H_2CO_3} \rightleftharpoons H^+ + \underset{\substack{\text{bicarbonate} \\ \text{ion}}}{HCO_3^-}$$

This is a reversible reaction and is useful for remembering the relationships between CO_2 and H^+. Note that as more CO_2 accumulates in the blood (which frequently is caused by reduced gas exchange in the lungs), the reaction moves to the right and more H^+ is produced, lowering the pH:

$$H_2O + \textbf{CO}_2 \rightarrow \underset{\substack{\text{carbonic} \\ \text{acid}}}{H_2CO_3} \rightarrow \textbf{H}^+ + \underset{\substack{\text{bicarbonate} \\ \text{ion}}}{HCO_3^-}$$

Conversely, as $[H^+]$ increases, more carbon dioxide will be present in the blood:

$$H_2O + \textbf{CO}_2 \leftarrow \underset{\substack{\text{carbonic} \\ \text{acid}}}{H_2CO_3} \leftarrow \textbf{H}^+ + \underset{\substack{\text{bicarbonate} \\ \text{ion}}}{HCO_3^-}$$

Disruptions of acid-base balance occur when the body's pH levels fall below or above the normal pH range of 7.35–7.45. When pH levels fall below 7.35, the body is said to be in a state of **acidosis.** When pH levels rise above 7.45, the body is said to be in a state of **alkalosis. Respiratory acidosis** and **respiratory alkalosis** are the result of the respiratory system accumulating too much or too little carbon dioxide in the blood. **Metabolic acidosis** and **metabolic alkalosis** refer to all other conditions of acidosis and alkalosis (i.e., those not caused by the respiratory system). The experiments in this lab will focus on these disruptions of acid-base balance and on the physiological buffer systems (renal and respiratory) that compensate for such imbalances (Figure 10.1b and c).

Respiratory Acidosis and Alkalosis

Respiratory acidosis is the result of impaired respiration, or *hypoventilation,* which leads to the accumulation of too much carbon dioxide in the blood. The causes of impaired respiration include airway obstruction, depression of the respiratory center in the brain stem, lung disease, and drug overdose. Recall that carbon dioxide acts as an acid by forming carbonic acid when it combines with water in the body's blood. The carbonic acid then forms hydrogen ions plus bicarbonate ions:

$$H_2O + \textbf{CO}_2 \rightarrow \underset{\substack{\text{carbonic} \\ \text{acid}}}{H_2CO_3} \rightarrow \textbf{H}^+ + \underset{\substack{\text{bicarbonate} \\ \text{ion}}}{HCO_3^-}$$

Because hypoventilation results in elevated carbon dioxide levels in the blood, the H^+ levels increase, and the pH value of the blood decreases.

Respiratory alkalosis is the condition of too little carbon dioxide in the blood. It is commonly the result of traveling to a high altitude (where the air contains less oxygen) or hyperventilation, which may be brought on by fever or anxiety. Hyperventilation removes more carbon dioxide from the blood, reducing the amount of H^+ in the blood and thus increasing the blood's pH level.

In this first set of activities, we focus on the causes of respiratory acidosis and alkalosis. From the drop-down menu, select **Exercise 10: Acid/Base Balance** and click **GO.** Then click **Respiratory Acidosis/Alkalosis.** You will see the opening screen for the Respiratory Acidosis/Alkalosis experiment (Figure 10.1). To familiarize yourself with the equipment, choose **Balloons On/Off** from the **Help** menu. This feature allows you to scroll around the screen and view equipment labels. You can turn off this feature by returning to the **Help** menu and selecting **Balloons On/Off.** If you have already completed Exercise 7 on respiratory system mechanics, this screen should look familiar. At the left is a pair of *simulated lungs,* which look like balloons, connected by a tube that looks like an upside-down Y. Air flows in and out of this tube, which simulates the trachea and other air passageways into the lungs. Beneath the "lungs" is a black platform simulating the diaphragm. The long, U-shaped tube containing red fluid represents blood flowing through the lungs. At the top left of the U-shaped tube is a pH meter that will measure the pH level of the blood once the experiment is begun. To the right is an *oscilloscope monitor,* which will graphically display respiratory volumes. Note that respiratory volumes are measured in liters (l) along the Y-axis, and time in seconds is measured along the X-axis. Below the monitor are three buttons: **Normal Breathing, Hyperventilation,** and **Rebreathing.** Clicking any one of these buttons will induce the given pattern of breathing. Next to these buttons are three data displays for P_{CO_2} (partial pressure of carbon dioxide in the blood)—these will give us the levels of carbon dioxide in the blood over the course of an experimental run. At the very bottom of the screen is the *data collection grid,* where you may record and view your data after each activity.

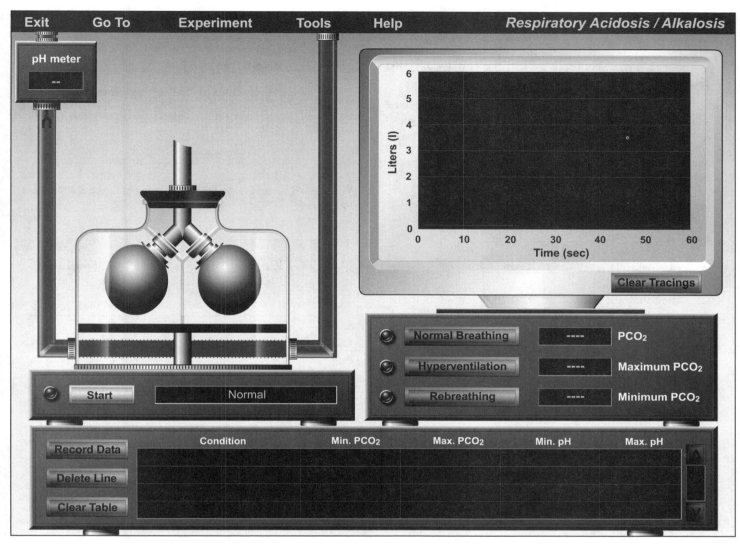

(a)

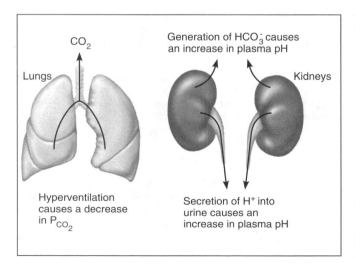

(b) Respiratory and renal response to acidosis

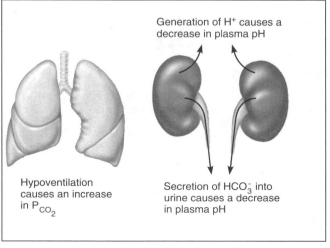

(c) Respiratory and renal response to alkalosis

FIGURE 10.1 Maintaining acid-base balance. (a) Opening screen of the Respiratory Acidosis/Alkalosis experiment. **(b)** Compensatory mechanisms for acidosis. **(c)** Compensatory mechanisms for alkalosis.

Normal Breathing

We will begin by observing what happens during normal breathing in order to establish baseline data.

1. Click **Start.** Notice that the **Normal Breathing** button dims, indicating that the simulated lungs are "breathing" normally. Also notice the reading in the pH meter at the top left, the readings in the P_{CO_2} displays, and the shape of the trace that starts running across the oscilloscope screen. As the trace runs, record the readings for pH at each of the following times:

At 20 seconds, pH = _____

At 40 seconds, pH = _____

At 60 seconds, pH = _____

2. Allow the trace to run all the way to the right side of the oscilloscope screen. At this point, the run will automatically end.

3. Click **Record Data** at the bottom left to record your results.

4. Select **Print Graph** in the **Tools** menu.

5. Click **Clear Tracings** to clear the oscilloscope screen.

Did the pH level of the blood change at all during normal breathing? If so, how?

_____

Was the pH level always within the normal range for the human body?

_____

Did the P_{CO_2} level change during the course of normal breathing? If so, how?

_____ ▬

Hyperventilation—Run 1

Next, we will observe what happens to pH and carbon dioxide levels in the blood during hyperventilation.

1. Click **Start.** Allow the normal breathing trace to run for 10 seconds; then at the 10-second mark, click **Hyperventilation.** Watch the pH meter display, as well as the readings in the P_{CO_2} displays and the shape of the trace. As the trace runs, record the readings for pH at each of the following times:

At 20 seconds, pH = _____

At 40 seconds, pH = _____

At 60 seconds, pH = _____

Maximum pH = _____

2. Allow the trace to run all the way across the oscilloscope screen and end.

3. Click **Record Data.**

4. Select **Print Graph** from the **Tools** menu.

5. Click **Clear Tracings** to clear the oscilloscope screen.

Did the pH level of the blood change at all during this run? If so, how?

_____

Was the pH level always within the normal range for the human body?

_____

If not, when was the pH value outside of the normal range, and what acid-base imbalance did this pH value indicate?

_____

Did the P_{CO_2} level change during the course of this run? If so, how?

_____

If you observed an acid-base imbalance during this run, how would you expect the renal system to compensate for this condition?

_____

How did the hyperventilation trace differ from the trace for normal breathing? Did the tidal volumes change?

_____

What might cause a person to hyperventilate?

_____ ▬

Hyperventilation—Run 2

This activity is a variation on Activity 2a.

1. Click **Start.** Allow the normal breathing trace to run for 10 seconds, then click **Hyperventilation** at the 10-second mark. Allow the hyperventilation trace to run for 10 seconds, then click **Normal Breathing** at the 20-second mark. Allow the trace to finish its run across the oscilloscope screen. Observe the changes in the pH meter and the P_{CO_2} displays.

2. Click **Record Data.**

3. Select **Print Graph** from the **Tools** menu.

4. Click **Clear Tracings** to clear the oscilloscope screen.

Describe the trace after the 20-second mark when you stopped the hyperventilation. Did the breathing return to normal immediately? Explain your observation.

_____

_____

_____

_____ ▬

Rebreathing

Rebreathing is the action of breathing in air that was just expelled from the lungs. Breathing into a paper bag is an example of rebreathing. In this activity, we will observe what happens to pH and carbon dioxide levels in the blood during rebreathing.

1. Click **Start.** Allow the normal breathing trace to run for 10 seconds; then at the 10-second mark, click **Rebreathing.** Watch the pH meter display, as well as the readings in the P_{CO_2} displays and the shape of the trace. As the trace runs, record the readings for pH at each of the following times:

At 20 seconds, pH = _____

At 40 seconds, pH = _____

At 60 seconds, pH = _____

2. Allow the trace to run all the way across the oscilloscope screen and end.

3. Click **Record Data.**

4. Select **Print Graph** from the **Tools** menu.

5. Click **Clear Tracings** to clear the oscilloscope screen.

Did the pH level of the blood change at all during this run? If so, how?

_____

_____

Was the pH level always within the normal range for the human body?

_____

_____

If not, when was the pH value outside of the normal range, and what acid-base imbalance did this pH value indicate?

_____

_____

Did the P_{CO_2} level change during the course of this run? If so, how?

_____

_____

If you observed an acid-base imbalance during this run, how would you expect the renal system to compensate for this condition?

_____

_____

How did the rebreathing trace differ from the trace for normal breathing? Did the tidal volumes change?

_____

_____

_____

Give examples of respiratory problems that would result in pH and P_{CO_2} patterns similar to what you observed during rebreathing.

_____

_____

6. To print out all of the recorded data from this activity, click **Tools** and then **Print Data.** ▬

In the next set of activities, we will focus on the body's primary mechanism of compensating for respiratory acidosis or alkalosis: renal compensation.

Renal System Compensation

The kidneys play a major role in maintaining fluid and electrolyte balance in the body's internal environment. By regulating the amount of water lost in the urine, the kidneys defend the body against excessive hydration or dehydration. By regulating the excretion of individual ions, the kidneys maintain normal electrolyte patterns of body fluids. By regulating the acidity of urine and the rate of electrolyte excretion, the kidneys maintain plasma pH levels within normal limits. Renal compensation is the body's primary method of compensating for conditions of respiratory acidosis or respiratory alkalosis. (Although the renal system also compensates for metabolic acidosis or metabolic alkalosis, a more immediate mechanism for compensating for metabolic acid-base imbalances is the respiratory system, as we will see in a later experiment.)

The activities in this section examine how the renal system compensates for respiratory acidosis or alkalosis. The primary variable we will be working with is P_{CO_2}. We will observe how increases and decreases in P_{CO_2} affect the levels of $[H^+]$ and $[HCO_3^-]$ that the kidneys excrete in urine.

Click on **Experiment** at the top of the screen, and select **Renal System Compensation.** You will see the screen shown in Figure 10.2. If you completed Exercise 41B on renal physiology, this screen should look familiar. There are two beakers on the left side of the screen, one of which is filled with blood, simulating the body's blood supply to the kidneys. Notice that the P_{CO_2} level is currently set to 40 and that the corresponding blood pH value is 7.4—both normal values. By clicking **Start,** you will initiate the process of delivering blood to the simulated nephron at the right side of the screen. As blood flows through the glomerulus of the nephron, you will see the

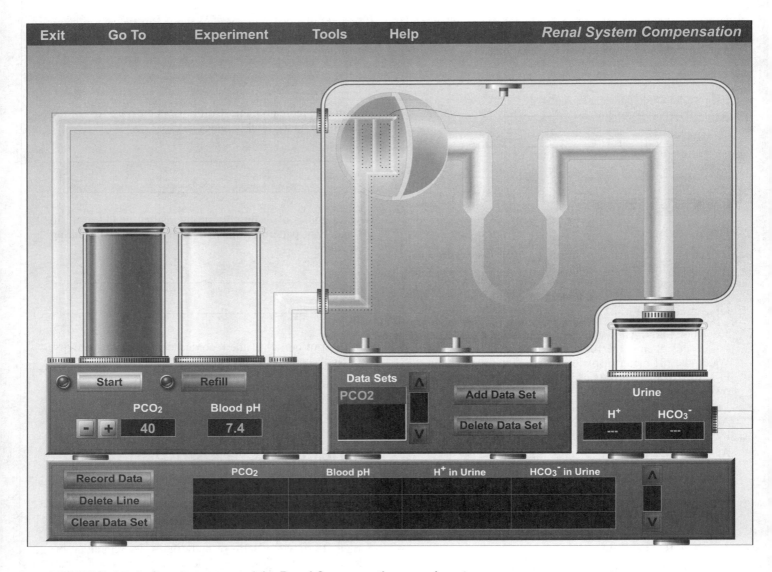

FIGURE 10.2 Opening screen of the Renal Compensation experiment.

filtration from the plasma of everything except proteins and cells (note that the moving red dots in the animation do *not* include red blood cells). Blood will then drain from the glomerulus to the beaker at the right of the original beaker. At the end of the nephron tube, you will see the collection of urine in a small beaker. Keep in mind that although only one nephron is depicted here, there are actually over a million nephrons in each human kidney. Below the urine beaker are displays for H^+ and HCO_3^-, which will tell us the relative levels of these ions present in the urine.

ACTIVITY 4

Renal Response to Normal Acid-Base Balance

1. Increase or decrease P_{CO_2} by clicking the (+) or (−) buttons. (Notice that as P_{CO_2} changes, so does the blood pH level.)

2. Click **Start,** and allow the run to finish.

3. At the end of the run, click **Record Data.**

At normal P_{CO_2} and pH levels, was the level of H^+ present in the urine normal? _____

What level of $[HCO_3^-]$ was present in the urine? _____

Why does the blood pH value change as P_{CO_2} changes?

_____

_____

_____

How does the blood pH value change as P_{CO_2} changes?

_____

_____

4. Click **Refill** to prepare for the next activity. ■

Renal Response to Respiratory Alkalosis

In this activity, we will simulate respiratory alkalosis by setting P_{CO_2} to values lower than normal (thus, blood pH will be *higher* than normal). We will then observe the renal system's response to these conditions.

1. Set P_{CO_2} to 35 by clicking the (−) button. Notice that the corresponding blood pH value is approximately 7.5.

2. Click **Start**.

3. At the end of the run, click **Record Data**.

4. Click **Refill**.

5. Repeat steps 1 through 4, setting P_{CO_2} to increasingly lower values (that is, set P_{CO_2} to 30 and then 20, the lowest value allowed).

What level of $[H^+]$ was present in the urine at each of these P_{CO_2} and pH levels?

_____

_____

What level of $[HCO_3^-]$ was present in the urine at each of these P_{CO_2} and pH levels?

_____

_____

Recall that it may take hours or even days for the renal system to respond to disruptions in acid-base balance. Assuming that enough time has passed for the renal system to fully compensate for respiratory alkalosis, would you expect P_{CO_2} levels to increase or decrease? Would you expect blood pH levels to increase or decrease?

_____

_____

_____

Recall your activities in the first experiment on respiratory acidosis and alkalosis. Which type of breathing resulted in P_{CO_2} levels closest to the ones we experimented with in this activity—normal breathing, hyperventilation, or rebreathing?

_____

_____

Explain why this type of breathing resulted in alkalosis.

_____

_____ ■

Renal Response to Respiratory Acidosis

In this activity, we will simulate respiratory acidosis by setting the P_{CO_2} values higher than normal (thus, blood pH will

be *lower* than normal). We will then observe the renal system's response to these conditions.

1. Make sure the left beaker is filled with blood. If not, click **Refill**.

2. Set P_{CO_2} to 60 by clicking the (+) button. Notice that the corresponding blood pH value is 7.3.

3. Click **Start**.

4. At the end of the run, click **Record Data**.

5. Click **Refill**.

6. Repeat steps 1 through 5, setting P_{CO_2} to increasingly higher values (that is, set P_{CO_2} to 75 and then 90, the highest value allowed).

What level of $[H^+]$ was present in the urine at each of these P_{CO_2} and pH levels?

_____

_____

What level of $[HCO_3^-]$ was present in the urine at each of these P_{CO_2} and pH levels?

_____

_____

Recall that it may take hours or even days for the renal system to respond to disruptions in acid-base balance. Assuming that enough time has passed for the renal system to fully compensate for respiratory acidosis, would you expect P_{CO_2} levels to increase or decrease? Would you expect blood pH levels to increase or decrease?

_____

_____

_____

Recall your activities in the first experiment on respiratory acidosis and alkalosis. Which type of breathing resulted in P_{CO_2} levels closest to the ones we experimented with in this activity—normal breathing, hyperventilation, or rebreathing?

_____

_____

Explain why this type of breathing resulted in acidosis.

_____

_____

7. Before going on to the next activity, select **Tools** and then **Print Data** in order to save a hard copy of your data results. ■

Metabolic Acidosis and Alkalosis

Conditions of acidosis or alkalosis that do not have respiratory causes are termed *metabolic acidosis* or *metabolic alkalosis*.

Metabolic acidosis is characterized by low plasma HCO_3^- and pH. The causes of metabolic acidosis include:

- *Ketoacidosis,* a buildup of keto acids that can result from diabetes mellitus

- *Salicylate poisoning,* a toxic condition resulting from ingestion of too much aspirin or oil of wintergreen (a substance often found in laboratories)

- The ingestion of too much alcohol, which metabolizes to acetic acid

- Diarrhea, which results in the loss of bicarbonate with the elimination of intestinal contents

- Strenuous exercise, which may cause a buildup of lactic acid from anaerobic muscle metabolism

Metabolic alkalosis is characterized by elevated plasma HCO_3^- and pH. The causes of metabolic alkalosis include:

- Alkali ingestion, such as antacids or bicarbonate

- Vomiting, which may result in the loss of too much H^+

- Constipation, which may result in reabsorption of elevated levels of HCO_3^-

Increases or decreases in the body's normal metabolic rate may also result in metabolic acidosis or alkalosis. Recall that carbon dioxide—a waste product of metabolism—mixes with water in plasma to form carbonic acid, which in turn forms H^+:

$$H_2O + CO_2 \rightarrow H_2CO_3 \rightarrow H^+ + HCO_3^-$$
$$\text{carbonic} \qquad \text{bicarbonate}$$
$$\text{acid} \qquad \text{ion}$$

Therefore, an increase in the normal rate of metabolism would result in more carbon dioxide being formed as a metabolic waste product, resulting in the formation of more H^+—and thereby lowering plasma pH and potentially causing acidosis. Other acids that are also normal metabolic waste products, such as ketone bodies and phosphoric, uric, and lactic acids, would likewise accumulate with an increase in metabolic rate. Conversely, a decrease in the normal rate of metabolism would result in less carbon dioxide being formed as a metabolic waste product, resulting in the formation of less H^+—raising plasma pH and potentially causing alkalosis. Many factors can affect the rate of cell metabolism. For example, fever, stress, or the ingestion of food all cause the rate of cell metabolism to increase. Conversely, a fall in body temperature or a decrease in food intake causes the rate of cell metabolism to decrease.

The respiratory system compensates for metabolic acidosis or alkalosis by expelling or retaining carbon dioxide in the blood. During metabolic acidosis, respiration increases to expel carbon dioxide from the blood and decrease $[H^+]$ in order to raise the pH level. During metabolic alkalosis, respiration decreases to promote the accumulation of carbon dioxide in the blood, thus increasing $[H^+]$ and decreasing the pH level.

The renal system also compensates for metabolic acidosis and alkalosis by conserving or excreting bicarbonate ions. However, in this set of activities we will focus on respiratory compensation of metabolic acidosis and alkalosis.

To begin, click **Experiment** at the top of the screen, and select **Metabolic Acidosis/Alkalosis.** The screen shown in Figure 10.3 will appear. This screen is similar to the screen from the first experiment; the main differences are the addition of a box representing the heart; tubes showing the double circulation of the heart; and a box representing the body's cells. The default "normal" metabolic rate has been set to 50 kcal/hr—an arbitrary value, given that normal metabolic rates vary widely from individual to individual. The (+) and (−) buttons in the Body Cells box allow you to increase or decrease the body's metabolic rate. In the following activities, we will observe the respiratory response to acidosis or alkalosis brought on by increases or decreases in the body's metabolic rate.

ACTIVITY 7

Respiratory Response to Normal Metabolism

We will begin by observing respiratory activity at normal metabolic conditions. This data will serve as a baseline against which we will compare our data in Activities 8 and 9.

1. Make sure the **Metabolic Rate** is set to 50, which for the purposes of this experiment we will consider the normal value.

2. Click **Start** to begin the experiment. Notice the arrows showing the direction of blood flow. A graph displaying respiratory activity will appear on the oscilloscope screen.

3. After the graph has reached the end of the screen, the experiment will automatically stop. Note the data in the displays below the oscilloscope screen:

- The **BPM** display gives you the *breaths per minute*—the rate at which respiration occurred.

- **Blood pH** tells you the pH value of the blood.

- **PCO₂** (shown as P_{CO_2} in the text) tells you the partial pressure of carbon dioxide in the blood.

- **H⁺** and **HCO₃⁻** tell you the levels of each of these ions.

4. Click **Record Data.**

5. Click **Tools** and then **Print Graph** in order to print your graph.

What is the respiratory rate (BMP)? _____

What is the blood pH? _____

Are the blood pH and P_{CO_2} values within normal ranges?

_____

6. Click **Clear Tracings** before proceeding to the next activity. ▪▪▪

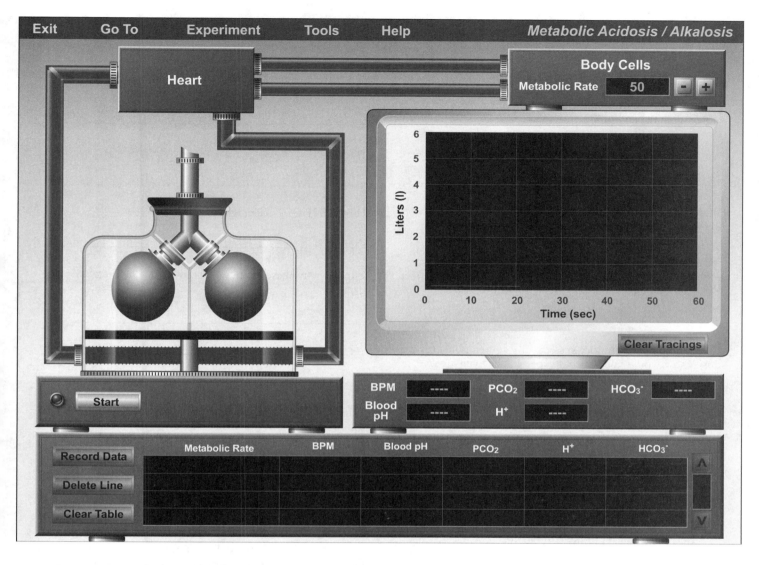

FIGURE 10.3 Opening screen of the Metabolic Acidosis/Alkalosis experiment.

<table>
<tr><td colspan="4">

ACTIVITY 8

Respiratory Response to Increased Metabolism

1. Increase the **Metabolic Rate** to 60 using the (**+**) button.

2. Click **Start** to begin the experiment.

3. Allow the graph to reach the end of the oscilloscope screen. Note the data in the displays below the oscilloscope screen.

4. Click **Record Data.**

5. Click **Tools** and then **Print Graph** in order to print your graph.

6. Repeat steps 1 through 5 with the **Metabolic Rate** set at 70, and then 80.

</td><td>

As the body's metabolic rate increased:

How did respiration change with respect to BPM and tidal volume?

_____

How did blood pH change?

_____

How did P_{CO_2} change?

_____

How did [H^+] change?

_____

</td></tr>
</table>

How did $[HCO_3^-]$ change?

_____

Explain why these changes took place as metabolic rate increased. Hint: Start with the formation of excess CO_2 waste and explain the changes.

_____

_____

Which metabolic rates caused pH levels to decrease to a condition of metabolic acidosis?

_____

What were the pH values at each of these rates?

_____

By the time the respiratory system fully compensated for acidosis, how would you expect the pH values to change?

_____

7.   Click **Clear Tracings** before proceeding to the next activity. ▬

Respiratory Response to Decreased Metabolism

1.   Decrease the **Metabolic Rate** to 40.

2.   Click **Start** to begin the experiment.

3.   Allow the graph to reach the end of the oscilloscope screen. Note the data in the displays below the oscilloscope screen.

4.   Click **Record Data.**

5.   Click **Tools** and then **Print Graph** in order to print your graph.

6.   Repeat steps 1 through 5 with the **Metabolic Rate** set at 30, and then 20.

As the body's metabolic rate decreased:

How did respiration change?

_____

How did blood pH change?

_____

How did P_{CO_2} change?

_____

How did $[H^+]$ change?

_____

How did $[HCO_3^-]$ change?

_____

Explain why these changes took place as the metabolic rate decreased.

_____

_____

_____

Which metabolic rates caused pH levels to increase to a condition of metabolic alkalosis?

_____

What were the pH values at each of these rates?

_____

By the time the respiratory system fully compensated for acidosis, how would you expect the pH values to change?

_____

7.   Click **Tools → Print Data** to print your recorded data. ▬

NAME _____

LAB TIME/DATE _____

Acid-Base Balance

Respiratory Acidosis and Alkalosis

The following questions refer to Activity 1: Normal Breathing.

1. What was the pH level during normal breathing? _____

2. Was this pH within the normal pH range? _____

The following questions refer to Activity 2: Hyperventilation.

3. In run 1, what was the maximum pH recorded with hyperventilation? _____

4. What acid-base imbalance occurred with hyperventilation? _____

_____

5. What happened to the tidal volume during hyperventilation?

_____

6. Describe the trace when hyperventilation stopped in run 2. _____

_____

The following questions refer to Activity 3: Rebreathing. _____

7. What was the effect on pH over time with rebreathing? _____

_____

8. Did rebreathing result in acidosis or alkalosis? Why? Hint: Specifically relate this to the level of CO_2.

_____

_____

9. List some potential causes that would mimic the patterns of pH and CO_2 levels seen in this rebreathing simulation.

_____

Renal System Compensation

The following questions refer to Activity 4: Renal Response to Normal Acid-Base Balance.

10. Describe how the pH of the blood changes with an increase in the level of CO_2.

_____

11. Why does this change occur? _____

The following questions refer to Activity 5: Renal Response to Respiratory Alkalosis.

12. What happened to the level of $[H^+]$ in the urine as the level of CO_2 decreased?

_____

13. Explain how the renal system compensates for respiratory alkalosis. _____

_____

14. Which type of breathing results in respiratory alkalosis? _____

The following questions refer to Activity 6: Renal Response to Respiratory Acidosis.

15. Explain how the renal system compensates for respiratory acidosis. _____

_____

16. Which type of breathing results in respiratory acidosis? _____

Metabolic Acidosis and Alkalosis

The following questions refer to Activity 8: Respiratory Response to Increased Metabolism.

17. What waste product is increased with an increased rate of metabolism? _____

18. Which metabolic rates results in metabolic acidosis? _____

19. List some other potential causes of metabolic acidosis. _____

_____

The following questions refer to Activity 9: Respiratory Response to Decreased Metabolism.

20. Which metabolic rates resulted in metabolic alkalosis? _____

21. List some other potential causes of metabolic alkalosis. _____

_____

Blood Analysis

O B J E C T I V E S

1. To become familiar with the "normal" values obtained with selected blood tests.
2. To understand how common laboratory procedures for examining blood can indicate pathology, or a state of disease.
3. To learn how the following blood tests are performed:
   hematocrit (packed cell volume) determination
   erythrocyte sedimentation rate
   hemoglobin determination
   blood typing
   total blood cholesterol determination
4. To understand what each of these procedures is measuring in a sample of blood.
5. To realize the importance of proper disposal of laboratory equipment that has come in contact with blood.
6. To understand the importance of matching blood types for blood transfusions.

Blood transports soluble substances to and from all cells of the body. Blood cells are also important in defense against pathogens. Laboratory analysis of the blood gives important information about how well these functions are being carried out.

This lab exercise consists of five common laboratory tests performed on blood: hematocrit determination; erythrocyte sedimentation rate; hemoglobin determination; blood typing; and total cholesterol determination.

Hematocrit Determination

Hematocrit refers to the percentage of red blood cells (RBCs) in a sample of whole blood. A hematocrit of 48 means that 48% of the volume of blood is red blood cells. Since the function of red blood cells is the transport of oxygen to the cells of the body, the higher the hematocrit, the more red blood cells are available to carry oxygen.

Hematocrit values are determined by spinning a microcapillary tube filled with a whole blood sample in a special microhematocrit centrifuge. This procedure separates the blood cells from the blood plasma and leaves a "buffy coat" layer of white blood cells between the heavier red blood cell layer and the lighter plasma.

The hematocrit value can be determined after centrifuging by measuring the height of the layer of red cells in millimeters and dividing that number by the height of the initial column of blood to obtain the percentage of red blood cells.

The percentage of white blood cells (WBCs) can also be determined after centrifuging by comparing the height of the buffy coat to the initial height of the blood column.

The average hematocrit value for males is 47%, and the average for females is 42%. The normal upper limit is 55%. A lower-than-normal hematocrit indicates *anemia*. A higher-than-normal hematocrit indicates *polycythemia*.

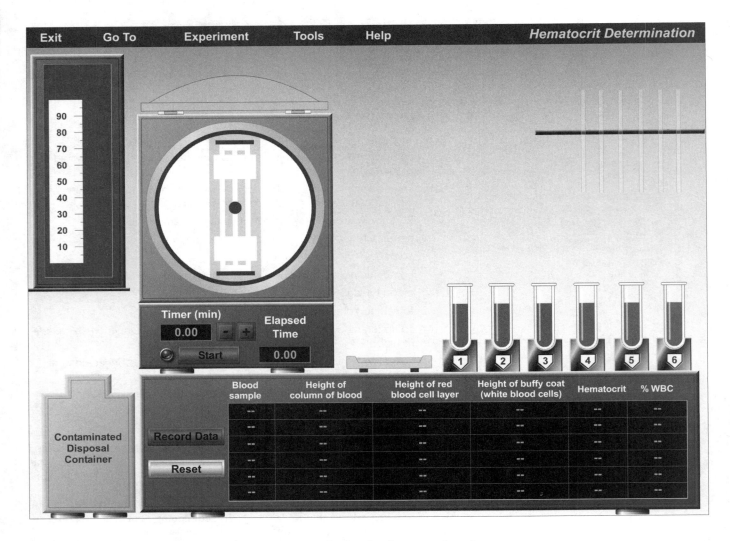

FIGURE 11.1 Opening screen of the Hematocrit Determination experiment.

Anemia is a condition in which insufficient oxygen is transported to the body's cells. There are many possible causes for anemia, including inadequate numbers of red blood cells, decreased amount of the oxygen-carrying pigment hemoglobin, and abnormal hemoglobin. The heme portion of hemoglobin molecules contains an atom of iron. If adequate iron is not available, the body cannot manufacture hemoglobin. This results in a condition called *iron-deficiency anemia. Aplastic anemia* is the result of the failure of the bone marrow to produce adequate blood cells. *Pernicious anemia* is due to a lack of vitamin B_{12}, which is necessary for cell division. Intrinsic factor, produced by the stomach, allows absorption of vitamin B_{12}. Individuals who do not produce adequate intrinsic factor, or individuals who do not have adequate vitamin B_{12} in their diet, will suffer from pernicious anemia. *Sickle cell anemia* is an inherited condition in which the protein portion of hemoglobin molecules is folded incorrectly. As a result, oxygen molecules cannot fit with the misshapen hemoglobin, and anemia results.

Polycythemia refers to a significant increase in red blood cells. There are many possible causes of polycythemia, including living at high altitudes, strenuous athletic training, and tumors in the bone marrow.

In the following activity, we will simulate the blood test that is used to determine hematocrit. From the drop-down menu, select **Experiment 11: Blood Analysis** and click **GO.** Before you perform the activities, watch the video **Blood Typing** to see how similar the simulation is to actual blood typing. Then click **Hematocrit Determination.** You will see the opening screen for the Hematocrit Determination experiment (Figure 11.1).

To familiarize yourself with the equipment, select **Help** from the menu bar and then select **Balloons On/Off.** This feature allows you to scroll around the screen and view equipment labels. You can turn the feature off by returning to **Help** and then selecting **Balloons On/Off.**

In the upper right portion of the screen is a dispenser containing six thin tubes, which are *heparinized capillary tubes.* Heparin is a substance that keeps blood from clotting. Below the capillary tubes are six test tubes containing samples of blood to be tested. When a capillary tube is dragged to a test tube of blood, it partially fills by fluid capillary action.

To the left of the samples of blood is a container of *capillary tube sealer* (a clay material, shown on-screen as an orange-yellow substance). The capillary tubes must be sealed on one end with this tube sealer so that the blood sample can be centrifuged without spraying out the blood.

When the tubes have been sealed, they are moved to slots in the *microhematocrit centrifuge*. When the **Start** button is clicked, the centrifuge will rotate at 14,500 revolutions per minute.

After the centrifuge stops and opens, the capillary tubes are moved, one at a time, next to the metric ruler on the upper left of the screen. When you click on the **Record Data** button next to the data table at the bottom of the screen, the following information about the sample will be recorded: the height of the column of blood in millimeters, the height of the red blood cell layer, the height of the buffy coat (white blood cells), the hematocrit (percentage of red blood cells) and the percentage of white blood cells.

In the lower left corner of the screen is a contaminated disposal container. Every piece of glassware that has come in contact with the blood must be disposed of by dragging it to this container for proper disposal.

ACTIVITY 1

Hematocrit Determination

The following individuals have contributed their blood for this test:

Sample 1: healthy male, living in Boston

Sample 2: healthy female, living in Boston

Sample 3: healthy male, living in Denver

Sample 4: healthy female, living in Denver

Sample 5: male with aplastic anemia

Sample 6: female with iron-deficiency anemia

1. Click and drag one heparinized capillary tube over to the test tube containing blood sample 1. Make sure the capillary tube is touching the blood. The capillary tube will fill itself by fluid capillary action.

2. Drag the capillary tube containing sample 1 to the container of capillary tube sealer to "seal" one end of the tube.

3. Drag the capillary tube to the microhematocrit centrifuge.

4. Repeat steps 1–3 for the remaining five samples of blood.

5. Set the timer for the centrifuge for 5 minutes by clicking the (+) button, and then click the **Start** button.

6. When the centrifuge stops and opens, click and drag capillary tube 1 to the metric ruler.

7. Click **Record Data** to record the information about sample 1.

8. Click and drag capillary tube 1 to the contaminated disposal container.

9. Repeat steps 6–8 for the remaining five capillary tubes in the centrifuge.

10. Click **Tools,** then **Print Data** to print the data from the table (or fill in Chart 1).

If you wish to restart or repeat the lab, click the **Reset** button next to the data table.

CHART 1	Blood Analysis Results				
Blood Sample	Total Height of Column of Blood (mm)	Height of Red Blood Cell Layer (mm)	Height of Buffy Coat (White Blood Cells) (mm)	Hematocrit	% WBC
Healthy male, living in Boston					
Healthy female, living in Boston					
Healthy male, living in Denver					
Healthy female, living in Denver					
Male with aplastic anemia					
Female with iron-deficiency anemia					

What is the hematocrit value of a healthy male living at sea level in Boston?

_____

What is the hematocrit value of a healthy male living at one mile elevation in Denver?

_____

Is there as much oxygen in the air in Denver as there is in Boston?

_____

How do your kidneys respond to a decrease in blood oxygen? (Review this section in your textbook if necessary.)

_____

_____

If your bone marrow is producing an elevated number of red blood cells, what happens to your hematocrit?

_____

What is the hematocrit value of the male with aplastic anemia?

_____

Would the red blood cell count for an individual with aplastic anemia be higher, lower, or the same as the red blood cell count of a healthy individual?

_____

What is the hematocrit value of a healthy female living in Boston?

_____

Explain the difference in hematocrit values obtained from a healthy female living in Boston and a female with iron-deficiency anemia.

_____

_____

Erythrocyte Sedimentation Rate

The **erythrocyte sedimentation rate (ESR)** measures the settling of red blood cells in a vertical, stationary tube of blood during one hour.

In a healthy individual, red blood cells do not settle very much in an hour. In some disease conditions, increased production of fibrinogen and immunoglobulins cause the red blood cells to clump together, stack up, and form a column (called a _rouleaux formation_). Grouped like this, red blood cells are heavier and settle faster.

This test is not a very specific or diagnostic test, but it can be used to follow the progression of certain disease conditions such as sickle cell anemia, certain cancers, and inflammatory diseases such as rheumatoid arthritis. When the disease worsens, the ESR increases; and when the disease improves, the ESR decreases. The ESR is elevated in iron-deficiency anemia. Sometimes a menstruating female will develop anemia and show an increase in ESR.

The ESR can be used to evaluate a patient with chest pains: the ESR is elevated in established myocardial infarction (heart attack) but normal in angina pectoris. Similarly, it can be useful in screening a female patient with severe abdominal pains because the ESR is not elevated within the first 24 hours of acute appendicitis but is elevated in the early stage of acute pelvic inflammatory disease (PID) or ruptured ectopic pregnancy.

Click **Experiment** on the menu bar, then select **Erythrocyte Sedimentation Rate.** You will see the opening screen for the Erythrocyte Sedimentation Rate lab (Figure 11.2). Use the **Balloons On/Off** feature from the **Help** menu to familiarize yourself with the equipment on the screen.

In the upper left portion of the screen is a shelf with six samples of blood that have been treated with the anticoagulant heparin. Also on the shelf is a dropper bottle of sodium citrate. The sodium citrate is used to bind with calcium to prevent the blood samples from clotting so they can easily be poured into the narrow sedimentation rate tubes (used later in the lab).

Below the shelf is a test tube dispenser and a test tube rack. To the right of the test tube rack is a cabinet that contains six sedimentation tubes. This cabinet will open when all six blood samples have been added to the test tubes and diluted with sodium citrate. Below this cabinet is a timer, a window showing elapsed time, and a **Start** button to start the timer.

In the upper right portion of the screen is a magnifying chamber that will help you read the millimeter markings on the sedimentation tubes.

In the lower right portion of the screen is a contaminated disposal container. All glassware that has come in contact with the blood must be placed in this container for proper disposal.

When you click on the **Record Data** button next to the data table at the bottom of the screen, the following information about the sample will be recorded: the distance that the RBCs have settled, time elapsed, and sedimentation rate.

ACTIVITY 2

Erythrocyte Sedimentation Rate

The following individuals have contributed their blood for this test:

Sample 1: healthy individual

Sample 2: menstruating female

Sample 3: person with sickle cell anemia

Sample 4: person with iron-deficiency anemia

Sample 5: person suffering from a myocardial infarction

Sample 6: person suffering from angina pectoris

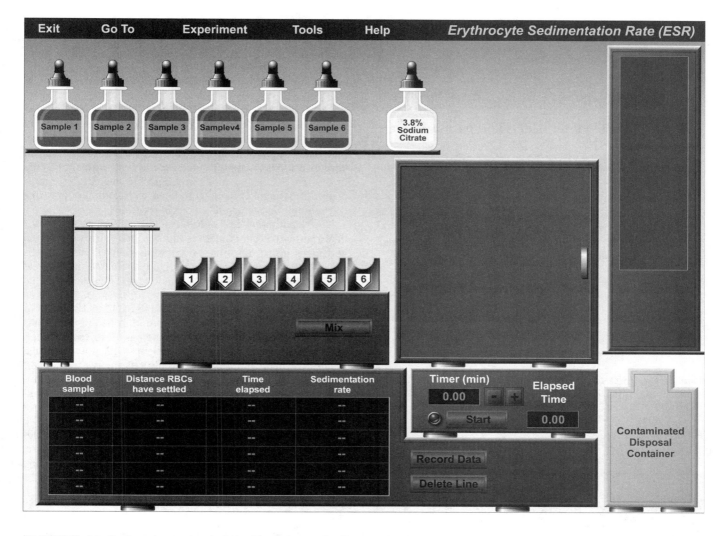

FIGURE 11.2 Opening screen of the Erythrocyte Sedimentation Rate experiment.

1. Individually click and drag six test tubes from the dispenser to the test tube rack.

2. Click on the dropper for blood sample 1, and drag it to the first test tube. One milliliter of blood will be dispensed into the tube.

3. Repeat step 2 for the remaining five samples of blood, using a different test tube for each sample.

4. Click on the dropper for the **3.8% sodium citrate,** and drag it over the test tube containing blood sample 1; 0.5 milliliter of sodium citrate will be dispensed into the tube.

5. The dropper will automatically slide over to each of the remaining samples.

6. Click on the **Mix** button. The samples will automatically mix for a few seconds.

7. After the samples have been mixed, the cabinet with six sedimentation tubes will open.

8. Click on the tube containing blood sample 1. Notice that the pointer is now a small test tube pointed to the left.

9. While still holding the mouse button down, move the mouse pointer to the first sedimentation tube in the cabinet.

The contents of the small test tube will pour into the sedimentation tube.

10. Click and drag the now empty test tube to the contaminated disposal container.

11. Repeat steps 8–10 with the other five samples of blood.

12. When the six sedimentation tubes are filled, set the timer for 60 minutes by clicking the (+) button, and then click the **Start** button.

13. After 60 minutes have elapsed, drag sedimentation tube 1 to the magnifying chamber at the top right of the screen. Examine the tube. The tube is marked in millimeters, and the distance between two marks is 5 mm. How many millimeters has the blood settled?

_____

What is in the beige-colored portion of the tube? _____

14. Click the **Record Data** button next to the data table. The distance in millimeters that the red blood cells have

settled, the elapsed time, and the sedimentation rate will be entered in the table.

15. Drag the sedimentation tube to the contaminated disposal container.

16. Repeat steps 13–15 with the other five sedimentation tubes.

17. Click **Tools,** then **Print Data** to print the data from the table, or fill in Chart 2.

Did the person with sickle cell anemia show an elevated ESR?

_____

How did the ESR for a person with iron-deficiency anemia compare to the ESR for a healthy individual?

_____

Explain the ESR for sample 2, the menstruating female.

_____

Explain the ESRs for samples 5 and 6 (the patients suffering from myocardial infarction and angina pectoris, respectively.)

_____

Hemoglobin

Hemoglobin (Hb), a protein found in red blood cells, is necessary for the transport of oxygen from the lungs to the body's cells. Anemia results when insufficient oxygen is carried in the blood.

Hemoglobin molecules consist of four polypeptide chains of amino acids, the "globin" part of the molecule. Each polypeptide chain has a heme unit—a group of atoms, which includes an atom of iron. When the polypeptide chain folds up correctly, it has an appropriate shape to bind with a molecule of oxygen. So, each hemoglobin molecule can carry four molecules of oxygen. Oxygen combined with hemoglobin forms oxyhemoglobin, which has a bright red color.

A quantitative hemoglobin determination is useful for determining the classification and possible causes of anemia and gives useful information on some other disease conditions. For example, a person can have anemia with a normal red blood cell count, if there is inadequate hemoglobin in the red blood cells.

Normal blood contains an average of 12 to 18 grams of hemoglobin per 100 milliliters of blood. A healthy male has 13.5 to 18 g/100 ml; a healthy female has 12 to 16 g/100 ml. Hemoglobin values increase in patients with polycythemia, congestive heart failure, and chronic obstructive pulmonary disease (COPD). They also increase at high altitudes. Hemoglobin values decrease in patients with anemia, hyperthyroidism, cirrhosis of the liver, renal disease, systemic lupus erythematosus, and severe hemorrhage.

The hemoglobin content of a sample of blood can be determined by stirring the blood with a wooden stick to rupture, or lyse, the cells. The intensity of the color of the lysed blood

CHART 2	Erythrocyte Sedimentation Rate Results		
Blood Sample	Distance RBCs Have Settled (mm)	Elapsed Time	Sedimentation Rate
Healthy individual			
Menstruating female			
Person with sickle cell anemia			
Person with iron-deficiency anemia			
Person suffering from a myocardial infarction			
Person suffering from angina pectoris			

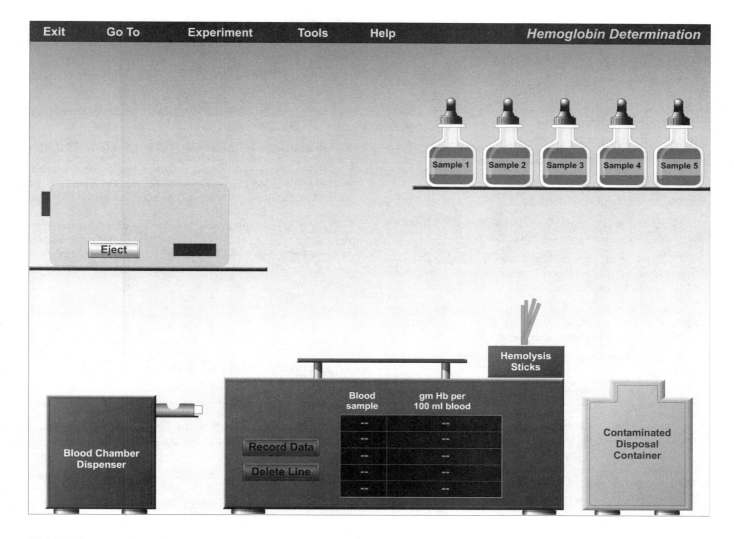

FIGURE 11.3 Opening screen of the Hemoglobin Determination experiment.

is a result of the amount of hemoglobin present. A *hemoglobi-nometer* compares the color of the sample to standard values to determine the hemoglobin content of the sample. The he-moglobinometer transmits green light through the hemolyzed blood sample. The amount of light that passes through the sample is compared to standard color intensities. Green light is used because the human eye is able to easily detect subtle differences in green colors.

From the **Experiment** menu, select **Hemoglobin Deter-mination.** You will see the opening screen for the Hemoglo-bin Determination lab (Figure 11.3). Use the **Balloons On/Off** feature from the **Help** menu to familiarize yourself with the equipment on the screen.

In the upper right portion of the screen is a shelf with five samples of blood.

In the middle of the screen is a lab table and a container of hemolysis sticks. The hemolysis sticks will be used to stir the blood samples to lyse the red blood cells, thereby releas-ing their hemoglobin.

At the bottom left of the screen is a blood chamber dis-penser that provides a slide with a depression to receive the blood sample.

Above the blood chamber dispenser is a hemoglobi-nometer. The hemoglobinometer has a black rectangular slot to receive the blood chamber and an **Eject** button to remove the blood chamber. When the loaded blood chamber is in-serted into the slot, the hemoglobinometer view will change to show a split screen that compares the color of the he-molyzed blood sample to a standard color for which given levels of hemoglobin are already known. A window on the hemoglobinometer displays the grams of hemoglobin per 100 milliliters of blood. A small handle on the top right of the hemoglobinometer can be slid down until the colors shown on the device match the colors of the sample of blood to be tested.

When you click on the **Record Data** button next to the data table at the bottom of the screen, the grams of hemoglo-bin per 100 milliliters of blood will be recorded.

In the lower right portion of the screen is a contaminated disposal container. All glassware and hemolysis sticks that have come in contact with the blood must be placed in this container for proper disposal.

Hemoglobin (Hb) Determination

The following individuals have contributed their blood for this test:

Sample 1: healthy male

Sample 2: healthy female

Sample 3: female with iron-deficiency anemia

Sample 4: male with polycythemia

Sample 5: female Olympic athlete

1.   Click and drag a clean blood chamber slide from the blood chamber dispenser to the lab table.

2.   Click on the dropper for blood sample 1, and drag it over to the depression on the blood chamber slide. A drop of blood will be dispensed into the depression.

3.   Click a hemolysis stick, and drag it to the drop of blood. The stick will stir the blood sample for 45 seconds, lysing the red blood cells and releasing their hemoglobin.

4.   Drag the hemolysis stick to the contaminated disposal container.

5.   Drag the blood chamber slide to the dark rectangular slot on the hemoglobinometer.

6.   You will see a pop-up window appear, displaying the view inside the hemoglobinometer. The left half of the circular field shows the intensity of green light transmitted by blood sample 1. The right half of the circular field shows the intensity of green light for known levels of hemoglobin present in blood.

7.   Click and hold the lever on the top right of the hemoglobinometer, and slowly drag it downward until the right half of the field matches the shade of green on the left side of the field.

8.   Click the **Record Data** button next to the data table to record the grams of hemoglobin per 100 milliliters of blood for blood sample 1. Click "X" to close the pop-up window.

9.   Click the **Eject** button to remove the blood chamber with blood sample 1 from the hemoglobinometer.

10.   Drag the blood sample 1 chamber to the contaminated disposal container.

11.   Repeat steps 1–10 for the remaining samples of blood.

Fill in Chart 3, using the grams of hemoglobin per 100 milliliters of blood that you obtained in this exercise. Use the packed cell volume (PCV) data provided in Chart 3 to calculate the ratio of PCV to Hb.

An individual might have a normal or near normal hematocrit value (packed cell volume) and still suffer from anemia if the red blood cells do not contain adequate hemoglobin. A normal ratio of packed cell volume to grams of hemoglobin is approximately 3:1.

What is the hematocrit value for the healthy male?

_____

What is the hematocrit value for the healthy female?

_____

What does the ratio of PCV to Hb tell you about the red blood cells of the female with iron-deficiency anemia?

_____

Does the male with polycythemia have a normal ratio of PCV

to Hb? _____

CHART 3	Hemoglobin Determination		
Blood Sample	Hb in grams per 100 ml of blood	Hematocrit (PCV)	Ratio of PCV to Hb
Healthy male		48	
Healthy female		44	
Female with iron-deficiency anemia		40	
Male with polycythemia		60	
Female Olympic athlete		60	

Based on these results, do you think his red blood cells contain adequate quantities of hemoglobin molecules? Why?

_____

_____

Does the female Olympic athlete have a normal ratio of PCV

to Hb? _____

Based on these results, do you think her red blood cells contain adequate quantities of hemoglobin molecules? Why?

_____

_____ ▪

Blood Typing

All of the cells in the human body, including the red blood cells, are surrounded by a *plasma (cell) membrane.* The plasma membrane contains genetically determined glycoproteins, called antigens, that identify the cells. On red blood cell membranes, these antigens are called *agglutinogens.*

It is important to determine blood types before performing blood transfusions in order to avoid mixing incompatible blood. Although many different antigens are present on red blood cell membranes, the ABO and Rh antigens cause the most vigorous and potentially fatal transfusion reactions. If a blood transfusion recipient has antibodies (called *agglutinins*) to the antigens present on the transfused cells, the red blood cells will be clumped together, or *agglutinated,* and then lysed. This results in a potentially life-threatening blood transfusion reaction.

The ABO blood groups are determined by the presence or absence of two antigens: type A and type B (see Figure 11.4b). These antigens are genetically determined so a person has two copies (alleles) of the gene for these proteins, one copy from each parent. The presence of these antigens is due to a dominant gene, and their absence is due to a recessive gene.

• A person with type A blood can have two gene alleles for the A antigen, or that person could have one gene allele for type A antigen and the other allele for the absence of either A or B antigen.

• A person with type B blood can have two gene alleles for the B antigen, or that person could have one gene allele for type B antigen and the other allele for the absence of either A or B antigen.

• A person with type AB blood has one gene allele for the A antigen and the other allele for the B antigen.

• A person with type O blood will have inherited two recessive gene alleles and has neither type A nor type B antigen.

Antibodies to the A and B antigens are found preformed in the blood plasma. A person has antibodies only for the antigens not on his or her red blood cells, so a person with type A blood will have anti-B antibodies. This is summarized in Chart 4.

CHART 4	ABO Blood Types	
Blood Type	Antigens on RBCs	Antibodies Present in Plasma
A	A	anti-B
B	B	anti-A
AB	A and B	none
O	none	anti-A and anti-B

The Rh factor is another genetically determined protein that may be present on red blood cell membranes. Approximately 85% of the population is Rh positive and has this protein. Antibodies to the Rh factor are not found preformed in the plasma. These antibodies are produced only after exposure to the Rh factor by persons who are Rh negative.

Separate drops of a blood sample are mixed with anti-sera containing antibodies to the types A and B antigens and antibodies to the Rh factor. An agglutination reaction (showing clumping) indicates the presence of the agglutinogen.

In this experiment, we will conduct blood typing tests on six blood samples. From the **Experiment** menu, select **Blood Typing.** You will see the opening screen for the Blood Typing lab (Figure 11.4a). Use the **Balloons On/Off** feature from the **Help** menu to familiarize yourself with the equipment on the screen.

In the upper right portion of the screen is a shelf with six samples of blood.

In the upper left portion of the screen is a shelf containing bottles of anti-A serum (blue color), anti-B serum (yellow color), and anti-Rh serum (white color). These bottles contain antibodies to the A antigen, B antigen, and Rh antigen, respectively.

In the center of the screen is a lab table for performing the blood typing. To the left of the lab table is a blood typing slide dispenser.

Above the blood typing slide dispenser is a container of stirring sticks. These sticks are color coded: the blue stick is to be used with the anti-A serum, the yellow stick is to be used with the anti-B serum, and the white stick is to be used with the anti-Rh serum.

To the right of the lab table is a *light box* for viewing the blood type samples. When you click on the **Light** button, the screen above unrolls to display the blood types.

To the left of the light box is a data table to record your results.

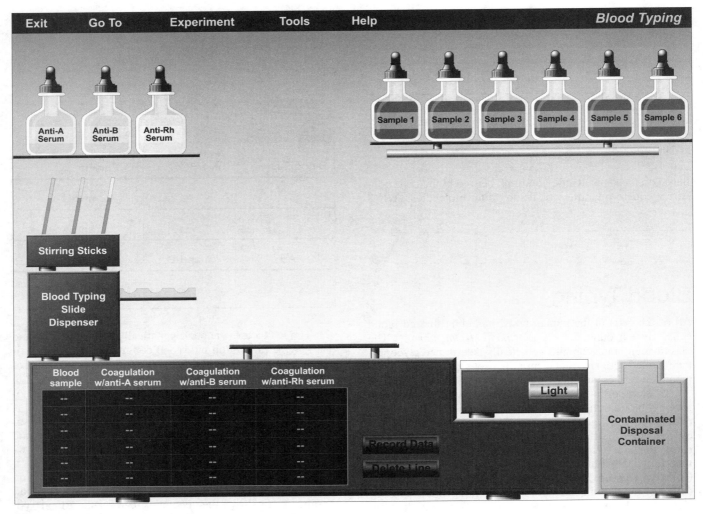

(a)

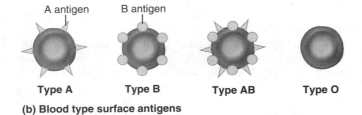

(b) Blood type surface antigens

A antigen   B antigen

Type A   **Type B**   **Type AB**   **Type O**

FIGURE 11.4 Blood typing. (a) Opening screen of the Blood Typing experiment. **(b)** Antigens determining ABO blood type, found on the surface of red blood cells.

In the bottom right portion of the screen is a contaminated disposal container. All glassware and sticks that have come in contact with blood must be placed in this container for proper disposal.

ACTIVITY 4

Blood Typing

Six individuals with different blood types have donated their blood for this exercise.

1. Click and drag a blood typing slide from the blood typing slide dispenser to the lab table. Note that the three wells on the slide are labeled "A," "B," and "Rh."

2. Click on the dropper for blood sample 1, and drag it over the well labeled A on the blood typing slide. A drop of blood will be dispensed into the well.

3. The dropper will automatically slide over to each of the remaining wells.

4. Click on the dropper for anti-A serum, and drag it over the well labeled A on the blood typing slide. A drop of anti-A serum will be dispensed into the well.

5. Repeat step 4 with the anti-B serum. Be sure to dispense it into the well labeled B.

6. Repeat step 4 with the anti-Rh serum. Be sure to dispense it into the well labeled Rh.

7. Obtain a blue-tipped stirring stick, and drag it to well A. It will mix the blood and anti-A serum.

8. Dispose of the stirring stick in the contaminated disposal container.

9. Select a yellow-tipped stirring stick, and drag it to well B.

10. Dispose of the stirring stick in the contaminated disposal container.

11. Select a white-tipped stirring stick, and drag it to well Rh.

12. Dispose of the stirring stick in the contaminated disposal container.

13. Drag the blood typing slide to the light box, and click the **Light** button. The screen will unroll, displaying the results of the blood typing.

14. Examine the results labeled A on the screen. If coagulation (agglutination, or "clumpiness") is present, click on **Positive.** If no coagulation is present (the sample will look smooth), click on **Negative.**

15. Repeat step 14 for the results labeled B and Rh. In each case, choose **Positive** if the sample is coagulated and **Negative** if the sample is not coagulated.

16. Click the **Record Data** button on the data table to record the results of blood sample 1.

17. Click and drag the blood typing slide to the contaminated disposal container.

18. Click the **X** at the top right of the scroll to close the scroll.

19. Repeat steps 1–18 for the remaining samples of blood.

Using the data you have collected in this activity, fill in Chart 5. (Indicate coagulation as either "positive" or "negative.")

Determine the blood type of each sample and fill in the last column. For Rh positive or negative, add $^+$ or $^-$ to the blood type; for example, AB^+.

If the anti-A antibody causes the blood to coagulate, which antigen would be present on the blood cells?

_____

If a person has type AB blood, which antigens are present on the red blood cells?

_____

Which antibodies are present in the plasma of a person with type AB blood?

_____

Does a person with type O blood have A or B antigens on the red blood cells?

_____ ▬

Blood Cholesterol

Cholesterol is a lipid substance that is essential for life. It is an important component of all cell membranes and is the basis for making steroid hormones, vitamin D, and bile salts.

Cholesterol is produced in the human liver and is present in some foods of animal origin, such as milk, meat, and eggs. Since cholesterol is a water-insoluble lipid, it needs to be wrapped in protein packages, called lipoproteins, to travel in the watery blood from the liver and digestive organs to the cells of the body.

CHART 5	Blood Typing Results			
Blood Sample	Agglutination with Anti-A Serum	Agglutination with Anti-B Serum	Agglutination with Anti-Rh Serum	Blood Type
1				
2				
3				
4				
5				
6				

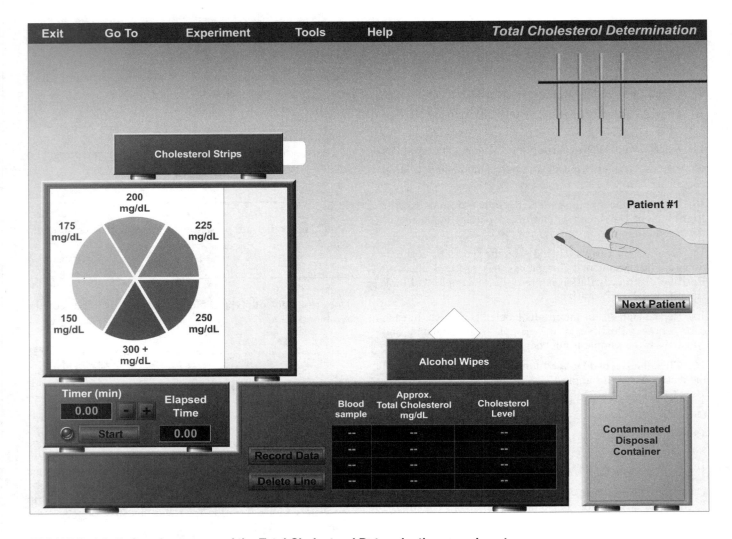

FIGURE 11.5 Opening screen of the Total Cholesterol Determination experiment.

One type of lipoprotein package, called LDL (low-density lipoprotein), has been identified as a potential source of damage to the interior of arteries because it can contribute to atherosclerosis, the buildup of plaque, in these blood vessels. A total blood cholesterol determination does not measure the level of LDLs, but it does provide valuable information about the total amount of cholesterol in the blood.

Less than 200 milligrams of total cholesterol per deciliter of blood is considered desirable. Between 200 and 239 mg/dl is considered borderline high cholesterol. Over 240 mg/dl is considered high blood cholesterol and is associated with increased risk of cardiovascular disease. Abnormally low blood levels of cholesterol (total cholesterol lower than 100 mg/dl) can also be a problem. Low levels may indicate hyperthyroidism (overactive thyroid gland), liver disease, inadequate absorption of nutrients from the intestine, or malnutrition. Other reports link hypocholesterolemia (low blood cholesterol) to depression, anxiety, and mood disturbances, which are thought to be controlled by the level of available serotonin, a neurotransmitter. There is evidence of a relationship between low levels of blood cholesterol and low levels of serotonin in the brain.

In this test for total blood cholesterol, a sample of blood is mixed with enzymes that produce a colored reaction with cholesterol. The intensity of the color indicates the amount of cholesterol present. The cholesterol tester compares the color of the sample to the colors of known levels of cholesterol (standard values).

From the **Experiment** menu, select **Total Cholesterol Determination.** You will see the opening screen for the Total Cholesterol Determination lab (Figure 11.5). Use the **Balloons On/Off** feature from the **Help** menu to familiarize yourself with the equipment on the screen.

In the upper right portion of the screen is a dispenser of *lancets,* sharp needlelike instruments that are used to prick the finger to obtain a drop of blood.

Beneath the lancet dispenser is a patient's finger. The patient can be changed by clicking the **Next Patient** button beneath the finger.

On top of the data table is a container of alcohol wipes for cleansing the fingertip before it is punctured with the lancet.

The left portion of the screen shows a cabinet containing a *color wheel* that is divided into sections showing different intensities of green. Each shade of green corresponds to a range of total cholesterol levels. Below the cabinet is a timer that can be set for 1 to 3 minutes.

In the upper left portion of the screen is a cholesterol strip dispenser. These cholesterol strips contain chemicals that convert, by a series of reactions, the cholesterol in the blood sample into a green-colored solution. These reactions take 3 minutes. By matching the color of the cholesterol strip to a color on the color wheel, we can determine the cholesterol level of a given blood sample. Higher levels of cholesterol will result in a deeper green color.

The bottom of the screen has a data table for recording the total cholesterol level of the blood samples.

In the lower right portion of the screen is a contaminated disposal container. Any piece of equipment that has come into contact with the blood must be disposed of properly by dragging it to this contaminated disposal container.

ACTIVITY 5

Total Cholesterol Determination

1. Click and drag an alcohol wipe over the end of patient 1's finger.

2. Click and drag a lancet to the tip of the finger. The lancet will prick the finger to obtain a drop of blood.

3. Drag the lancet to the contaminated disposal container.

4. Drag a cholesterol strip to the finger. The blood should transfer to the strip.

5. Drag the cholesterol strip to the rectangular area to the right of the color wheel.

6. Set the timer for 3 minutes, and click **Start.** Notice that the strip begins to change color.

7. After 3 minutes, decide which color on the color wheel most closely matches the color on the cholesterol test strip. Click on that color. It is sometimes difficult to match the color on the cholesterol strip with the appropriate color on the color wheel. If the color you have chosen is not an exact match, you will see a pop-up window asking you to try again.

8. Click on **Record Data** to record this information in the data table.

9. Drag the cholesterol test strip for patient 1 to the contaminated disposal container. Record your results in Chart 6.

10. There are a total of four patients. Click **Next Patient** and repeat steps 1–9 until you have collected data for all four patients.

What health problems might be in store for patient 2, based on these results?

_____

What advice about diet and exercise would you give patient 4?

_____

CHART 6	Total Cholesterol Determination	
Blood Sample	**Approximate Total Cholesterol**	**Cholesterol Level**
1		
2		
3		
4		

Blood Analysis

NAME _____

LAB TIME/DATE _____

Hematocrit Determination

The following questions refer to Activity 1: Hematocrit Determination.

1. List the following values from Chart 1:

   Hematocrit value for healthy male living at sea level in Boston = _____

   Hematocrit value for healthy female living at sea level in Boston = _____

2. Were the values listed in question 1 within normal range? _____

3. Describe the difference between the male and the female hematocrit for an individual living in Boston. _____

   _____

4. List the following values from Chart 1:

   Hematocrit value for healthy male living in Denver = _____

   Hematocrit value for healthy female living in Denver = _____

5. How did these values differ from the values for Boston? _____

   _____

6. Describe the effect of living at high elevations on a person's hematocrit. _____

   _____

7. Describe how the kidneys respond to a decrease in oxygen and what effect this has on hematocrit. _____

   _____

8. List the following values from Chart 1:

   Hematocrit value for male with aplastic anemia = _____

   % WBC for male with aplastic anemia = _____

9. Were the values listed in question 8 within the normal range? Why or why not?

   _____

   _____

10. List the following value from Chart 1:

Hematocrit for female with iron-deficiency anemia = _____

11. Was the value in question 10 normal or not? Explain. _____

_____

Erythrocyte Sedimentation Rate

The following questions refer to Activity 2: Erythrocyte Sedimentation Rate.

12. Describe the effect that sickle cell anemia has on the sedimentation rate. _____

_____

13. Why do you think that it has this effect? Hint: Sickle cell anemia alters the shape of red blood cells. _____

_____

14. Record the sedimentation rate for a menstruating female. _____

15. How did this value compare to the healthy individual? Why? _____

_____

16. What was the sedimentation rate for the iron-deficient individual? _____

17. What effect does iron deficiency have on ESR? _____

_____

18. Record the following values from Chart 2:

ESR for person suffering from a myocardial infarction = _____

ESR for person suffering from angina pectoris = _____

19. Compare the values in question 18 and explain how they might be used to monitor heart conditions. _____

_____

20. List some other conditions that ESR is used to monitor. _____

_____

Hemoglobin

The following questions refer to Activity 3: Hemoglobin (Hb) Determination.

21. Describe the ratio of packed cell volume to Hb (hemoglobin) obtained for the healthy male and female subjects. _____

_____

22. Describe the ratio of packed cell volume to Hb (hemoglobin) for the female with iron-deficiency anemia. _____

23. Is the female with iron-deficiency anemia deficient in hemoglobin? _____

24. Is the male with polycythemia deficient in hemoglobin? _____

25. Is the female Olympic athlete deficient in hemoglobin? _____

26. List conditions in which Hb would decrease. _____

_____

27. List conditions in which Hb would increase. _____

_____

Blood Typing

The following questions refer to Activity 4: Blood Typing.

28. Which blood sample contained the rarest blood type? _____

29. Which blood sample contained the universal donor? _____

30. Which blood sample contained the universal recipient? _____

31. Which blood sample did not coagulate with any of the antibodies tested? _____

    Why? _____

32. What antibodies would be found in the plasma of blood sample 1? _____

33. When transfusing an individual with blood that is compatible but not the same type, it is important to separate packed cells

    from the plasma and administer only the packed cells. Why do you think this is done?_____

    _____

34. List which blood samples in this experiment represent people who could donate blood to a person with type B$^+$. _____

    _____

Blood Cholesterol

The following questions refer to Activity 5: Total Cholesterol Determination.

35. Which patient had desirable cholesterol levels? _____

36. Which patient(s) had an elevated cholesterol level? _____

37. Describe the risks for the patient identified in question 36. _____

_____

38. Which advice would you give patient 4? Why? _____

_____

39. Describe some reasons why a patient might have abnormally low blood cholesterol.

_____

_____

Histology Atlas and Review Supplement

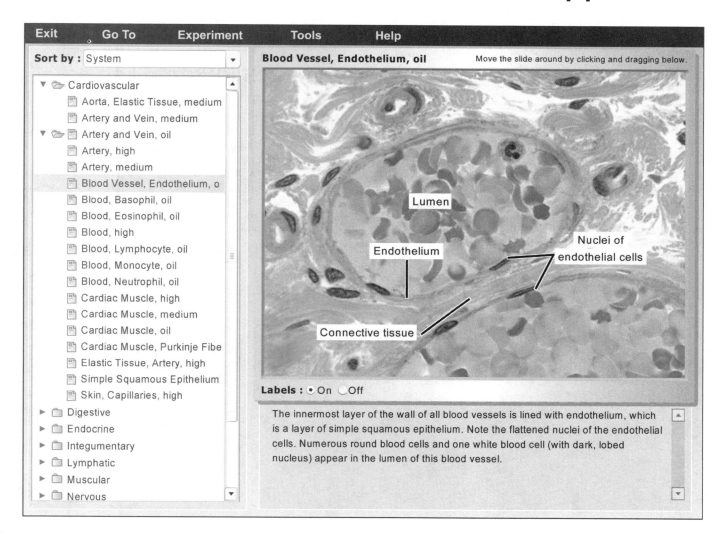

| Exit | Go To | Experiment | Tools | Help |

Sort by : System ▼

▼ 📂 Cardiovascular
   📄 Aorta, Elastic Tissue, medium
   📄 Artery and Vein, medium
▼ 📄 Artery and Vein, oil
   📄 Artery, high
   📄 Artery, medium
   📄 Blood Vessel, Endothelium, o
   📄 Blood, Basophil, oil
   📄 Blood, Eosinophil, oil
   📄 Blood, high
   📄 Blood, Lymphocyte, oil
   📄 Blood, Monocyte, oil
   📄 Blood, Neutrophil, oil
   📄 Cardiac Muscle, high
   📄 Cardiac Muscle, medium
   📄 Cardiac Muscle, oil
   📄 Cardiac Muscle, Purkinje Fibe
   📄 Elastic Tissue, Artery, high
   📄 Simple Squamous Epithelium
   📄 Skin, Capillaries, high
▶ 📁 Digestive
▶ 📁 Endocrine
▶ 📁 Integumentary
▶ 📁 Lymphatic
▶ 📁 Muscular
▶ 📁 Nervous

Blood Vessel, Endothelium, oil   Move the slide around by clicking and dragging below.

Lumen

Endothelium

Nuclei of endothelial cells

Connective tissue

Labels : ● On ○ Off

The innermost layer of the wall of all blood vessels is lined with endothelium, which is a layer of simple squamous epithelium. Note the flattened nuclei of the endothelial cells. Numerous round blood cells and one white blood cell (with dark, lobed nucleus) appear in the lumen of this blood vessel.

Examining a specimen using a microscope accomplishes two goals: first, it gives you an understanding of the cellular organization of tissues, and second—perhaps even more importantly—it hones your observational skills. Because developing these skills is crucial in the understanding and eventual mastery of the scientific method, using this histology tutorial is not intended as a substitute for using the microscope. Instead, use it to gain an overall appreciation of the specimens and then make your own observations using your microscope.

The Histology Atlas can be used independently of this lab manual to explore the different tissue types found in the human body. Or, it can be used in conjunction with the printable Histology Review Supplement worksheets found in Exercise H on the PhysioEx website, for a review of histology slides specific to topics covered in the PhysioEx lab simulations.

To begin, choose **Exercise H: Histology Atlas and Review Supplement** from the drop-down menu and click **GO.** Then click **Histology Atlas** to browse the library of histology images. There are four main components of the tutorial. The *Sort by* drop-down menu is located at the top left. After you select a sorting option, the *slide menu* below will display all the folders and slide listings that are available. The *image viewer* is located on the right side with the *description box* directly below it.

Sorting and Locating Slides

You can search for slides by selecting any of the four sorting options from the *Sort by* drop-down menu. Click on the white menu bar to select from the following sorting options:

- **A-Z** Organizes slides alphabetically by title. Contains all of the slide listings in the tutorial.

- **System** Organizes slides into folders based on the body system they represent.

- **Tissue Type** Organizes slides into folders based on the tissue type(s) they represent.

- **Histology Review** Calls up the images used in the Histology Review Supplement worksheets that are available on the PhysioEx web site.

Certain histology images demonstrate more than one system or tissue type; therefore, an image might be found in multiple locations with different titles, labels, and descriptions, depending on the categories it is listed under.

All slide listings include magnification information at the end of the title. Because the exact magnification is variable depending on screen resolution, we have provided approximate magnifications instead:

- **Low** originally photographed at **40×**

- **Medium** originally photographed at **100×**

- **High** originally photographed at **400×**

- **Oil (immersion)** originally photographed at **1000×**

Viewing Slides and Labels

Click on any listing in the *slide menu* to call up an image and description in the viewing area. The image may take a few seconds to load if you are using the web version. You can move the slide around in the viewer by clicking and dragging directly on the image.

You can show or hide the labels at any time by selecting the **On** or **Off** buttons in the *Labels* menu below the viewer. If a label appears to be out of the viewing area, keep in mind that you can see more of the image by clicking and dragging it in the *image viewer*.